Kylie
The Biography

D1144336

Kylie
The Biography

'You [Kylie] are a multi-faceted chameleon woman.'
SAM TAYLOR-WOOD

*'God is in his heaven, Kylie's at number one, surely
nothing really bad can happen now.'*
BRYAN APPLEYARD

SEAN SMITH

POCKET
BOOKS

LONDON · SYDNEY · NEW YORK · TORONTO

This edition first published in Great Britain by Pocket Books, 2006
An imprint of Simon & Schuster UK Ltd
A CBS COMPANY

5 7 9 10 8 6

Simon & Schuster UK Ltd
Africa House
64–78 Kingsway
London WC2B 6AH

www.simonsays.co.uk

Simon & Schuster Australia
Sydney

A CIP catalogue record for this book
is available from the British Library

ISBN-13: 978-1-8473-9030-1

Typeset in Baskerville by M Rules
Printed and bound in Great Britain by
Cox & Wyman Ltd, Reading, Berks

Acknowledgements

Thanks to everyone who helped me with this book, both the original and new editions, and made them such fun to do. They include Paul Marcolin, Peter Holt, Jane Oddy, Spencer Bright, Alison Jane Reid, Rick Sky, Frank Thorne and Cassandra Hooper. Some people wanted to remain anonymous because of the very small world nature of the record business and I have respected their wishes. I hope they enjoy the book.

Doug Booth was an enormous help in Melbourne and Lizzie Clachan did invaluable research in London. There have been quite a few books about Kylie over the years – that's not surprising considering what a long and varied career she has enjoyed. *Kylie Fever* by Trevor Baker is full of lovely photographs while my own personal favourite is *Kylie la la la* compiled by William Baker and Kylie herself. It's full of fascinating insights and pictures not available anywhere else. Many excellent websites are devoted to all things Kylie. LiMBO is, in my opinion, the best of them.

At Simon & Schuster, for this new edition, my thanks to Jonathan Atkins for his commitment to the book, Stuart Polson for his stunning cover design, Jo Edgecombe for overseeing production and Christianna Ingram-Hofer for helping me update the story. My editor Rumana Haider has brought great skill, patience and good humour to the project.

Finally, a special thank you to my wife Zoë Lawrence for her excellent advice and support.

Contents

Acknowledgements   v

Introduction   1

Life and Times   7

PART ONE: **HAPPY ACCIDENTS**

1   **Dannii's Big Sister**   33

2   **One Night with Kylie**   42

3   **The Henderson Kid**   55

4   **Especially Jason**   64

5   **Locomotion**   73

6   **London Calling**   83

7   **Media Relations**   98

PART TWO: **THE WILD ROSE**

8   **The Sexual Revolution**   113

9   **Coolification**   132

10   **Goodbye Yellow Brick Road**   145

11   **A French Connection**   157

12   **Thirty Up**   171

13   **Gay Old Times**   182

PART THREE: **SHOWGIRL**

14 **Small, Beautiful and Portable** 193
15 **Gold Hot Pants** 208
16 **Kylie's Wrecked My Life** 223
17 **French Connection II** 235
18 **Langoustines in Portofino** 246

Heard and Seen 257
Photo Credits 270
Index 271

Introduction

I always like to listen to recordings of my subject when I am writing about them. It puts me in the mood to hear Justin, Robbie or Britney coming out of the speakers. And Kylie. I am always trying to strip away the image a little bit to see what's underneath. Image is built up like varnish, layer by carefully applied layer. Hearing their music is invigorating because it's image free. The songs are either good or bad. You can't see what new tattoo Robbie is sporting when you are listening to him sing Frank Sinatra. Similarly you don't know what Kylie is wearing, or how she has styled her hair when you put 'Slow' or 'Can't Get You Out Of My Head' in the CD player or iPod. Instead, you have a picture in your mind of them and it is individual to you.

For Kylie that picture may be of Charlene Mitchell in greasy overalls, or of her bubble hair cut singing 'I Should Be So Lucky' or in gold hot pants for 'Spinning Around'. I change the image of Kylie in my mind practically every song. She has so many of them. That's why I love Sam Taylor-Wood's description of Kylie as a 'multi-faceted chameleon woman'. I have all those pictures of Kylie in my head – as well as the one of her wearing little red devil horns but we had better not go there. The image I don't have of Kylie is the one of her as cancer victim, desperately ill, stick thin, her hairless head covered in a washer-woman scarf. That's a bit too much reality where Kylie is concerned. Pop princesses don't get cancer, do they?

The other singer I have been listening to a lot while updating my biography of Kylie is Edith Piaf. Her sobriquet of 'little sparrow' is one that could nicely fit Kylie. Predictably, my favourite Piaf track is the timeless classic 'La Vie En Rose' – life in pink. I see Kylie as a bit of a pink person, a girly girl, not in the least like her tomboy television persona. I like to think that 'La Vie En Rose' translates as 'life through rose-tinted spectacles' and that's how I see Kylie, which is why I chose journalist Bryan Appleyard's words as my second introductory quote for this book: 'God is in his heaven, Kylie's at number one, surely nothing bad can really happen now.' Edith Piaf's life was full of genuine tragedy, despair and heartbreak. Kylie once memorably said, while discussing her status as a heroine of gay culture, 'I don't have any tragedy in my life, only tragic outfits.' It's a great quote but one that circumstances have rendered too flippant.

Bizarrely, contracting cancer has given Kylie a substance she previously lacked. Surviving in the pop business is not exactly the same as surviving life threatening illness. I can remember one of the first things I ever wrote about Kylie was when she went to the theatre in the West End with Michael Hutchence and he spent the entire time twanging her bra strap. I failed to take her seriously which was my error. The main thrust of my first book on Kylie was that she was and never had been a girl next door. I found a contemporary of hers in Melbourne who, shortly after they had met, had lost his virginity to Kylie in a garden shed. I remember speaking to someone after the book was published who told me he had read the book lots of times. 'Really', I said, pleasantly surprised. 'Well, not exactly', he confessed. 'Just the bit with her having sex in the shed.'

'Kylie Minogue' is a coat Kylie hangs on a peg by her front door. She puts it on and poses for us. She takes it off, snuggles up on the sofa and watches *Bridget Jones's Diary* on DVD. Occasionally over the years she puts on the wrong coat and is caught in tears after a row with her boyfriend, wearing an old anorak and not looking much like Kylie Minogue at all. Michael Hutchence told Kylie to always wear an 'ego jacket' when she was being a star and that nothing could touch her when she had it on. Rob Williams from Stoke-on-Trent puts one on when he becomes Robbie Williams. Britney Spears from Kentwood, Louisiana puts one on when she becomes Britney snogging Madonna on stage. Similarly, Kylie is a middle-class girl from a suburb of Melbourne who can transform herself into a Showgirl for us. She is an actress superbly playing a star.

Kylie was driven by ambition at an early age. I believe that she and her sister Dannii fed off a perfectly natural sibling rivalry as children and that, quite possibly, neither would have made it without the other. Once, however, performing got in their blood it became a lifelong addiction. The thrill of performance, applause and adulation is a drug that is practically impossible to shake off – the more you get, the more you want. Over the years we have tried to define Kylie by the unsatisfactory men in her life and her perceived desire to play happy families. It really is only because she is female and, even in these modern times, we want to put celebrities in pretty patterned, perfect boxes. We wanted Kylie to settle down with Jason and produce a family of singing stars – the von Trapp family of Melbourne. We wanted Kylie to tame Michael Hutchence and turn him into a devoted husband and father and change the name of his band to NOXS.

We still want Kylie to live a fairytale, happy-ever-after life and so in her first major interview after being given the all-clear from breast cancer, she was asked yet again about children. In 1989, aged twenty-one she said she wanted a church wedding and three children – two girls and a boy, just like her own parents. In 2006, she told Cat Deeley she would just 'love kids', no specifics. She will be asked again in her next interview, just as she will be questioned about her relationship with French actor Olivier Martinez. I prefer to look at the very simple facts. At the moment they are still together and, as far as I can see, he is the longest standing proper boyfriend she has had since her teens. Usually her boyfriends last no more than two years and then she heads back to Melbourne and the comfort and protection of her very loving family. Martinez strikes me as being an interesting man of some substance but, he may be history by the time the ink is dry on this page. Who knows? All I can say is that Kylie's family are full of admiration for the way he has helped her through the past eighteen months and that's an important seal of approval.

Certainly, newspaper and magazines are full of so-called experts giving their views on Kylie and Olivier. Here's a selection of the best of them:

'Kylie falls in love quite easily. She is in the first flush of romance, enjoying something new. She is smitten by Olivier.' – *Who* magazine, June 2003.

'Maybe when we see her having a heart to heart with her mum over a coffee in Melbourne, we'll know it's finally over with Olivier . . . Kylie's no victim. She's in control of her life and is very strong minded. It suits her needs to have relationships which don't threaten her independence.' – *Grazia*, March 2005.

'For the first time in twenty years, she has had a chance to simply hang out with a boyfriend – and has found true love. I'm sure that if Kylie were to marry Olivier, everyone around her would be thrilled.' – *Daily Mirror*, April 2006.

I say these are the best of them but they might also be the worst of them, depending on your point of view. They are, in fact, all quotes from the same Kylie expert – me. I really must stop being so gobby where Kylie is concerned. I do get asked about Kylie a lot. Lately I have been quizzed on why she is bothering to make a come-back after her cancer. I think that's a genuinely easy one. Touring and performing is normality for Kylie and I can't think of anything more natural, after such a health scare, than wanting to do again something which is so funda-mentally part of your life. Money and fame are irrelevant in this context. I also expect everybody to be ecstatic when she resumes centre stage. She may never be a 'pop princess' again. She looks a million dollars but her brush with death – because that is what it is – has given her a mature beauty that she never had in skimpy gold hot pants.

There was one occasion when I had nothing to say about Kylie. The day after she announced she had been diagnosed with breast cancer, I was phoned by a magazine and asked if I would like to send a message to Kylie. I declined. What could I say that wouldn't be trivial, unhelpful and pointless? I told the journalist that I thought it was a private matter for Kylie and I wanted to leave it there. My own mother died of breast cancer and, as Forrest Gump would have said, 'That's all I have to say about that.' If I had been given no choice in the matter, I would have said, 'I hope God is smiling on Kylie.' I still hope so.

Sean Smith
October 2006

Life and Times

28 May 1968 Kylie Ann *Minogue* born in Melbourne.

1970 Brendan Minogue born.

1971 Danielle (Dannii) Minogue born.

1979 KM attends her first TV audition and lands role as Dutch girl Carla in the Australian series *The Sullivans.* Dannii appears for the first time on *Young Talent Time.*

1980 KM starts at Camberwell High School, Melbourne. Appears as Robin in an episode of the Australian TV series *Skyways;* on set, meets Jason Donovan for the first time. First visit to Britain, with her family to see relatives in Wales and go sightseeing in London. Dannii becomes a permanent team member of *Young Talent Time* and is temporarily the more famous of the two sisters.

October 1984 KM wins role as Charlotte (Char) Kernow in TV mini-series *The Henderson Kids.* Goes on location for the first time during the five months of filming in New South Wales.

May 1985 Aged nearly seventeen, plays a 12-year-old, 'Yvonne the Terrible', in an episode of children's TV programme *The Zoo Family*. Beats fifty other hopefuls to win female lead as Samantha Collins in six-part TV mini-series *Fame and Misfortune*. First episode of *The Henderson Kids* shown on Australian TV.

January 1986 Leaves Camberwell High School having passed her Year 12 exams in Art and Graphics. Auditions for *Neighbours* and is cast as Charlene Mitchell. Initial contract is for thirteen weeks but that is quickly extended to twenty-six weeks when bosses sense screen chemistry between Charlene and Scott Robinson (Jason Donovan).

April 1986 First episode of *Neighbours* featuring KM shown on Australian TV. She has begun a relationship with Jason which is kept secret from the public.

August 1986 Sings in public for the first time at a benefit for an Australian Rules Football team. Performs 'I Got You Babe' and 'The Loco-Motion'.

October 1986 First screening of *Neighbours* on British TV.

December 1986 Jason and Kylie slip away for a private holiday on Bali.

April 1987 Becomes youngest ever artist to be

crowned Most Popular Actress in Australia at the annual Logie Awards; Jason is named Best New Talent. Sings a duet with Dannii, 'Sisters Are Doing It For Themselves', at an anti-drugs concert in Melbourne.

July 1987 Releases first single in Australia, 'The Loco-Motion', which reaches No. 1 and stays there for seven weeks. The wedding of Charlene and Scott in *Neighbours* is the TV event of the year. Meets Michael Hutchence for the first time at a party after a music awards ceremony in Sydney. Appoints Terry Blamey as her manager.

October 1987 During a break in filming *Neighbours*, flies to London to record with Stock, Aitken and Waterman. They write 'I Should Be So Lucky' while she waits in reception.

December 1987 Sings 'I Should Be So Lucky' on Noel Edmonds's BBC TV Christmas Special.

January 1988 BBC decides to screen *Neighbours* twice a day; UK viewing figures top 15 million per episode. 'I Should Be So Lucky' is KM's first single release in UK, where it reaches No. 1. It also tops the charts in Australia, Germany, Finland, Hong Kong, Israel and Switzerland. Meets the Prince and Princess of Wales in Sydney during Australia's Bicentennial celebrations. KM later admits to being tongue-tied in front of the Princess.

March 1988 Wins four Logie awards including the top Gold Logie as Most Popular Personality on Australian TV.

April 1988 Savaged in print by famous British columnist Jean Rook for arriving at Heathrow looking like a 'slept-in Qantas blanket'. Ms Rook suggests KM should try to emulate the style of Joan Collins.

May 1988 'Got To Be Certain', her second single in Britain, reaches No. 2 where it stays for six weeks. In Australia it is the first ever single to debut at No. 1.

June 1988 Films her last scenes for *Neighbours*. Cries at a leaving party at a Melbourne restaurant where she is presented with an antique mahogany mirror and a framed montage of her magazine covers.

August 1988 Her first album, *Kylie,* released in the UK and Australia. Its success will make her the youngest ever female to top the UK album charts. 'The Loco-Motion' released for the first time in UK but just misses the No. 1 spot.

September 1988 Becomes known as 'The Loco-Motion Girl' after the single becomes her first hit in the USA. It will remain her biggest hit there until 'Can't Get You Out Of My Head' in 2002.

October 1988 'Je Ne Sais Pas Pourquoi', Pete

Waterman's favourite Kylie song, is her third consecutive single to reach No. 2 in the UK. It was originally intended to be a double A-side with 'Made in Heaven'.

November 1988 In response to public demand records a duet, 'Especially For You', with Jason.

December 1988 *Kylie* is the biggest-selling album of the year in the UK. The accompanying *Kylie – The Videos* also reaches No. 1. 'Especially For You' misses the Christmas No. 1, kept off the top by Cliff Richard's 'Mistletoe and Wine'. Becomes the first artist to have four consecutive No. 1s in Finland.

January 1989 'Especially For You' finally reaches No. 1 in the UK. It will be her biggest-selling record until 'Can't Get You Out Of My Head'. Has three simultaneous worldwide No. 1s when 'Turn It Into Love' reaches the top in Japan and 'The Loco-Motion' matches it in Canada.

April 1989 'Hand On Your Heart', the first single from her second album, *Enjoy Yourself,* becomes her third UK No. 1. Begins work on *The Delinquents,* her first movie, playing Lola Lovell.

May 1989 Celebrates her 21st birthday with a champagne party for 150 at the trendy Red Eagle Hotel in Sydney. An over-eager bouncer slams the door in Jason's face.

July 1989 Her seventh single in the UK, 'Wouldn't Change A Thing', reaches No. 2. Her first seven singles in the UK have gone 1-2-2-2-1-1-2.

September 1989 While in Hong Kong, preparing for her first international tour, has dinner with Michael Hutchence, who has a home in the colony.

October 1989 *Enjoy Yourself* is released in the UK and reaches No. 1.

November 1989 'Never Too Late', the second single from the album, spoils Kylie's run by only reaching No. 4 in the UK charts. She had wanted to release the track 'Enjoy Yourself' but was overruled by Waterman.

December 1989 Switches on the Christmas lights in London's Regent Street. Joins Bob Geldof and other Stock, Aitken and Waterman stars to record Band Aid II's version of 'Do They Know It's Christmas?', which becomes the Christmas No. 1. *Enjoy Yourself,* complete with free Kylie poster, tops 1 million sales in Britain. At the Australian première of *The Delinquents* KM is barely recognizable in blonde wig and microskirt. Attends the première of *The Delinquents* in Leicester Square and is greeted by a huge crowd of fans. The film is not well received by the critics, however. Voted Best Female Vocalist of 1989 at the Japan Radio Music Awards.

January 1990 'Tears On My Pillow', from *The Delinquents* soundtrack, is Kylie's fourth British No. 1 from her first nine singles.

February 1990 First concert tour – with, for the first time, a live backing band – in Australia is praised by both critics and fans. Receives the UK Video Industry's Top Music Video of 1989 award for *Kylie – The Videos*.

March 1990 First signs of a break from Stock, Aitken and Waterman when KM records four songs in Los Angeles with different producers. She dedicates one, 'Count the Days', to boyfriend Michael Hutchence.

April 1990 Takes control of her image for the first time with the video for her next single, 'Better The Devil You Know'; she is seen to writhe provocatively in the arms of a naked black man almost twice her size.

May 1990 'Better The Devil You Know' reaches No. 2 in the UK, and becomes an anthem for a generation of gay fans. It is widely assumed that the song is about her relationship with Hutchence.

June 1990 Moves to London with Hutchence, who also buys a farmhouse in the South of France which she helps to furnish.

November 1990 Third album, *Rhythm Of Love*, is her least successful so far, peaking at No. 9 in the UK and

No.10 in Australia. A single from it, 'Step Back In Time', reaches No. 4 in Britain. The video features Kylie in seventies disco gear cruising the streets in an open-topped car.

December 1990 For the first time spends Christmas away from her family in Melbourne, preferring to celebrate with Hutchence at the farmhouse in Roquefort-les-Pins.

February 1991 Splits with Hutchence amid rumours of his philandering on tour 'What Do I Have To Do?', another Waterman favourite, reaches No.6 in the UK (Dannii appears in the video) and becomes one of the most popular of all Kylie songs live.

May 1991 Wins Bestselling Australian Artist at the World Music Awards in Monte Carlo.

June 1991 'Shocked', which boasts a raunchy video, becomes her thirteenth consecutive Top 10 hit, a record. It places her ahead of Elvis Presley, The Beatles and Madonna.

August 1991 Her first flop: 'Word Is Out' manages a lowly No. 16, the first time a Kylie release fails to make the UK Top 10. Davina McCall, later the presenter of *Big Brother*, plays one of Kylie's friends in the video.

October 1991 Releases her fourth album, *Let's Get To It*. The second single from it, 'If You Were With Me

Now', with Keith Washington, is much better received and reaches No. 4 in the UK. The album is also praised in the music press. Begins her second sellout tour of the UK.

January 1992 Releases her first cover since 'The Loco-Motion': 'Give Me Just A Little More Time', a 1970 hit for Chairmen of the Board, takes her back to her favourite chart position, No. 2.

April 1992 Her new video, *Kylie Live*, recorded at a concert in Dublin, is released and enters the UK video chart at No. 2.

June 1992 Takes part in the Rhythm of Life charity fashion gala in London, joining models and other celebrities at the Grosvenor House Hotel, recruited by Sting to support his Rainforest Foundation.

July 1992 Her name is linked in the British press with superstar Prince after they are seen leaving a London nightclub together.

August 1992 Her final Stock, Aitken and Waterman release is a compilation of twenty numbers entitled *Kylie's Greatest Hits*. It is a runaway success, reaching No. 1 in both the album and video charts. Not so her final Pete Waterman single, 'Celebration', which only reaches No.20 in the UK chart.

February 1993 Signs to independent British dance label deConstruction, responsible for pop soul favourites M People. The year marks key restyling of KM – she meets William Baker for the first time.

October 1993 Invited by Baz Luhrmann to pose at Universal Studios for world-famous photographer Bert Stern. The '60s-style spread' fills twenty-one pages of Australian *Vogue.*

January 1994 Bridesmaid to Dannii at her wedding to Julian McMahon, soap actor and son of a former prime minister of Australia. The marriage is over within a year.

February 1994 Performs 'What Do I Have To Do?' at the gay Mardi Gras in Sydney.

June 1994 In Thailand for the start of filming for *Street Fighter*, in which she takes the female lead, Cammy, alongside Jean-Claude Van Damme.

August 1994 Releases her first deConstruction single. 'Confide In Me', five minutes long, is a radical departure from Stock, Aitken and Waterman but receives a thumbs-up from fans, reaching No. 2 in Britain, kept off the top spot by Whigfield's 'Saturday Night'.

October 1994 Her first deConstruction album, *Kylie Minogue,* is released to critical acclaim. It features arrangements and mixes by producers Brothers in Rhythm – one half of that team, Steve Anderson, becomes a long-term friend and collaborator.

November 1994 One of her most famous videos accompanies 'Put Yourself In My Place'. She is seen floating in a spacecraft slowly undressing until completely naked. The single, however, only reaches No. 11 in the UK. Plays herself in guest appearance on *The Vicar of Dibley*.

December 1994 Wins Best Female Solo Singer at the *Smash Hits* awards. *Street Fighter* proves to be big Christmas box office, but does nothing for KM's movie career.

January 1995 Records 'Where The Wild Roses Grow', a dark and brooding duet with Nick Cave, in Melbourne.

February 1995 Films short art-house film *Hayride to Hell* in Sydney. KM plays a psychotic girl who terrorizes a man who gives her a lift home.

April 1995 Spends three months making *Bio-Dome*, playing Petra Von Kant, in Los Angeles, during which she has a fling with co-star Pauly Shore. The film is a turkey, however.

June 1995 Features on the front cover of *Loaded*, the definitive British lads' magazine.

July 1995 Meets photographer Stephane Sednaoui at a party. Shortly afterwards spends three weeks driving across the USA with him. The final single from the *Kylie Minogue* album, 'Where Is The Feeling?', only reaches No. 16 in the UK.

August 1995 Performs live at a rock festival for the first time when, backed by a 9-piece band, she performs in front of 30,000 at the 'T in the Park' in Glasgow. Cave joins her on stage to perform 'Where The Wild Roses Grow'.

October 1995 'Where The Wild Roses Grow' released; reaches No.11 in UK but does better in Australia, climbing to No. 2. The video features an apparently dead Kylie floating face up in a lake. Appears on stage for an AIDS benefit at the Royal Albert Hall to perform a duet with Elton John (in drag) of 'Sisters Are Doing It For Themselves'.

January 1996 KM has no record releases in 1996 but performs live throughout the year, beginning with the 'Big Day Out' concerts in Australia with Nick Cave and his band, The Bad Seeds.

July 1996 Kylie reads words to 'I Should Be So Lucky' at the Poetry Olympics at the Royal Albert Hall.

August 1996 Hard at work on her next album, taking her most active role to date in the material and writing all the lyrics. In London, performs 'Where The Wild Roses Grow' with Nick Cave at the Brixton Academy.

October 1996 'Where The Wild Roses Grow' wins Best Single, Best Pop Release and Best Song of the Year at the Australian Record Industry Awards.

December 1996 Appears on stage in London with Manic Street Preachers, performing their song 'Little Baby Nothing'.

January 1997 Her second deConstruction album was due for release this month, but is put back. The original plan for exclusive collaboration with Brothers in Rhythm is scrapped in favour of KM working with a number of producers, including Manic Street Preachers.

February 1997 Appears on British TV in a special episode of comedy series *Men Behaving Badly* in aid of Comic Relief.

May 1997 Makes a special appearance with Ray Charles and Australian rock legend John Farnham at the opening of world's largest casino in Melbourne. Elton John is among 1,500 guests.

August 1997 Performs 'Some Kind of Bliss', written by Manic Street Preachers, at the *Radio 1 Roadshow* in Newquay, Cornwall. Song will be first single released from her new album *Impossible Princess*. However, the death of Diana, Princess of Wales in Paris prompts a radical rethink of album title and marketing.

September 1997 'Some Kind of Bliss' flops, only

reaching No. 22 in the UK chart. James Dean Bradfield of Manic Street Preachers later says he failed Kylie. Records MTV special *Some Kind of Kylie.* Wins award for Most Stylish Female Pop Star at the *Elle* magazine style awards in London. Release of the new album is put back until after Christmas.

October 1997 Goes ahead with filming video for 'Did It Again', the second single from the new album. It features four Kylie 'personas' in battle with each other.

November 1997 Relationship with Sednaoui ends. Michael Hutchence found dead in a Sydney hotel room. Kylie attends funeral at St Andrew's Cathedral, Sydney.

December 1997 'Did It Again' is another disappointment, only reaching No. 14 in the UK.

February 1998 Performs at the Sydney gay Mardi Gras. Sister Dannii does the 2 a.m. show while Kylie goes on at 4 a.m. to perform 'Better The Devil You Know'.

March 1998 'Breathe', the third single from the new album, also only reaches No. 14. Album finally released in UK under the title *Kylie Minogue In Europe.* It just scrapes into the album chart at No.10.

May 1998 Kylie turns thirty.

June 1998 A new-look Kylie starts tour in Australia. The 'Intimate & Live' Show, with its camp, Las Vegas-show atmosphere, is received rapturously.

August 1998 Leaves deConstruction by 'amicable agreement'. London concerts grab rave reviews in the national press.

December 1998 Kylie is honoured at the annual Australian Export Awards in Sydney where she receives a special award for selling more than 30 million records up to that point.

March 1999 Plays Miranda in a version of Shakespeare's *The Tempest* in Barbados.

April 1999 In New York to record 'The Reflex' with Ben Lee for a Duran Duran tribute album.

May 1999 In Adelaide, shoots cameo role in teen horror movie *Cut*, in which she suffers a grisly death. Signs for The Beatles' old record label, Parlophone, the start of a carefully planned musical comeback.

July 1999 In Vienna for the annual Life Ball, takes to the catwalk in the Imperial Palace to raise money for AIDS charities.

October 1999 Publication of acclaimed book *Kylie*, a photographic journey through images of KM and her life.

December 1999 Wearing a revealing Santa outfit, entertains 10,000 Australian troops who are part of a peacekeeping force in East Timor and who will not be home for Christmas.

January 2000 Meets British model James Gooding at a pool party in Los Angeles.

June 2000 Photo of her bottom appears on the front page of the *Sun*.

July 2000 'Spinning Around', her first release on Parlophone, becomes the first of her singles to debut at No. 1 on the UK chart.

August 2000 Special guest on Robbie Williams's *Top of the Pops* special performing their duet 'Kids'.

October 2000 Performs 'Dancing Queen' and 'On A Night Like This' at the closing ceremony of the Olympic Games in Sydney. The global audience is estimated at 3.7 billion. Less than three weeks later she sings at the opening ceremony of the Paralympics. The album *Light Years* reaches No. 2 in the UK album chart, but fills the top spot in Australia. 'Kids' reaches No. 2 on the UK chart.

November 2000 Kylie and Robbie duet at the MTV Europe Awards in Stockholm before a worldwide TV audience of 1 billion.

December 2000 Films her role as The Green Fairy in

Moulin Rouge.

February 2001 Makes Pepsi commercial in Australia. Appears as a guest on *An Audience with Ricky Martin*, sharing a duet on his biggest hit, 'Livin' La Vida Loca'.

March 2001 The 'On A Night Like This' world tour opens in Glasgow. KM performs nineteen songs, opening with 'Loveboat' and closing with 'Spinning Around'.

April 2001 Launches her own brand of lingerie, 'Love Kylie x'. Performs a record nine sellout nights at the Sydney Entertainment Centre. Ticket sales in Australia alone net $8 million.

August 2001 Stars at the V2001 Festival in Weston Park, Staffordshire and Chelmsford, Essex. At the latter she performs twelve numbers to an audience that had been drenched in the rain. An Australian album called *Corroboration* features a duet between KM and Aussie folk singer Jimmy Little. The song, 'Bury Me Deep In Love', had been the background music in *Neighbours* when Charlene's mother Madge married Harold Bishop.

September 2001 'Can't Get You Our Of My Head' races to the top of the Australian charts, displacing 'Bob the Builder'. Her seventh No. 1 in her home country, it sells 140,000 copies in its first week of release. A week later it becomes her sixth UK No. 1, selling 77,000 copies on its first day on sale. KM sells more records (306,000) than the rest of the Top 10 combined, including Victoria Beckham, who languishes at No. 6. Makes her first British TV advertisement as the face of Eurostar. She is seen catching a train from London to Paris. Wins *GQ* magazine's Services to Mankind Award.

October 2001 *An Audience with Kylie Minogue* is broadcast in the UK. Kermit the Frog and Adam Garcia appear as guest stars; Brendan, Dannii and Pete Waterman are in the 'audience'. 'Can't Get You Out Of My Head' stays as the UK No. 1 for four weeks, keeping Michael Jackson's long awaited 'You Rock My World' off the top spot. Tickets for her 2002 British tour sell out in one hour. Sings the theme tune for the new TV soap *Night and Day*. Named Best Female Solo Artist at the Australian Record Industry Awards, the Arias.

November 2001 Wins a Bambi, Germany's top pop award, for Best Comeback of the Year. A pair of her knickers raises £4,000 as part of a fashion package auctioned in aid of BBC *Children In Need*. Kylie tops the list of 100 greatest Welsh women. *Fever*, Kylie's second Parlophone album, reaches No. 1 in the UK album charts.

December 2001 Wins two of the inaugural *Top of the Pops* awards for Best Single and Best Tour. 'Can't Get You Out Of My Head' is placed third in the Record of the Year contest on UK TV; the winner is S Club 7's 'Don't Stop Moving'. Her advertisement for underwear firm Agent Provocateur is considered too sexy for a TV audience.

February 2002 'Can't Get You Out Of My Head' tops the US dance charts and enters the *Billboard* Top 100. Appears on the *Tonight Show with Jay Leno* as part of US publicity campaign. *Fever* released in the USA. 'In Your Eyes' enters UK chart at No. 3. Wins two Brit awards for Best International Album and Best International Female.

March 2002 *Fever* debuts on US chart at No. 3, selling 107,000 copies in first week. It is her highest ever album position in the US. Crowned Bestselling Australian Artist at the World Music Awards in Monaco. She performs at the ceremony wearing a short red dress by Dolce & Gabbana and thigh-high black boots. Allegedly, Prince Albert of Monaco gropes her bottom.

April 2002 Kylie begins her most ambitious world tour to date at the Cardiff Arena. Twenty-five UK dates would be followed by a further thirteen in Europe leading up to twelve in August in Australia. William Baker and Kylie devised a show borrowing style from *Dr Who*, *Star Trek*, David Bowie's *Diamond Dogs*. Photos of Kylie in a white boiler suit and black bowler hat also revealed a link to the notorious film *A Clockwork Orange*. Kylie's break-up from James Gooding becomes public.

July 2002 Madame Tussaud's unveils Kylie waxwork

which forms centre point of new interactive exhibition. Kylie is on all fours and breathes seductively 'I Can't Get You Out Of My Head' at passers-by. Visitors ignore the 'Do Not Touch' sign. Her DVD/video 'Live In Sydney' is banned in Malaysia where authorities consider it too hot. She cancels US tour claiming she wants to devote more time to private life. She admits to having 'faint' cellulite.

October 2002 The awards keep coming...Kylie is named Woman of the Year at *Elle* style awards. She is also second in a VH1 poll of the 100 most important women in music history. She is named 29th most powerful person in the music industry – for once ahead of Madonna. She is nominated for four MTV Europe music awards and six Arias. Travels with mother Carol to a remote retreat in Western Australia for complete rest following reported breakdown. Kylie attends Paris Motor Show as the face of Ford Streetka and is paid £350,000 for a five minute appearance. She signs a special pedal car version for the Great Ormond Street Children's Hospital in London.

Feb 2003 Steals the headlines at the Brit Awards when Justin Timberlake grabs the Minogue bottom during their duet of the Blondie classic 'Rapture'. Launches her *Love Kylie* lingerie range in the UK. Meets actor Olivier Martinez in a hotel lobby after the Grammy Awards.

March 2003 James Gooding claims in the Sunday

newspapers that Kylie had ruined his life, complaining that the public never saw the 'real' Kylie. He admits cheating on Kylie and also reveals they enjoyed wild sex in a tent.

May 2003 The rumours are true. Kylie holds the hand of her new boyfriend Olivier Martinez, as they arrive at the Laureus World Sports Awards in Monaco. Their dramatic entrance was enhanced by Kylie's fireball red outfit and Olivier dressed head to toe in black.

November 2003 Achieves her seventh No. 1 in UK singles chart with the very sensual 'Slow', accompanied by sexy video of Kylie writhing on a towel. Album *Body Language* peaks at No. 6.

January 2004 At the age of thirty-five Kylie is placed first in *heat* magazine's sexiest bodies list. She beats Beyoncé into second.

July 2004 Earns £200,000 for a half hour set at the pre-wedding banquet in Paris of billionaire's daughter Vanisha Mittal and Amit Bhatia. Serenades couple with 'Slow' and 'Spinning Around'.

October 2004 Tickets for 'Showgirl' tour sell out in two hours. Takes to the floor at a charity ball in London with Jake Shears of Scissor Sisters. Jake wears gold pants – Kylie is in jeans.

November 2004 Guest stars in an episode of the cult

Australian comedy, *Kath and Kim,* as a character called Epponnee Rae. She wears a bridal outfit as part of a spoof of her famous *Neighbours* wedding. *Ultimate Kylie,* a new greatest hits package, reaches No. 4 in the UK album chart.

March 2005 £5 million 'Showgirl' world tour begins in Glasgow with six costume changes. Most of the attention is focused on her handmade corset reducing her waist to an eye-watering sixteen inches. 'Giving You Up', second single from *Ultimate Kylie* reaches No. 6 in UK – her last single release to date.

April 2005 Splits with Creative Director William Baker but maintains they are still the best of friends. All three experts in *heat* magazine's 'Surgery Spy' column conclude that Kylie has had cosmetic surgery. The *heat* verdict is 'Yes': 'With fuller lips, a new nose and no lines, seems Kylie can't get the surgeon's scalpel out of her head.'

May 2005 Cancels the rest of her 'Showgirl' tour after being diagnosed with breast cancer while staying at her parents' home in Melbourne. Kylie says, 'Hopefully all will work out and I'll be back with you all soon.' Undergoes surgery in which a tumour is removed from her left breast in a partial mastectomy.

July 2005 Begins chemotherapy in Paris because she 'wants a life' with Olivier. Mother Carol accompanies her. Her weight will drop to six stone during the treatment.

December 2005 Final chemotherapy session in Paris is followed by anxious wait to see if the cancer has gone into remission. Faces six months further radiation treatment and decides to receive that back in Australia when she is well enough to travel.

March 2006 Wearing a floor length bright blue silk dress and a garland of white flowers, Kylie visits a Sri Lankan theatre troupe formed in the aftermath of the terrifying Tsunami which devastated the region. She is pictured waving and smiling on top of an elephant.

April 2006 The first pictures of Kylie after the all-clear appear on her web site. They were taken by Olivier in Portofino and reveal that her hair is growing back and that she is relaxed and happy.

July 2006 Sits in front row at Karl Lagerfeld's Chanel show in Paris. Full of sparkle and smiles while being interviewed by Cat Deeley for Sky television. Describes her cancer ordeal in full, revealing there were times when she could not bear to look in the mirror, and says 'It's no picnic.'

August 2006 Starts gruelling rehearsals for resuming tour in November in Australia. Confirmed as the headline act for the Sunday night of Glastonbury 2007.

PART ONE

HAPPY ACCIDENTS

1

Dannii's Big Sister

Kylie Minogue wearily picked up another pile of fan mail and spread it out on the kitchen table. Mostly it would be requests for photographs so she would select one, write the person's name at the top and underneath sign it, 'Love Dannii'. Her little sister was a big star and received so much mail that Kylie was drafted in to forge her signature. She did hundreds every week. One day she might be doing it for real but, for the moment, she was just an ordinary schoolgirl in the neighbourhood.

Casting off the shackles of suburbia would be a long drawn-out process for Kylie. She was born in the Bethlehem Hospital in Melbourne on 28 May 1968 on a cool winter day. That's a cool day by Australian standards – at fifty-four degrees it would almost be summer in the UK. Rather aptly, considering her future persona as a woman-child, the UK number one single was the haunting 'Young Girl' by Gary Puckett and the Union Gap. They would be replaced after a few weeks by The Rolling Stones with 'Jumpin' Jack Flash', the number with which they opened their most recent British tour in August 2006. The Stones are probably the only pop act that Kylie will fail to match in the longevity stakes. Kylie's parents, Ron and Carol, were always great fans of The Stones and The Beatles but, to a large extent, the swinging sixties had passed them by in suburban Melbourne. They had moved down from Townsville in Queensland, where Ron had grown up a fifth generation Australian, and to where Carol and her parents had moved from Wales.

Carol Jones was from Maesteg, a small town not far from Swansea in South Wales, and lived there until she was ten. This was 1955 and a long time before air travel shrunk the world. When her parents, Dennis and Millie Jones, decided to uproot their family for a new life in Australia, it was a momentous decision. They had a vision of something better for their four children than the gloom and austerity of post war Britain.

The family of six quickly became a family of eight when Millie had two more sons and they all settled down to an idyllic life in Melbourne before eventually moving north to Townsville where Carol spent her teenage years. It's easy to see where Kylie's very distinctive looks came from. The fashions may have changed but Carol and Kylie could almost be twin sisters. They are exactly the same height and a similar slender shape, as well as sharing the well-scrubbed look of the girl-next-door which would be Kylie's passport to public affection. The teenage Carol, however, was a shy girl who was a talented young ballet dancer but never wanted to pursue it professionally.

Carol's ambitions began and ended with the Townsville Theatre Royal where she won many of the local dancing competitions. She recalled, 'I was a bit quiet. I never really had the drive to go any further. I danced until I was eighteen or nineteen but then I lost interest. I think dancing is a hard life but I loved it while I was doing it.' Part of her lack of ambition was due to falling in love with Ron Minogue, a young trainee accountant. After they married they moved to Melbourne where the now qualified Ron set about looking for a job.

Ron Minogue has always enjoyed a reputation for being a very level-headed, both feet on the ground sort of man. He has coped with his mercurial offspring in a very capable manner, making sure right from the start that they would use their money wisely. Not much gets under his skin, although he did get cranky at Kylie's annoying childhood habit of raising the inflection at the end of a sentence. It is a common trait among Australians, particularly women, to rise to a higher pitch when speaking, so that everything sounds like a question. Ron understood that it would not aid his daughter's acting career to have a pronounced 'Strine Twang', as it is called.

By the time she was twenty-five, Carol Minogue was a full time housewife and mother to three children. Kylie was two when her brother Brendan was born to be followed a year later by the irrepressible Danielle. Kylie is officially half Welsh, which more than qualified her for an entry in the book *One Hundred Great Welsh Women*. She was placed at number one. While she will always be a Melbourne girl at heart, Kylie has been mindful of her strong Welsh roots. Her great uncle, Dennis Riddiford, still lives near Maesteg but tries to be discreet about his family association, mainly to stop kids singing 'I Should Be So Lucky' outside his front gate. Dennis actually emigrated to Australia at the same time as his sister Millie but disappointingly, could not stay in the hot climate after he contracted a bad bout of malaria.

The Minogue family moved around various suburbs of Melbourne in the 1970s which was a little unsettling for the children trying to make new friends at different schools. One of Kylie's primary schools, Studfield Primary in Wantirna South, closed a couple of years ago despite a campaign by local parents, who contacted Kylie's management in London to ask for her support. Unfortunately Kylie was unable to help because she was recording at the time.

Kylie enjoyed her early school days, even though being so small meant she rarely spoke up in class. Despite this early reticence the image of Kylie as a shy little flower is well wide of the mark. Just ask Carol, who revealed that her eldest daughter was a bit of a poser even when she was a tiny girl. Kylie actually thought she was a shy kid until her mother put her right. At this early stage of her life Kylie was not dreaming of being a superstar. Her chief ambition was to get a car like Fred Flintstone, one with her feet poking out the bottom.

The family eventually settled in the Camberwell district of the Melbourne suburb of Canterbury, handy for Ron's new job in the finance department of the local council. Named after Viscount Canterbury, a nineteenth century Governor of Victoria, the suburb lies about six miles (ten kilometres) east of the city and is staunchly middle class, with spacious houses and plenty of green areas. The easiest way of getting into the city is by tram, a half hour journey from Camberwell Station.

The Melbourne suburbs were a relaxed and easygoing environment in which to grow up. The most upsetting thing that happened to Kylie in her early days was when her pet terrapin ate the family goldfish. She also had

Gabby, a large black 'Bitsa' dog (bitsa this, bitsa that), which she missed terribly when she came to London. At Camberwell Primary School she developed her first crush on a boy called Grant. Kylie was all of a dither when they were seated next to each other for a spelling test. 'I was terribly excited,' she later recalled. 'I was a bit confused about spelling bicycle so Grant and I cheated together – the start of a blossoming romance.'

Kylie was a natural performer from an early age. Normally one might take such precociousness with a pinch of salt. It sounds good to think of Kylie and younger sister Dannii, as Danielle was called, as suburban Shirley Temples spurring each other on to even more glorious heights of cuteness. When Kylie was still in pigtails her mother Carol took her to a small annual festival of music and art at a country town called Dandenong, just outside Melbourne. It was a showcase for serious local talent but, as a diversion, there was a piano competition for talented tots. Kylie bounced on stage, played 'Run, Rabbit, Run' and carried off second prize. She gave the judges one of her perkiest smiles and they were completely charmed by her, even though her feet barely reached the pedals and her hands certainly could not spread to an octave.

Even though Dannii was three years younger than Kylie, she was, if anything, even more precocious than her big sister. They had singing and dancing lessons and learnt to play the piano. Both girls have always been at pains to point out that Carol was never a Hollywood-style pushy mother. Carol herself confirmed, 'I was never very keen on them taking up dancing because I knew how hard it was. But when they started I didn't try and stop them because I had to let them do what they felt was right.

'I wanted them to learn the piano because I think the piano is something that you have for life. As for singing, I can't sing a note. I couldn't even sing in church.'

The earliest audience for the all-singing, all-dancing Minogue sisters were grandparents Dennis and Millie who would babysit whenever their parents went out for the evening. They would be treated to impromptu performances of the girls' favourite songs of the time. Usually the choice would be Abba. The Swedish group were massively popular in Australia and *Abba: The Movie* was set against a backdrop of an Australian tour. Kylie admitted, 'I wanted to be Agnetha, the blonde one, when I grew up. We'd put on dresses and dance to Abba records in the lounge, singing into hairbrushes.'

Kylie's other great favourite was the singer Olivia Newton-John. Like a million other girls she dreamt of being Sandy from the film *Grease* singing 'You're The One That I Want' to John Travolta. She later confided that she loved the scene where the prim and proper Sandy is transformed into a leather-clad rock chick, a piece of fiction that would later strangely mirror Kylie's real life. She too dramatically changed her image from the virginal girl-next-door on the arm of Jason Donovan to raunchy babe on the arm of rock star Michael Hutchence. Kylie actually fulfilled that childhood fantasy.

As a young teenager Kylie was quite a homey sort of schoolgirl, much preferring sewing and needlework to netball. Melbourne is often considered to be the sporting capital of Australia and Camberwell High was geared towards sport which did not interest Kylie one bit. She always hated 'games' because her 'little legs could not go fast enough'. At least the school had a progressive music department where Kylie flirted briefly with the violin before resuming the piano.

Dannii was always the more exuberant of the sisters, a characteristic easily misconstrued as being cocky. Another popular Minogue misconception is that the two are, and always have been bitter rivals and do not get on. Admittedly, their rivalry is what drives them on, particularly in their early years when they tried to match each other's success. Poor Dannii seems eternally to be half a step behind but it was not always so. Until Kylie joined the cast of *Neighbours* at the age of seventeen, Dannii was by far the more famous of the two. And Kylie owed her start in showbusiness to her younger sister. Thanks to family connections – Aunt Suzette was an actress – Dannii was asked to audition for a large independent production company, Crawford's, and, in order to keep the peace, their mother decided to take Kylie along as well. They both did their best but Dannii was too young for the part they had in mind, so they cast ten-year-old Kylie.

The show was *The Sullivans*, a popular if dire soap of the seventies set in World War Two. Kylie played Carla, a Dutch orphan girl, who befriended a group of Australian troops. Mercifully she was killed off after a few episodes. That did not stop *The Sullivans* being rerun in the late eighties, purely so that a devoted audience could witness Kylie's television debut. All she could recall of her first audition was that she had to try and speak in a Dutch accent. 'I wasn't very good at it', she said. Most of the fun of *The Sullivans* is in trying to spot a famous face of the future. Other than Kylie, both Mel Gibson and Sam Neill cut their acting teeth on the show.

Carol Minogue had to soothe Dannii's disappointment

but her chance came later when, in the same series, they needed a Kylie lookalike to play the part of Carla in a soldier's dream sequence. After *The Sullivans*, Kylie landed another inconsequential part in a show called *Skyways*, set in and around an airport. It was one of those wonderfully naff shoestring dramas. 'We have a plane crash', recalled Kylie. 'You can see the tissue paper on the model plane as they're rocking it. In one scene another character asks me something and you can see that I have absolutely no idea what I'm supposed to do.' The role only required a few weeks' work but did allow for a key event in Kylie's young life – on set she met for the first time a goofy child called Jason Donovan. They played brother and sister, but all Kylie remembers is that he was 'really chubby with a bowl haircut.'

Perhaps unsurprisingly, *The Sullivans* and *Skyways* did not lead to Kylie becoming the most popular child actress in the land. She started senior school at Camberwell High where, much to her disgust, she had to wear a bottle green uniform and watch in awe as her sister became one of the most famous children in Australia. Dannii was the number one star of *Young Talent Time*, a hugely popular light entertainment show. It was a much bigger show in Australia than *Neighbours* ever was, and cynical pop fans in the UK have no idea what a big star Dannii was at the time. One of the girls who danced on the show observed, 'Dannii was so popular. I can't believe Dannii has not made it as big as Kylie. She was always the favourite on *YTT*.'

Dannii was always chaperoned by her mother when the show went on the road. Carol was a permanent fixture in the audience, proudly watching her daughter perform and encouraging her to do her best – just as she continues to do for both of her daughters to this day. Dannii's star was shining so brightly that she even started her own clothing label, something which Kylie, a keen dressmaker, had always wanted to do. The Dannii label consisted of her name with two little love hearts above the 'i's. When she, too, became famous Kylie would often use a love heart next to her name. She now has her own range of products under the 'Love Kylie x' banner.

While Dannii basked in the fame of *YTT*, Kylie had to make the best of her mundane existence at school. She had no choice but her ambition was burning no less brightly. She could do nothing at this stage to match her sister's success. Instead, she became used to being introduced as Dannii's elder sister. She even started introducing herself as Kylie, sister of Dannii. An early boyfriend recalled, 'There was no hint of jealousy. The impression I got was that they were great mates and that she was quite enthused about it.' Kylie did manage some reflected glory when she appeared with Dannii on *Young Talent Time*. They sang 'Sisters Are Doing It For Themselves'. It was Kylie's only appearance on the show while Dannii was back for more the following week.

The most important quality Ron and Carol Minogue gave their children growing up was the opportunity to express themselves. From an early age Kylie was prepared to take a chance, particularly where her career was concerned.

'My sister was the famous one.'

2

One Night with Kylie

The tall, athletic schoolboy footballer was delighted when Kylie scribbled down her telephone number before giving him a little peck on the cheek goodnight. It had been a memorable party. It had been a memorable night. First they had kissed passionately, then she had told him her name was Kylie just before they had made love on a cold, concrete floor. And now the phone number. What a way for him to lose his virginity!

Kylie has always had a rebellious streak. She freely admits that she went through a wild stage as a teenager, smoking, drinking and giving her parents a tough time. A streak of defiance is a key ingredient of her survival. It goes a long way to explaining why she revelled in her relationship with Michael Hutchence, why she ditched Stock, Aitken and Waterman and why, throughout her astonishing career, she has continued to shock and surprise. When she found success, she admitted that she had had a 'really good upbringing' and that her parents, Ron and Carol, handled a recalcitrant girl with hormones flying in all directions in the way that most parents would have done: 'I used to think, I'm fourteen or fifteen and I'm old enough to do whatever I want. We used to have terrible fights. Nowadays, I can understand the things they did and I'd probably be the same if I had kids. I thought they were being incredibly unreasonable, and all my friends seemed to have so much more freedom.'

For the young Kylie, the two main places to meet boys were the local bowling alley and the swimming pool. Although she was hopeless at sports, Kylie proved more than a match for anyone at bowling, once winning a first prize of Aus $15 in a ladies' competition. 'I was pretty stoked', she recalled. She may hate sports but Kylie is expert at pursuits like bowling and pool, which are normally associated with bars and having a good old sociable time. One of her recent boyfriends, James Gooding, invited her bowling when he met her for the first time, little realizing that it was a quick and easy way to her heart.

At the pool Kylie met her first serious boyfriend, an older local boy called David Wood. A group of teenagers, including Kylie and her school friend Georgina Adamson, would hang around the pool where the boys would jump off the high board to try and look impressive. David thought Kylie was 'stunning' although quite reserved which meant it was difficult to break the ice. David had no idea that Kylie had fancied him for ages and failed to ask her out on a date when they eventually got chatting.

Fate, however, intervened when David was put on 'trash duty' for being a nuisance at the pool by 'bombing'. Kylie saw her opportunity and went round with him picking up the rubbish. It led to a first, very romantic kiss for which Kylie had practised diligently on the back of her hand. David, who is now a hairdresser, enjoyed a typical teenage on/off relationship with Kylie throughout her schooldays. He was a bit of a Jack the Lad, which led to several rows and bitter break-ups after he failed to pick her up when he said he would.

David has revealed a side to Kylie which she has kept hidden over the years. She is very emotional: 'She doesn't like to expose her emotions – but she can get mad', he recalled. That volatile side to Kylie's nature is one that future boyfriends have had to face and cope with.

Kylie grew up fast as a teenager. Many of the kids, especially the girls, at Camberwell High School were quite advanced for their age. At the age of sixteen Kylie used to work in a video store in Burke Road, Camberwell, on Saturday mornings to earn a few dollars to spend on clothes or, more often, the material to run up her own creations on the sewing machine at home. She had a real aptitude for dress-making and her interest in fashion stems from that time. She might well have made a successful career out of fashion if acting, and then singing, had not snared her first.

At weekends she would join friends for parties or a night out at the pubs they knew would serve underage drinkers. One in particular was a hundred metres from the police station in the Kew district of Melbourne and, on the occasions when the local constabulary popped in to check IDs, it was always amusing to see the number of girls who would have an urgent need to visit the toilets.

Unusually within her circle, the teenage Kylie was into funky, black music, like Donna Summer and especially Prince, her musical hero. Her favourite record, however, was 'Sexual Healing' by Marvin Gaye, one of the most erotic tracks of all time and perennially favourite background music for making love. Kylie clearly has always enjoyed sex. That was the strong impression she gave Paolo Marcolin on the unforgettable night when she became his first lover. She was also, at the age of sixteen years and two months, fully experienced in the ways of pleasing a man.

It was a cool August Friday night in the middle of an Australian winter and Paolo was in high spirits. Earlier he had played in the final match of the schools' football season in the state of Victoria. This was Australian Rules Football, a game that's best described as a combination of soccer and basketball. It can be very physical, although the participants do not wear all the padding and paraphernalia associated with gridiron. You have to be fit, and Paolo had the physique of a young man who took his sport seriously. His parents were first-generation immigrants from Italy and he had the advantage, as far as the young female population of Melbourne was concerned, of a traditional Latin look of dark hair and olive skin. Despite his obvious good looks, Paolo had spent his school years more interested in sport than girls and, as a result, was quite innocent for his age of just eighteen.

Everyone was on a high this particular evening because Marcellin College, his exclusive, Catholic private school in Melbourne's eastern suburbs, had won the match of the season against their arch rivals, Assumption College, and, as a result, were unofficial Victorian grammar school champions. Paolo, an attacking wingman, had played a blinding game, so was more than up for the celebrations planned for that night. It was party time. The venue for the festivities was the home of team-mate Damian Bonser, who lived just a few doors down from Paolo in the relatively new and up-and-coming district of Templestowe, about five miles from Kylie's house. By the time she arrived with a group of schoolfriends, the beer was well and truly flowing. As well as the victorious players, there were supporters and a number of parents. Paulo's mother even popped in for a while to toast his team's success.

Paolo settled himself in a chair in the lounge and was chatting to the boys, drinking beer and generally basking in the glory of their win, when he spotted a girl in an armchair across the other side of the room, surrounded by half a dozen eager boys. She was slender, with blonde curly hair and a winning smile. There were only a very few girls at the party, so she stood out and caught the attention of most of the boys there, especially Paolo: 'There was a lack of female options, so I bit the bullet and just wandered over to where she was and sat on the arm of the chair.' Paolo started listening to the conversation, hoping he would get the chance to say more than two words to the girl, when he was joined by another friend, Nick, who was one of the biggest and loudest guys in the team. Nick was also very inebriated and leaned on Paolo's left shoulder to hold himself upright: 'His weight started to push me down towards the girl,' recalled Paolo. 'I am basically a shy sort of person and not the sort who hits on women. I turned around and looked at her to almost apologize but, before I could say anything, we started kissing. It all happened so spontaneously.' The spark was instantaneous and obvious to the other suitors, who, disgruntled, moved away to try their luck elsewhere.

By this stage it was past 11 o'clock and the parental

presence was thinning out. Paolo was feeling self-conscious snogging the girl because his mates would make loud and gormless comments every time they walked past the chair. He suggested they went somewhere more private: 'She agreed without question, so we got up and went outside into the backyard where there was a fire going in an old drum. It wasn't that cold for an August night – perhaps about twelve degrees, but we kept each other warm by kissing and cuddling. There were a few people walking around, but it was quite dark and there wasn't as much comment as there had been in the living room.

'By this stage my hands were wandering a bit and we were getting even hotter by the fire. Out of the blue she said to me, "Do you want to go somewhere even more private?" Of course I agreed. It sounded great to me. We walked down the driveway of the house, around the front and up the other side. She had no idea where she was going, but eventually she took me to the opposite side of the house. There were a few people catching taxis, so we walked round the corner to be out of sight – or so I thought. We started kissing again and I remember that I actually told her my name at this point and she said she was called Kylie. Before that point I hadn't a clue who she was. The next thing I knew her hands had gone down and she had undone my fly, got the old fella out, and dropped to her knees. I thought it was pretty amazing for a sixteen-year-old.'

Paolo found himself in a state of bliss as Kylie went into action: 'She was fantastic and knew exactly what she was doing. I just shut my eyes and let her get on with it.' Alas, his ecstasy was short-lived when he opened his eyes and realized they were in full view of other party guests: 'I don't think they were watching Kylie in action but I'm sure a couple of them would have wondered what was going on in the dark. I felt very conspicuous and more than a little uneasy that we might be spotted.'

Fortunately, he spied a tiny door next to him, grabbed the door handle and was relieved when it opened, so that he could bundle Kylie inside, away from prying eyes. It was not exactly five-star luxury. The room appeared to be a small workshop underneath the front of the house. The first problem was that neither of them could find the light switch and it was very dark inside, with just a small window at the front letting in a chink of light. The young lovers didn't cared too much as passion got the better of them. Nor, remembers Paolo, did it matter to Kylie that he had no protection with him. He later discovered, when it came up in conversation, that she was not on the Pill.

That was in the future. For the moment it was important to take off as few clothes as possible because the dingy room was absolutely freezing. Fortunately, Kylie was wearing a skirt, which made things easier, although Paolo had to remove his jeans. They had sex first on the chair: 'I was on top but this wasn't very comfortable so I took hold of her again and we laid on the floor.' Paolo, ever the gentleman, took off his jacket and laid it on the ice-cold floor for Kylie to lie on, before they started again. 'It was freezing but I had enough alcohol in my veins for me not to notice. I was really enjoying myself because Kylie was so nice, but then we heard some voices sniggering outside the door.'

Suddenly passion died in a desperate flurry to get dressed. Too late: 'The door burst open just as Kylie was putting her panties back on and my mate Nick, the same one who had leaned on me in the lounge, walked in: 'He just said, "Oh *here* you are," but I was embarrassed. Fortunately, the darkness hid my red face and I just mumbled, 'Yeah, yeah.' But there was enough light showing through the open door for him to see exactly what we had been up to. Kylie was standing behind me, so I couldn't see whether she was as embarrassed as me. But she followed us outside.' If Paolo had been able properly to see his teenage temptress, he would have noticed how upset she was. He was soon in no doubt: 'All of a sudden she started crying. Real sobs. I just didn't know what to do, so I tried to reach out and reassure her but she just brushed me off. She was wailing: "You've just used me." I assured her that wasn't the case and asked for her phone number. That seemed to cheer her up a bit, because she stopped crying although she was still tearful.'

In his excitement and youthful pride at having had sex for the first time, Paolo let slip exactly what had happened when another team-mate came over to ask what was going on. 'I said, "Don't say anything but I just shagged her."' That was all the encouragement the friend needed to announce the fact at the top of his voice. Paolo was aghast: 'There was a balcony where everybody had gathered, and they all must have heard what my mate said. Kylie didn't appear to react, so perhaps she didn't realize what he had said.'

Back inside the house, Paolo found a pen and a scrap of paper so that Kylie could write down her name and phone number. Shortly afterwards, Kylie's friends shouted out that they were leaving and that she should go with them. She told Paolo that she had to go to work the next morning. Once more, his sporting mates were less than tactful. One asked if he was going to ask Kylie out – to which another blurted out, 'Don't worry, he's already been there.' Kylie must have heard, because she was standing right next to Paolo at the time. But, after a little goodnight kiss, she was gone and Paolo returned to drink beer and talk with his friends.

When he went in to school on the following Monday, Paolo discovered his exploits were still the talk of his set. He thought he had better find out a little more about Kylie. He learned that she went to Camberwell High School and that she was the sister of Dannii Minogue, whom everybody in Australia had heard of at the time because of her starring role in the TV series, *Young Talent Time.* He discreetly asked around and was pleased to discover that none of his friends, or even acquaintances, had enjoyed a sexual encounter with Kylie. Perhaps she was not what his friends would call an easy lay. Perhaps he was special.

Now that they had had sex, it was time to think about a first date. Playing it cool, Paolo waited until the middle of the week to call up. They chatted briefly and Kylie mentioned that she was a fan of Prince, so he asked her if she fancied going to see his movie *Purple Rain* at the Hoyts Midtown cinema the following weekend. He could not have come up with a more appealing idea, because Prince was Kylie's pop idol and she was dying to see his first film.

Kylie suggested he take the bus from Templestowe to Camberwell Junction and meet her there. They could then take the tram into the city. By Saturday, Paolo was full of anticipation at seeing his first lover for the second time. Kylie was clearly excited, too, because, as soon as she caught sight of him, she ran over and planted a big, exuberant kiss on his lips. They hopped on a tram and spent the thirty-minute journey talking non-stop all about themselves, as people always do on a first date. Kylie told him she had just been hired to appear in a new television series called *The Henderson Kids* and also confided that she helped Dannii reply to her fan mail. 'Kylie had a nice bubbly personality,' recalled Paolo. 'She was very easy to talk to and get along with.'

It was after they had got off the tram and were walking to the cinema that Paolo had his first misgivings. 'I suddenly noticed how tiny she was. I am close on six foot and she was literally a foot shorter than me. I felt very awkward and self-conscious. People have asked me what it was like and the only way I have been able to put it is that it was like taking out my little sister. She was sixteen, but I realized she looked much younger than that because of her size – even though she was so mature for her age in other ways.' Kylie, meanwhile, was happily unaware of her date's growing unease: 'She was saying things like, "I can't wait to introduce you to all my friends." She was being very chatty and I was listening, but at the same time I was thinking, "I'm not sure about this. Do I really want to be with this girl?"'

Paolo has no idea if Kylie was beginning to pick up on his negative vibes at this point, but he was becoming quieter and quieter. They went in to watch the movie together and, just like every other young couple, bought popcorn and enjoyed a little kiss and a cuddle before the film started. There was no groping in the back row! After the movie, they caught the tram back to Camberwell. By this time, Paolo had decided that he did not want to take things any further with Kylie, and set about trying to let her down gently. He used the old excuse that he would have far too much work to do in the coming months, as he had been neglecting his studies to play football, and he had his Year Twelve exams (the Australian equivalent of A-levels in the UK). 'I told her I would not have a great deal of time to socialize, which was actually true. I genuinely didn't have time for a girlfriend, even one as brilliant sexually as Kylie.'

Eventually, poor Kylie got the heavy hint and agreed that this would be their first and last serious date together. 'She had gone from a long-term relationship to a casual fling in half an hour.' The ability to make hard, even painful, decisions is one of Kylie's great strengths, one that has been important to her throughout her life and career. Perhaps this early teenage setback enabled her to identify when it is time to walk away with your dignity intact. Paolo will never know if Kylie was crestfallen or not, as she made the last leg of her journey home by herself from Camberwell Junction. He took a bus which conveniently passed The Harp pub in Kew where, through the window, he spotted some of his mates drinking. He got off at the next stop to go back and join them until it was chucking-out time.

And that was pretty much it, although he had mentioned that he had a ticket for her to a school social in a couple of weeks' time. It was a typical school disco, where the girls all talk to each other about boys and the lads all talk to each other about sport. Kylie turned up, Paolo gave her the ticket, but as soon as they went inside they split up and spent the evening with their respective friends. If Kylie was hurt by what had happened, she did not let on to him. He was pleased to see that she went home by herself and did not immediately go on to the next likely guy.

The Paolo saga puts to bed much of the myth of Kylie as an innocent girl-next-door. Her behaviour with him was hardly unusual for teenage girls in Melbourne at the time. Paolo himself observed, 'A lot of the girls we all knew at the time were sexually active. Kylie was mature sexually, but we knew of girls of thirteen and fourteen who were having sex with boyfriends. I am not saying they had multiple partners – just with their boyfriends.' Maybe Kylie saw Paolo as boyfriend material. If so, she was quickly disillusioned, because he was not ready for that. Instead, it was an enjoyable fling. And it exposes the lie that Kylie was 'corrupted' by sex Svengali Michael Hutchence, as has been portrayed time and time again. She may even have taught *him* a thing or two between the sheets. His ungallant and oft-reported boast that Kylie was the best f*** in the world does not seem quite so incredible. The other intriguing 'first' in the Templestowe knee-trembler was that it was the first time that Kylie took a risk in being discovered *in flagrante*. It would not be the last.

Paolo now prefers to be known as Paul. He still lives in Melbourne, where he is happily married with two children and has a successful career as a graphic designer, after a brief spell as a personal fitness trainer. He saw Kylie once more when he was twenty, and she was the star of *Neighbours*. He was driving home from university and saw her walking down the street before going into the video store she used to work in. He decided against stopping to catch up on old times: 'I don't have any regrets about breaking up with Kylie or missing out on being part of her career, because I just don't think it would have worked.'

'If you meet a boy, you know pretty soon if he's any good for you or not.'

3

The Henderson Kid

On her last day of school, Kylie joined two other girls on the
second floor of the main building where they found a hose,
turned the taps full on, and proceeded to drench everybody
walking below. When a teacher arrived to sort things out, Kylie
ducked and hid, while her two friends took the rap and were
expelled.

Hollywood-style breaks seldom happen in real life. It did
happen to Daniel Radcliffe when he sat next to the producer David Heyman at the cinema. Heyman was in the
middle of seeing literally hundreds of possible candidates
to play Harry Potter when he found Daniel in these
unlikely surroundings. Nothing like that ever happened to
Kylie Minogue. Like a million other aspiring actors, she had
to trudge around to auditions, hoping to catch the casting
director's eye. Even though she was still at school, she had
not forgotten her ambitions. Kylie was never put under any
pressure by Ron and Carol to go to auditions. It was entirely
her own motivation. On one occasion, she saw a newspaper
advertisement seeking young actors aged between eleven
and sixteen for a new television series. Auditions are poten-
tially soul-destroying but Kylie had an inner self-belief.

The Henderson Kids had a substantial budget for an Australian series at the time – Aus $3 million – and was going to be filmed on location in the countryside around Melbourne. If Kylie landed a role, it would mean time away from school. Now that she was sixteen, she did not need her mother, Carol, to hold her hand at an audition. Instead, she put on one of the dresses she had made at home, did her own make-up and presented herself for consideration to the producer Alan Hardy and the director Chris Langman.

Hardy could not believe that the girl auditioning was the same one who had appeared in *The Sullivans* four years earlier. Kylie may still have been small in stature but, in other ways, she was a mature girl for her age. Young actress Nadine Garner, who was fourteen at the time, and would become Kylie's co-star observed that Kylie was very aware of her femininity and was much worldlier than she: 'She had a great sense of herself. There was this determination and quiet ambition.'

Hardy and Langman decided to take a chance on Kylie. Both were impressed by her naturalness and thought she had the right personality for the part of Charlotte Kernow, one of nine roles that required young actors. Langman admitted that they cast her on a whim rather than on any more substantial consideration. They were concerned about her high-pitched voice and her tendency to lose her words somewhere in her teeth, but they hoped that a voice coach could sort that out. Kylie was more worried by the fact that she had to dye her hair a bright shade of red for the role. On the few occasions that she did pop into Camberwell High, she was greeted with general astonishment. She once told *Smash Hits* magazine: 'I went to school and my hair was bright red, especially in the sunlight because it had just been done, and, as you can imagine, bright red dye onto blonde hair was pretty shocking. I was so embarrassed. I had to tell everyone that I hadn't done it of my own free will.'

Kylie never felt comfortable as a redhead and could not wait to return to her natural dark blonde. It worried her so much that she even confessed to Paolo Marcolin that she was a 'little worried' about her new role because they wanted to dye her hair bright red. More importantly, however, she also told him that she saw *The Henderson Kids* as her 'big break'

The plot of *The Henderson Kids* was hardly *War and Peace*, but it did allow Kylie to improve her acting skills and she worked very hard on the clarity of her speech and her emotional range. She put an enormous amount of energy into her role, something which, even at this early stage of her career, took its toll physically. She would burst into tears if anyone shouted at her on set and Nadine Garner described her as 'fragile'.

Nadine played the lead role of Tamara Henderson who, with her brother Paul, was taken in by their uncle after their mother died in a car crash. Their uncle was a policeman in a country town and the twelve-part series followed their adventures. Kylie's character, known as Char, lived in the town and became Tamara's best friend. She wore bright orange pants, colourful shirts that clashed horribly and spent most of her time chewing pink bubblegum: 'I'm so sick of this stuff, but it's part of my character,' admitted Kylie, making an early concession to complete professionalism. That quality impressed her director, Langman: 'She was always prepared, always on time, always focused and

very much aware of her image and her look.' It is an observation of the 1984 vintage Kylie that could fittingly
describe her at any point in her career.

The Henderson Kids led directly to Kylie being able to do
something for the very first time – she had the confidence
to tell an interviewer not to describe her as Dannii's elder
sister. 'Call me Kylie', she said.

Also, for the first time in her life Kylie spent a night
away from home when the production went upstate for
some outdoor filming. She was given about Aus $10 a day
for meals. Kylie and her young co-stars were able to bond
and make friends. In particular, she and Nadine became
close when they discovered they both loved singing and
would sit around between scenes practising their har-
monies. They would listen to each other's records and try
and copy the tunes. They even proudly announced to the
rest of the cast that when they were older, 'We are going
to be great singers.' Alan Hardy would never forget his
on-set opinion that the two girls had great voices. In the
not too distant future that opinion would be of great benefit to Kylie. Nadine never pursued a singing career but
she has been one of Australia's most popular actresses for
the past twenty years, although little known outside her
home country.

After filming the first series, Kylie was determined not
to waste the opportunity. Coincidentally, Kylie's wild stage
of fighting with her parents, smoking because she
thought it made her look tough, and generally playing
the difficult teenager did not last past *The Henderson Kids*.
She became more focused about acting. Her school even
noted that she was 'sensible' about juggling acting and
studying. After *The Henderson Kids* she immediately starred

in a one-off episode of another Crawford's series, *The Zoo Family*. She played Yvonne, an abused child, who is given a temporary home by a zoo caretaker. The episode was entitled 'Yvonne the Terrible' which is exactly what the child was. She lived up to her name by letting all the animals out of their cages and generally wrecking the zoo. At the end of the episode, she had a Damascene moment when she saw a young roo, which had also been a battered infant, return to mother kanga. Kylie impressed everybody. She would soon be seventeen, but convincingly played a twelve-year-old. Kylie was proving to be as adaptable in her acting career as she would be later as a singer. Gwenda Price, her producer on *The Zoo Family*, was convinced that Kylie would be a 'stayer'.

Kylie learnt at an earlier age one of the most important lessons of show business – you are only as good as your last performance. So, after *The Zoo Family*, Kylie was back on the audition trail and this time she beat fifty rivals to the leading female role in a six-part mini series, *Fame and Misfortune*. Kylie had to play a scheming minx called Samantha, which she managed to do successfully, demonstrating that she was expanding her acting range. But, secretly, she still hankered after a career as a singer, an ambition sharpened by her energetic sister's continued exposure.

So strong was Kylie's desire to be a performer that she paid her own money – part of her fee from *The Henderson Kids* – to record two demos for the executives of *Young Talent Time*. She chose 'Dim All the Lights', a 1979 dance hit by Donna Summer and 'New Attitude' by Patti LaBelle, which featured on the *Beverly Hills Cop* soundtrack in 1984. The choices were quite removed from the

Abba and Olivia Newton-John music that the pre-teen Kylie had loved so much. Instead, they reflected an early interest in black disco which in many ways is derivative of much of the music the latter day Kylie is producing. Donna Summer was the brazen Queen of Disco whose UK number ones, 'I Feel Love' and 'Love to Love You Baby' were hardly girl-next-door songs. Coincidentally, Donna was to enjoy a career revival under the guidance of Stock, Aitken and Waterman who would be so instrumental in taking Kylie to the very top. The pop world is always a labyrinth of connections. Patti LaBelle had sung the original version of 'Lady Marmalade' in 1975. In 2001 it was a number-one hit for Christina Aguilera, Mya, Pink and Li'l Kim, whose version was recorded for the film *Moulin Rouge* which featured Kylie in a cameo role as The Green Fairy.

During this period of her career, Kylie's verve and drive were forever being underestimated by people who could not see past a little girl trying to overcome her shyness. Kylie had true grit. She certainly needed it when she was called in to a meeting with Alan Hardy who was putting *The Henderson Kids II* into production. He sat her down and gently explained that she was being dropped because her character Char was being written out of second series. Kylie was bitterly upset, of course, and went away to consider her options.

She was sixteen and ready to leave Camberwell High, having passed the obligatory Higher School Certificate in art and graphics. While away on location she had on-set teachers and had managed to pass a compulsory English exam. Kylie describes herself as being of average intelligence, much preferring the arts to sciences, which she loathed, almost as much as sport. At this stage she was seriously considering taking a secretarial course. The suburban side of Kylie was still drawn to what would have been a normal path for a young woman with her background – marriage, children and looking after house and home. Perhaps there was always a nagging feeling that her mother had somehow missed out on fulfilling her destiny which decided Kylie against this career path. Instead, she decided she would stick to acting for the moment and so followed the best course of action for a million wannabes – she signed on the dole.

Kylie has often said that much of her career was a 'happy accident'. One of her favourite observations about her success comes from her father who told her she was lucky she always skipped steps one to eight and went straight to numbers nine and ten. 'Miraculously I get away with it,' she confessed. It is a nice story but its flippancy masks the drive and ambition, and the hours of hard graft she has devoted to learning lines, practising dance steps until her feet are covered in blisters and plasters, and grappling with difficult melodies, so that her performances are never less than completely polished.

She may not have known it at the time but being killed off in *The Henderson Kids* was 'a happy accident' because her career might have been entirely different. Instead, she was free to go along to an audition for a part in a Melbourne-based soap opera. The casting director for *Neighbours,* Jan Russ, was one of Australia's most respected talent spotters. She remembered seeing Kylie in *The Zoo Family* and thought she was a possible for a new role that had just come up, a tomboy teenager called Charlene Mitchell.

Jan immediately thought Kylie had the right look and attitude for the part acknowledging that the petite teenager had a certain spark, an 'extra charisma' that lifted her above the competition. When she read for the character, Kylie was transformed from a shy girl into a 'wonderful presence'. Jan had no hesitation in recommending Kylie for the role despite competition from forty other girls because, she observed, 'The camera loved her.'

Alan Hardy has always enjoyed telling the story of how he made Kylie famous by killing her off in *The Henderson Kids II*. 'It turned out to be the best thing for her,' he acknowledged.

Neighbours was the brainchild of Reg Watson, head of drama for the Grundy Organisation and the man responsible for such kitsch classics as *Prisoner Cell Block H* and *The Young Doctors*. He had also launched the soap *Crossroads* on an unsuspecting British audience before he moved back to Australia, so he had early experience of wooden sets filled with wooden actors. *Neighbours* was a brilliant idea because it was such a simple one, a story of everyday families and their ordinary lives. Reg had a lot of trouble convincing his bosses that it was not as dull as it sounded: 'When I told them about it, eyebrows were raised and thumbs were turned down. They had doubt about a concept which was simply about communication between parents and their children.'

Neighbours, which was originally to be called *One Way Street*, first hit television screens on Channel Seven in March 1985 when Kylie was just finishing filming *The Henderson Kids*. It was very innocent and non-controversial and seemed ideal daytime fodder. Watson was trying to recreate the warm feeling of life in a Brisbane suburb, where he grew up: 'If you were at the beach when it started raining, your neighbour would dash out, take your washing off the line and fold it ready for your return.' Sad things would happen in Ramsay Street, Erinsborough, but very few bad things.

One common observation about Kylie's early life is that her upbringing in suburban Melbourne was very *Neighbours*-like. The Minogue family could have lived in Ramsay Street. That's only true up to a point. Yes, theirs was a household which was very normal on the outside, with pets and barbecues, chores and sibling squabbling and yet both Kylie and Dannii led extraordinary lives as children and, subsequently, teenage stars. Picture the scene at the breakfast table: over a bowl of cornflakes, or vegemite on toast, Ron Minogue inquires what his daughters are doing today before he sets off for a day's auditing of the housing department. The reply: 'We're going to be singing "Sisters Are Doing It For Themselves" on national television.' Show business became such a normal part of their lives that nobody seemed to realize how unusual it was to have two young daughters 'on the stage'. This was nothing like Ramsay Street.

Surprisingly, Channel Seven dropped *Neighbours* after just six months, but rival Channel Ten picked it up almost immediately and began airing it the following January, with a brief to Grundy that there should be a greater emphasis on younger characters. The target audience was teenage schoolgirls. That was the decision that would give Kylie her chance and would ultimately provide her with the fan base for musical stardom.

'I would have made a great secretary.'

4

Especially Jason

It was an innocent question. The blonde journalist was chatty and friendly and simply asked Kylie, over a bowl of pasta, if she had a boyfriend. Kylie 'confessed' that she had not had a boyfriend for more than two years, roughly the entire time she had been in *Neighbours*. She had conveniently forgotten that for the majority of that period she had been virtually shacked up with Jason Donovan.

When Kylie was young and impressionable she had a crush on a minor American singer called Leif Garrett. He was a child actor turned teenie heartthrob in the late 1970s who had one decent hit, the disco-lite 'I Was Made For Dancin'. Garrett was blond with perfect, shiny white teeth and a ghastly mullet. When Kylie met up with Jason again four years after meeting him on *Skyways* he was no longer a podgy kid. He was transformed into a blond heartthrob with perfect, shiny white teeth and a ghastly mullet. The attraction was inevitable.

Kylie made the first move. She enlisted the help of an old friend Greg Petherick, who had become friendly with the Minogue family when he worked as the floor manager on *Young Talent Time*. He was also one of the few people at this stage to have heard Kylie's original demo. Greg agreed to act as a go-between to find out if there was any spark of reciprocal interest. She was thrilled to discover there was indeed and, as a thank you for his help, later gave Greg a photograph of herself and her new man Jason on the set of *Neighbours*. She had handwritten a little message and embellished it with love hearts.

Jason had joined *Neighbours* just before Kylie. He played Scott Robinson, the youngest son of Jim Robinson. The character had been in the show from the start, but played by another actor. When *Neighbours* changed from Channel Seven to Channel Ten, it was decided that Scott would change, too. Enter Jason. Like Kylie, he had been a child actor but he came from more of a show business background. His father is the well-known Australian actor Terry Donovan, who would later play builder Doug Willis in *Neighbours*, and his mother, Sue McIntyre, was a glamorous television newsreader and actress. His parents divorced when he was five and, as a teenager, Jason always remained closer to his father, geographically as well as emotionally. Jason lived at the bottom of Terry's garden in a one-room bungalow, a teenage grunge paradise where he could strum guitar and dream of being Michael Hutchence. Kylie loved hanging out at Jason's place, not having to bother to wear make-up or smart clothes, just being able to relax, away from the pressure of being a celebrity. It is the lifestyle she still favours today and, when not on show, Kylie is barely recognizable as a singing superstar. She is certainly not a fashion icon when she pops out to buy a loaf of bread or have a cappuccino with her friends.

Gradually, the camera picked up the chemistry

between Jason and Kylie. Her character, Charlene, was originally booked for a thirteen-week run but this was quickly extended when the programme's bosses realized that the couple represented a marketing gold mine. The romance between Scott and Charlene 'made' the show. The programme's creator Reg Watson was never in any doubt that Scott and Charlene would be a big success with the viewers.

Jason observed, 'There was just a feeling between us that probably happens once in a million times.' Their first screen kiss was front-page news not just in Australia but also in the UK, where *Neighbours* first went on air in October 1986. It became a phenomenon of British television when artful schedulers decided to show it twice a day. Mothers watched the lunchtime episode while it was nice and peaceful at home, and then the kids would switch on the early evening repeat when they arrived back from school. Kylie and Jason did not appear on British screens until the following summer, but soon were just as popular in the UK as in Australia. They were described as Britain's most idolized teenagers, loved by both young and old.

Meanwhile, the pair had made a decision back home in Melbourne which would have an enormous effect on their future together. They had agreed to a demand from *Neighbours'* bosses to keep their off-screen relationship absolutely secret. Brian Walsh, the Promotions Manager for Channel Ten, warned them that if their romance became public knowledge it would ruin the show, and their own popularity. The view was that, while the audience loved the fictional love affair between Charlene and

Scott, they might not be able to handle Kylie and Jason arguing in the supermarket over which brand of cereal to buy. Kylie's decision was almost Faustian in the way it coloured her future life. She was putting her career before her private relationship. She has continued on the same path ever since. She has never abandoned her working commitments for love. She did not do it even for Michael Hutchence, one of the greatest loves of her life. And she has continued to keep parts of her life secret from her adoring fans. This air of mystery remains part of her appeal. Later, in a fairly candid interview after her duet with Jason, 'Especially For You', had been the first number one of 1989, Kylie said, 'Everyone believes we are [together] and I suppose it's quite obvious but no one can be 100 per cent sure, can they? If they knew all about us, where we slept, what we did together, and so on, wouldn't it spoil the mystery?'

Kylie is not the first, and certainly will not be the last star to manipulate the facts to suit the image that, at any given moment, she wants to convey. It literally happens all the time. The commonest 'lie' is the old Hollywood chestnut that promotes a leading man as the world's greatest heterosexual when he is, in fact, gay. To a lesser extent, it also applies to women. At least one female superstar has it written into her contract that she cannot reveal her true sexuality. It might well ruin her image. Obviously, Kylie is not gay, far from it, but the principle of cheating the public, in order to promote a carefully conceived image, remains the same. The character of Charlene Mitchell was a curiously asexual girl-next-door, far too nice to be getting steamy over the cocoa every night.

With their secret safe, the public continued to lap up

the romance between Charlene and Scott. In one memorable episode, Charlene was going to 'give' herself to Scott in a hotel room. Everything was going well, until Scott found out that Lenny, as she was popularly known, was not a virgin. He stormed out leaving her crying on the bed. For that, he received a much applauded punch on the jaw. The PR people never missed a trick and a story promptly appeared in the media that Kylie was now known on the set as 'Bruiser' because she had laid Jason out with one punch. A more likely scenario would have been that, had she connected, Kylie would have suffered a broken hand.

And then there was *the* wedding in July 1987. It was episode number 523. Charlene had been unable to persuade her mother to give the seal of approval to her living in sin with Scott, so had decided to marry him. Scott had rolled up on his skateboard, still wearing his school uniform, and proposed. Jason said, 'It was a really nice natural scene. I didn't feel stupid at all. Sometimes you look at a script and you think, "Oh God! I've got to tell her she's the most gorgeous person in the world and that I can't live without her and here I am on this stupid skateboard trying to drag her out from underneath an oily car engine."'

Kylie and Jason were mobbed at a shopping mall in Sydney while they were filming the wedding reception scenes. Somehow, 4,000 fans found out where it was taking place and some ended up in hospital as a result of the mêlée. Unsurprisingly, the following day, the newspapers were full of reports of a 'riot'. Kylie complained that the wedding scene itself was very tiring, and that she had to walk up the aisle some twenty times before everyone was happy – ironically, despite much speculation over the years, she has never been close to being a bride in real life. Once again, the public confused fact and fiction, and Kylie found people coming up to her in the street, congratulating her on her 'marriage'.

That wedding remains one of the most popular moments in the history of soap, and the pinnacle of Kylie's acting career – so far. Charlene and Scott were the most popular couple in Australia, regularly appearing on the cover of *TV Week*. Even the Australian edition of *Time* magazine was caught up in the hype. They featured Charlene and Scott on the front cover inside a pink heart, with the headline, 'Aussie Soaps Capture The World'. *Time* was trying to make sense of the cult of niceness, in which *Neighbours* played a leading role. It was, the magazine argued, soap as 'social engineering', an antidote to modern melodrama. The characters were the embodiment of comfy armchairs – the unbearable niceness of being.

In an interview Jason Donovan acknowledged, 'A lot of people get us muddled up with Charlene and Scott, but we're really quite different.' Kylie was not Charlene Mitchell at all. She was not a bit like her. But when the cameras rolled she was transformed into the tomboy who left school to become a car mechanic, and seemed to spend most of her life in a pair of unflattering overalls that completely disguised the fact that there was a future sex symbol underneath. Lenny was a spitfire with a machine-gun tongue, which she would unleash should any man try to patronise her by calling her 'love' or, even worse, 'babe'. As we know from Kylie herself, her lack of height may have been a disadvantage on the sports field, but it was a definite plus when it came to playing young, spunky types.

As always, Kylie was determined to extract every last drop of opportunity from her five days a week exposure in a popular soap. The big advantage the young stars of *Neighbours* had over other familiar television faces was that promoting them was part of the public strategy to force the programme into the consciousness of the nation's youngsters. As a result, Kylie was out in the community right from the start, with personal appearances at shopping malls and youth centres. It is a tactic well-tried and tested in the pop world as a means of raising public awareness. Kylie was determined to get what she could get out of *Neighbours* and was always the complete professional, even when her singing career took off. One of the show's directors, Andrew Friedman, told author Dino Scatena, 'Even at the height of her career with the music and the publicity, she was always there; always early, always keen and always willing to learn. She was always aware of her work.'

Kylie as the complete professional is a recurring theme, but it would be wrong to say that she was naïve enough to think of *Neighbours* as great art. Former pop columnist Peter Holt remembered Kylie telling him that she could not wait to get out of the series and move to London. She revealed: 'It opened the showbiz door for me, but I can't wait to get out of it as soon as possible. I never liked soaps whether home-produced or imported and, to be honest, in spite of its success *Neighbours* is a bit rough. It's only the story of three families but everything happens to them! It's all rather implausible and sometimes I have to grit my teeth when I film an unlikely situation. I shudder at the speed it is turned out day after day. The writers are still working on the script when we start filming.

'Of course I am not complaining. *Neighbours* has been marvellous for me. I am just amazed that so many people are attracted to it. The trouble is that it gives a completely distorted view of normal life in Australia.'

Those are hardly the words of a woolly-headed pop poppet. Kylie was completely focused during her time with *Neighbours* and, not for the last time, she demonstrated a willingness to push her body to the limit of its fragile capabilities. As any actor in soap will testify, it is always a punishing schedule. Her alarm clock would sound an unwelcome hurrah at 5.30am, a quick shower, breakfast on the run, make-up at 6.30am, rehearsals at 7.30am, a fifteen minute run through, twenty minutes of filming and all that for one minute of the show. It would be an exhausting schedule for an Olympic athlete. And then there was publicity and the recording career she was so desperate to progress.

Jason was certainly right about the differences between his screen character and real life because when he and Kylie returned home, tired after a day's filming, he would abandon his clean-living, surfer-boy image and pretend he was a rock star. In the future he would extol the virtues of cannabis, declaring he would rather walk into a room full of dope smokers than one filled with alcoholics: 'It just puts a smile on your face at the end of the day.'

Some observers believe that the issue of drugs became a divisive element in the relationship between Kylie and Jason. That did not appear to be the case between Kylie and Michael Hutchence, a much more serious drug user, a few years later. It was not, however, the most destructive element for Kylie and Jason. The amount of time they spent apart pursuing their own ambitions was much more critical. As Jason would observe, 'I found it really hard to deal with her fame at the time. I was extremely jealous of Kylie.'

A curious interview with Kylie appeared in *TV Week* in October 1988, in which she admitted how much she missed Jason when she was away from him. She also confessed that she did not live at home all the time. Nobody told Jason about the interview, which seemed very indiscreet of Kylie, so when he appeared on television three days later to plug a record, and denied any relationship with Kylie, he was made to look a complete idiot. Kylie's team denied that she had ever given the interview, in order not to destroy the myth about her and Jason. But, if she did say it, what a sad admission of how she really felt. It certainly did not sit comfortably on the shelf next to the souvenir magazine from the same year, *Kylie and Jason: Just Good Friends.* Within a year, she and Jason had drifted apart. Perhaps the killer punch was when Jason declared that he had not yet experienced true love and was still looking.

For a while, they were happy.

'Jason and I lived in each other's pockets.'

5

Locomotion

The crowd was ecstatic. Someone on stage said 'Let's do another one' and stepping into the limelight was the most popular actress on TV, Kylie Minogue aka Charlene Mitchell. The band knew how to play it, she knew all the words and she could really hold a tune. It was the first time an audience heard Kylie sing 'The Loco-Motion' but within a year it would be the biggest selling Australian single of the decade.

One of Charlene's early story-lines in *Neighbours* involved Scott and Mike, played by future Hollywood star Guy Pearce – getting together to form a band and make a demo. They ask Lenny to sing backing vocals. And with the delicious irony of art imitating life, they play the demo for a record company boss who thinks the boys are rubbish but loves Lenny's singing.

In August 1986, five months after Kylie had joined the cast, she was approached by Alan Hardy, who had remembered her passion for singing on location with *The Henderson Kids*. He was organising a special fund raiser for his favourite Australian football team, Fitzroy, at the Dallas Brooks Hall in Melbourne. He was delighted that she was enthusiastic, not knowing that she had already been preparing for just such an opportunity with secret musical sessions organised by Greg Petherick.

Several of the cast shared Kylie's dreams of musical stardom. Jason, of course, as well as Guy Pearce and Craig McLachlan. In that rather macho Aussie way, the guys decided to form Ramsay Street's answer to INXS. They thought it might be fun to invite some of the girls along for decoration and occasional vocals, which is how Kylie became involved. They had absolutely no idea that Kylie would soon leave them in the starting blocks while she ran the whole 100 metres.

There already was a *Neighbours* band of older actors, who would enjoy a 'jam session' once a week after filming had finished on a Thursday. They were Peter O'Brien (Shane Ramsay), Alan Dale (Jim Robinson) and Paul Keane (Des Clarke). Greg Petherick was the Mr Fixit who would book a downtown rehearsal room for the boys to use. He invited Kylie and Jason down to join them. Kylie sat quietly, watching, taking everything in, playing a little tambourine while Jason sang, strummed guitar and did his impersonation of Michael Hutchence. 'It was interesting, to say the least' said Greg. Jason, however, soon got bored. Not so Kylie, who started to sing along a little. Then one week she asked Greg if he could find a song specifically for her to sing with the band. He rummaged around in his record collection and produced 'The Locomotion', performed by Little Eva (the stage name of a young black singer from Bellhaven, North Carolina, called Eva Boyd), a bit of a one-hit-wonder. The song was a product of the great songwriting team of Carole King and Gerry Goffin and had been a huge hit in 1962. Kylie loved it instantly. Every week she would practise and everyone agreed it was a show-stopper.

For the fundraiser, Alan Hardy asked Kylie to perform the Sonny and Cher classic 'I Got You Babe' with another local actor called John Waters. On the night, he recalled, Kylie was very nervous about performing. But one of the outstanding qualities Kylie possesses is the determination to overcome any nerves to give a great performance – the true art of being a star. She was a sensation and when she sang 'The Loco-Motion' she was the star of the show.

The benefit show displayed all the hallmarks of another 'happy accident' for Kylie – a lucky break. There is a famous saying in golf: 'the more I practise, the luckier I get.' There was nothing accidental about Kylie's polished on-stage performance. She had worked to get it right. Now was not the time to step back and admire her efforts. It was a good start but she needed to secure a record deal and, in order to do that, she needed to cut a much more professional demo. Once again she turned to Greg Petherick.

Greg knew just the man to help – an engineer called Kaj Dahlstrom who ran a small recording studio in Melbourne. They decided that 'The Loco-Motion' was a good place to start and Dahlstrom laid down a backing track which had a funkier feel than Little Eva's version. There is nothing quite like the thrill of a trip to a studio to make a real record. Kylie was so excited when she made the journey across Melbourne to where the aptly named 'Sing Sing' studios were situated. The only problem was that when she arrived Kylie realized she could not sing in the same key as the backing track, so she had to go away again while Dahlstrom set about changing everything to the higher E Minor key. It took him a week and then Kylie came back. It was all new to her, but she responded well as he nursed her through the song line by line. Many artists – even very famous chart-toppers – have to record their songs line by line because their pitch is not perfect. But this was Kylie's first go and she would soon make sure she was as professional in this sphere as she was in every other aspect of her career. Pete Waterman, who would become her early pop Svengali, observed, 'She'd be exhausted half the time, but when she had to work, her whole personality would transform and she would light up. We would literally only get an hour at a time to work with her, but we always got things done.'

Dahlstrom hawked the demo around various record companies before there was a glimmer of interest from the Melbourne-based Mushroom Records. Michael Gudinski, the company chairman, sent a memo to two executives asking them to listen to the demo because he thought it was 'kinda cute' and might be worth taking a chance on. The crucial selling point for Mushroom was that Kylie had swiftly become one of the most recognizable faces in Australia. By the time they signed her up in the spring of 1987 Kylie, on the eve of her nineteenth birthday, had been voted Most Popular Australian Actress at the annual Logies, the premier TV awards. The award was voted for by readers of the magazine *TV Week*, so it accurately reflected the strength of Kylie's following in the country. Afterwards, wearing a bright red leather skirt she had made herself, she admitted, 'I wish I had been better prepared. I was so nervous I forgot to thank all the people in the show.' It was a huge accolade for such a relative newcomer and, in her moment of triumph, Kylie had chastised herself for a lack of professionalism.

The executives at Mushroom were very smart where Kylie was concerned. Firstly, they wanted to introduce a sound similar to the one that had been dominating the British charts. They asked Pete Waterman if he could send someone to Melbourne to work with their engineers. Waterman and his partners Mike Stock and Matt Aitken already had an impressive list of UK hits to their name. Waterman agreed to 'loan' them Mike Duffy, a Canadian employee. The managing director of Mushroom, Gary Ashley, had met up with Waterman at MIDEM, the international music trading conference held annually in Cannes, and had told him that they had signed up Kylie Minogue. Amusingly, Pete did not have a clue who she was.

Secondly, Amanda Pelman, who was in charge of Mushroom's promotion, and who was responsible for signing Kylie to the label, realized that the singing Kylie should complement the acting Kylie. There was a ready-made audience of young girls who could identify with the character of Charlene Mitchell and could will her to be successful as a popstar. Pelman wanted a million girls in a million bedrooms to sing 'The Loco-Motion' into their hairbrushes, just as Kylie herself had done when she imagined she was Olivia Newton-John or Agnetha from Abba. The character of Charlene was gearing up to the most famous episode of all time in *Neighbours* – her marriage to Scott. In the eyes of a spellbound viewing public, the wedding of these two fictional characters would be the biggest event since Prince Charles married Lady Diana Spencer. It is no coincidence that the executives at

Mushroom were desperate for the first Kylie record to be released in tandem with this episode. This was cold-hearted, dead-eyed opportunism that was practically guaranteed to be a successful strategy. It was no 'happy accident' that Mike Duffy's version of 'The Loco-Motion' was released in mid-July 1987, just two weeks after millions of potential record buyers had watched the 'wedding of the year'.

Mike Duffy had only started work on the track the previous month so it had all been a bit of a rush, but they were able to use Kylie's original vocal from the 'Sing Sing' session. Pete Waterman, who had loved the Little Eva version, had encouraged Duffy to have a go at copying his sound. He conceded, 'It sounded roughly, very roughly, like one of ours.' Waterman gave him his blessing but was astonished a few short weeks later to be woken at 3am by an excited Duffy shouting down the phone that 'The Loco-Motion' was number one. He was so surprised he got up and put on the track. Duffy had sent him a final copy but he had not yet got round to listening to it. He played it through: 'It was rubbish, so I went back to bed.'

'The Loco-Motion' was number one in Australia for seven weeks, the biggest-selling record there of both 1987 and of the entire decade. The Australian public had already been suckered into confusing Kylie with Charlene. In the eyes of the record buying public it was Charlene, the girl-next-door with a feisty edge, who was singing 'The Loco-Motion'. Practically anyone on television can have a hit record, whether it's Robson and Jerome or Orville the Duck. Practically nobody, however, builds a singing career on the back of TV success.

It was time for Kylie to step into the international

market place and, in order to do that, she needed some-one else in her corner. She would always have her father protecting her interests but Ron Minogue was never going to give up his life in Melbourne to court the music business. She was fortunate to find a man to stick by her through good and bad times, a former drummer called Terry Blamey.

In January 1986, when Kylie auditioned for her role in *Neighbours*, a new board game called 'So You Want To Be A Rockstar' went on sale around Australia. The idea was that each player represented a band and followed its ups and downs from first gig to, hopefully, a number one album. The game was devised by Simon Young, director of business affairs at Mushroom Records, and his friend Terry Blamey, who was working as the music talent co-ordinator for the TV programme, *Hey, It's Saturday* and also managed a novelty act featuring a former Australian Rules Footballer called Jacko. Blamey had been in bands in the late 1960s but had decided that 'it was more lucra-tive to be a manager or an agent.' Young and Blamey resolved not to include anything that involved sex and drugs in the board game, but just stuck to the rock and roll.

Blamey explained the philosophy of the game: 'You can lie, but then people can lie back to you. You don't have to tell the truth, you can charge whatever you like, you can give things away free, you can hire them, you can lease them, you can swap them. It is as wide open in terms of bargaining as it is in the real world, but it all comes back to you when you are in a less favourable position. The winner does extremely well. He ends up with a lot of money and a lot of chart success.'

With exquisite timing, barely six months would pass before Blamey took control of Kylie Minogue's career. They have both done extremely well, ending up with lots of money and chart success – enough to have easily won any board game. Blamey's 20 per cent of all things Kylie has made him a multi-millionaire, but they are still a strong partnership twenty years later and he remains fiercely protective of his famous client. Blamey was practically part of the family at Mushroom and was in a strong position to take over the reins of Kylie Minogue's career when she needed personal day-to-day handling of her life. Mushroom had taken her to number one with 'The Loco-Motion' but she would need something more than shared responsibility if the next phase of her career – the international years – was to be a success.

Before he became her manager Terry Blamey had to get the seal of approval from her father, rather like a hapless schoolboy on a first date. Ron Minogue was naturally cautious, very shrewd and had maximized all the opportunities for both Kylie and Dannii up until this point. He was most definitely not the sort of man who would be seduced by the glamour of the pop business. His feet were so firmly on the ground, he had lead in his boots. From the very outset, he had set up a limited company, Kaydeebee, to control the finances of his children, and had a reputation for being thrifty. Kay was for Kylie, Dee was for Dannii and Bee stood for their brother Brendan. It was an amusing reminder of when the three children used to squabble over which television programmes they wanted to watch, and so a rota for using the remote control was posted in the kitchen – Monday K, Tuesday D, Wednesday B, and so on.

The success of his daughters meant that Ron no longer felt able to commit full time to his job as the Director of Finance of Camberwell Council. He went on to work as a consultant for three days a week, before finally quitting for good in 1989 to devote himself to the family business. Evidence of his financial acumen came to light when it was disclosed that he had managed to secure a car valued at Aus $17,000 for just $2,000 as part of a severance package. He also took three months' pay and a long service bonus away with him. The car was sold a few months later to a local dealer for an undisclosed price.

Ron has always had a solid contractual arrangement with Kylie who, as a result, has never had any financial concerns of any kind over the money she has earned. She is not at all mean with money, but has just inherited a natural prudence, so that she will always go for the bargain in a supermarket – even today, when she is one of the richest women in entertainment. Like Ron, her mother Carol goes on the payroll when Kylie is on tour. She works backstage helping the dancers, a legacy of her own training as a dancer when she was younger. Although Kylie is very close to her mother, she admits she has always been a daddy's girl. It was, therefore, essential that Terry Blamey pass the 'Ron' test before he could be accepted into the Minogue inner sanctum. Gary Ashley, of Mushroom Records, described Blamey as a 'straight-up guy', and it was this quality that Minogue Senior liked and thought he could work with in the future. The longevity of 'Kylie Minogue Limited', the team behind the public Kylie, is proof of what a mutually beneficial decision that was. While Ron remained in Melbourne in the 1990s, Terry Blamey upped sticks and moved close to Kylie, rather like a sensible elder brother looking after a vulnerable sister. Even today, record company insiders marvel at the way he rules Kylie with a 'rod of iron'. That is not strictly true, but he certainly enjoys a reputation as a hard man with whom to do business.

'My life has always been geared to my career.'

6

London Calling

The crowd outside Melbourne's Red Eagle Hotel surged forward to wish Kylie a Happy Birthday as she clamboured out of the Mercedes in a semi see-through black silk dress. It was her twenty-first birthday and she was the centre of attention. So much so that Jason Donovan was completely forgotten as he scrambled out the back of the car. As soon as someone had escorted Kylie though the door of the hotel, a bouncer promptly slammed it in poor Jason's face.

Kylie Minogue, popular soap actress, and now fledgling pop star, waited patiently, curled up on the sofa. Terry Blamey was there to keep an eye on things. They had enjoyed their week together in London, sightseeing from the top of a tourist bus and getting in line for the Tower of London and Madame Tussaud's. But these outings had just been a pleasant bonus. The real reason they had used up Kylie's short filming break from *Neighbours* in October 1987 was to meet with Pete Waterman and proceed with the master plan for international stardom. The only problem was that this was their last day and they had yet to clap eyes on the chart wizard. Instead, they were apparently wasting their last afternoon in London in the reception area of the unpretentious Vine Yard studio complex behind Borough tube station, near London Bridge.

Fortunately, Kylie had no idea of the bedlam behind closed doors. Waterman was not even in London that day. He was relaxing at his mansion in Newton-le-Willows, Merseyside, when his partner Mike Stock rang up to enquire if a small Antipodean rang any bells – a small Antipodean called Kylie Minogue. Waterman had forgotten to mention that he had agreed to a joint venture with Mushroom Records to help Kylie's recording career. He had never watched *Neighbours,* so the whole thing had gone straight out of his head. 'She's in town,' he told Stock, helpfully, only to be told that she was actually sitting in reception and had to be on her way back to the airport in a few hours: 'She's expecting to do something with us, now!' Without thinking, Waterman replied, 'She should be so lucky.' The rest, as they say, is history. It is a great story, and one that Waterman never tires of telling.

The biggest-selling record of 1988 was written by fax between London and Merseyside in about half an hour – although Stock does not give Waterman much credit for the song. Later in the day, Waterman rang the studio to find out how Kylie's vocal was coming along. Matt Aitken, the other member of the famous Hit Factory triumvirate, came on the line and announced, 'This girl's got a really good voice.' The record done, the Hit Factory promptly forgot all about Kylie Minogue. At this stage, Pete Waterman had never even met the girl who would take over his commercial life. He had yet to hear the record.

Six weeks later, at the PWL (Pete Waterman Limited) Christmas party at the Natural History Museum in London, a record came on that he did not recognize:

'I thought it was fantastic, so I ran over to the DJ and asked him what it was. He said, "It's Kylie Minogue, 'I Should Be So Lucky'."' Waterman turned to Mike Stock and told him the track would be a smash. Waterman, who has an uncanny sense of the commercial, was absolutely right. He was the glue that joined together the songwriting skills of Mike Stock, the musicianship of guitarist, Matt Aitken, and the talent of their singers. Kylie once compared the Hit Factory to a Hollywood Studio – if that's the case, then Pete Waterman is Sam Goldwyn ('I am willing to admit that I may not always be right – but I am never wrong').

Waterman did not fully appreciate just how popular *Neighbours* was becoming in the UK, and how everybody wanted to hear 'Charlene's' record. *Neighbours* was watched regularly by 15 million viewers a day, which was a considerable potential record-buying market. Waterman confessed that he had absolutely no conception of the 'power of Kylie's presence in the market-place.' It was an intangible power that she has always possessed. There is a little of the chicken and the egg about *Neighbours* and Kylie's pop career. Would *Neighbours* have been an enduring commercial success without 'I Should Be So Lucky', or would Kylie have made it as a singer without *Neighbours*? It is probably a bit of both. The exposure given to the record because it was 'Charlene' was huge – but then, at the time, Stock, Aitken and Waterman could have turned their grannies into stars. In 1987, before Kylie, they had sold thirty-seven million records worldwide. One of the famous trio reportedly said that Kylie could have burped into the microphone and it would have been a hit.

The BBC was instrumental in the speed with which the nation knew that Kylie had made a record. She may have been number one in Australia, New Zealand and Hong Kong, but that did not mean a thing in Oxford Street. But *The Noel Edmonds Christmas Day Special* sent a film crew out to Australia to film Kylie singing 'I Should Be So Lucky'. This was significant exposure and neatly coincided with *Neighbours* being shown twice daily. In those days, Noel Edmonds was one of the biggest names on British television, so it was a big break for Kylie. The single was finally released on 23 January 1988. It was the month of the Australian bicentennial celebrations. Kylie was in Sydney as one of the celebrity guests invited to meet Prince Charles and Princess Diana. Charles met her first and gave her the tried and tested royal enquiry: 'And what do you do?' Kylie timidly replied that she worked on *Neighbours,* and Charles smilingly told her he would make sure he watched an episode. When it came to speaking to Diana, six feet tall in high heels, and the most famous woman in the world, Kylie was completely tongue-tied. For a minute, she was Minnie Minogue, the little girl from the Melbourne suburbs, and not the performer who was a blink away from international fame.

Three weeks after the single was released, Kylie, back home in Melbourne, was awoken by her mother with the news that there was a phone call from England. She was grumpy at first, fearing it was a British journalist after an early morning scoop. Instead, it was the PWL office congratulating her on reaching number one. It would be the first single in a decade to stay at the top of the charts for five weeks. Far from being a 'happy accident', each step in Kylie's proposed world domination was being carefully planned. When she gave interviews about her latest success, she admitted that her future with *Neighbours* was uncertain, even though she still had six months to go on her contract: 'I've done *Neighbours* since I left school. I'd obviously like to do other things. I'd be in London right now if I could, but I have commitments to *Neighbours*.' The reality was that, in eighteen short months, Kylie had outgrown the homespun Aussie soap. When she left the series in June 1988, she was given as a leaving present a mahogany mirror and a framed montage of her magazine covers. Her last episode, when Charlene drove off to a new life in Queensland, was broadcast in the UK in October when 'Je Ne Sais Pas Pourquoi' (Pete Waterman's favourite among his Kylie songs) was her third consecutive top three hit. Kylie had done even better in Finland, where her first four releases reached number one – a record.

Kylie was still a teenager. But, at nineteen, she was positively an old lady next to the girl she knocked off the number one spot, sixteen-year-old Tiffany with 'I Think We're Alone Now'. Great things were predicted for the auburn-haired girl from Oklahoma, but she managed just two more top ten hits and was on the chart scrapheap within a year. Her demise is a salutary lesson in just how hard it is to stay at the top in such a fickle business for one year, let alone for almost twenty. Kylie, however, had probably had the best first year in the singles chart of any female artist ever.

Stock, Aitken and Waterman were unlikely candidates to have become the British equivalent of Tamla-Motown. They had met in 1984, when none of their careers were particularly soaring. Waterman was a brash yet sociable ex-Mecca Ballroom DJ, Aitken a former cruise-line guitarist and Stock used to play in a hotel band – hardly pop royalty. Yet, for a few years, they gelled into the most formidable hit-making team in the world. According to Mike Stock, the confident Waterman had told his partners, 'Stick with me, boys, and I'll show you how to make a hit record.' And he did. Their roster of stars at the time read like a who's who of unhip: Samantha Fox, Sinitta, Sonia, Hazell Dean, Mel & Kim, Rick Astley, Bananarama . . . and the bubble-haired soap star Kylie Minogue. Their aim was to produce classic three-minute hit singles. It was not rocket science. Waterman explained, 'We have taken pop music back to the people who buy records, not the journalists who preach to people.' They set out to appeal to listeners with 'Woolworth's Ears'.

It is easy to underestimate the craftsmanship of a Stock, Aitken and Waterman record, and just as facile to suggest they all sound the same. They constructed energetic records around one catchy melody. Music author Spencer Bright recalled, 'Like everyone else at the time, I found Stock, Aitken and Waterman pretty gruesome. But you could not deny the hummability of their music, or their skill.'

And the lyrics were canny. They did not seek to save the world in three minutes. Instead they focused on key emotions, which would appeal to the young, impressionable, record-buying public. There are, for instance, an astonishing number of SAW records which have the word 'heart' in the title. Kylie released 'Hand On Your Heart', Jason – 'Too Many Broken Hearts'; Rick Astley – 'Take Me To Your Heart'; Sinitta – 'Cross My Broken Heart';

Kylie and her sixteen inch waist dazzle at the Birmingham NEC on her 'Showgirl' tour

Above and **below:** Kylie with her sister Dannii, three years her junior – for a time in the early 80's Dannii was the more famous of the two

With her younger brother Brendan

Above: With her mother, Carol Minogue, and **right**, with Anne Charleston, who played her screen mother, Madge in *Neighbours*

Bad hair days – with Jason 'Scott Robinson' Donovan

Kylie and Jason sing their 1988 No. 1 duet 'Especially For You'. They kept their passionate relationship a secret from their fans

On stage with Elton 'Donatella' John, at the Stonewall Fund Gala at the Royal Albert Hall, in October 1995

With Pete Waterman, who had a huge influence on Kylie's pop career

Posing with Nick Cave, with whom she recorded 'Where The Wild Roses Grow'

A dramatic change of image: Kylie and escort Michael Hutchence at the Sydney première of her film *The Delinquents*, December 1989

Her three year relationship with Jason was already over when Kylie and Michael became lovers

At Michael's funeral at St Andrew's Cathedral, Sydney, November 1997. They had spilt early in 1991

Sonia – 'Listen To Your Heart'; Dead Or Alive – 'My Heart Goes Bang'; Cliff Richard – 'I Just Don't Have The Heart'. Besides this simplistic approach, anything that might offend was banned, so there was no sex, no bottoms. And no 'baby', which Mike Stock considered the most clichéd word in popular music. The satirical magazine *Punch* devised a spoof Stock, Aitken and Waterman song for their Winter Special in 1989. They called it 'Your Arms Are In My Heart'.

The 1988 bestselling roster for Stock, Aitken and Waterman in the UK reads:

	Artist	Song	Sales
1.	Kylie Minogue	I Should Be So Lucky'	672,568
2.	Kylie Minogue	'The Loco-Motion'	439,575
3.	Kylie Minogue	'Je Ne Sais Pas Pourquoi'	315,201
4.	Kylie Minogue	'Got To Be Certain'	278,000
5.	Jason Donovan	'Nothing Can Divide Us'	266,194
6.	Brother Beyond	'The Harder I Try '	232,000
7.	Rick Astley	'Together Forever'	223,112
8.	Brother Beyond	'He Ain't No Competition'	202,000
9.	Rick Astley	'She Wants To Dance With Me'	182,793
10.	Bananarama	'I Want You Back'	175,000

Kylie had already completely eclipsed the competition in the Stock, Aitken and Waterman stable. According to Waterman, Kylie's success was the worst thing that ever happened to him: 'I don't mean that against Kylie, but merely that she was so successful that I had to fall in line with that success. I didn't want my company to become one artist, as much as I loved that artist, as much as now history shows what a wonderful artist she is, and how proud I am of her.'

There is a fashion for instant nostalgia in New Millennium Britain, and the Kylie Minogue of the Stock, Aitken and Waterman era is no exception. As Spencer Bright acknowledged, 'We are less judgmental today of commercial sounds.' At the time, there was a great wave of anti-Kylie feeling with 'I Hate Kylie Minogue' pins and satirical versions of 'I Should Feel So Yucky' and 'I'm a Lucky Ducky'. A great deal of the criticism was fuelled by jealousy, especially as PWL was an independent label formed specifically to make Kylie records, and independents were traditionally the home of more cutting-edge sounds like The Smiths and, later, Oasis. Waterman explained, 'We were pissing people off incredibly because every record we had released dominated the independent chart. Kylie Minogue was number one in the independent chart! That was unpopular.'

Jason Donovan meanwhile was desperate for a slice of the fame his girlfriend was enjoying. From the moment that Kylie had released a record, there was speculation that 'Scott' would follow suit. He came over with Kylie on one of her recording trips to London, and Pete Waterman took them out for a Chinese meal and asked Kylie whether she wanted him to work with Jason. She said yes, and the deal was done. It is quite telling that this deal was agreed on Kylie's say-so.

Whenever Kylie and Jason were in London at the same time they would stay together but, just as in *Neighbours* and at Mushroom Records, their true relationship was kept secret. By this time, it was one of the worst-kept secrets in show business but, amazingly, nobody printed it, even though pictures of the couple holidaying in Bali had been published. A PWL insider explained, 'It was quite bizarre, because everyone knew. They were always holding hands and kissing in the car.' Contrary to popular belief, it was Jason who had a roving eye, well before Michael Hutchence turned Kylie's head. He was like a kid in a candy store when he first came to London on a promotional tour. The insider observed, 'She [Kylie] was totally into it [their relationship] and I remember him saying that she was really keen and everything. But he was saying "I'm a young man and I just want to enjoy myself while I'm here – and she wants to get more serious." I think that probably caused friction between them. It was inevitable it wasn't going to last.'

Intriguingly, the decision to keep their relationship secret at this time was just as much to protect Jason's career as Kylie's. For two years Jason was the ultimate teen-girl fantasy. He was eligible, and every girl studying for her exams or working behind the counter in a store felt they had a chance of going out with him. Fantasy is what it's all about and, unlike Jason, the more street-wise Kylie has never lost sight of that, whether as girl-next-door or as a wet dream.

The ultimate fantasy coupling of Jason and Kylie was on their number one 'Especially For You', which is either cheesy and cynical or the best love song ever, depending on whether you like fluffy, cuddly toys, or not. This was 'pop noodle' – popular, but not to everyone's taste. 'We didn't want to do it,' said Waterman, fearing it might be considered too tacky. In the end he was persuaded by public pressure, and because Kylie thought it was a good idea. She described the duet merely as an extension of work for her and Jason: 'We'd done everything else together.' Waterman and Matt Aitken flew to Sydney to record the pair's vocals, caught the next flight home, and went straight to the studio to work on the mix in time to turn the track into a Christmas hit. It took only three days, from start to finish.

Professionally, there was nowhere for Jason and Kylie to go together, and soon their private life was rocky as well. Meanwhile her sister Dannii was keen to follow in her footsteps, something she has had to do, at a respectful distance, since her initial success in *Young Talent Time*. Kylie was a star in *Neighbours;* Dannii landed the part of rebel Emma Jackson in rival Aussie soap *Home and Away*. Kylie's first UK record in 1988 went to number one. Two years later Dannii followed her, but her debut 'Love And Kisses' only reached number eight. Dannii also has Terry Blamey as her manager, but there is just a hint that this is more to keep an eye on little sister than anything else. Dannii did not join the Stock, Aitken and Waterman Hit Factory. Waterman has said that they could have signed Dannii but Kylie preferred them to pass. Instead, the younger Minogue joined MCA.

The most important commodity Kylie has had throughout her career is not her voice, her face, her hair or even her bottom – it is her image, of which they are all a part. Nothing can be allowed to deflect from the strict control of that image, whether it be her relationship with Jason Donovan or the subtle changes in her clothes, her videos or her music. The songs she released after she left *Neighbours*, 'Better The Devil You Know', 'Shocked' and 'What Do I Have To Do?' were more sophisticated than her 'Charlene' songs 'I Should Be So Lucky' and 'Got To Be Certain', reflecting a more mature Kylie. She has often cited the fact that her fan base has 'grown up with her' as one of the reasons for her enduring appeal.

So it was not at all helpful to her changing image that, a year after she left *Neighbours*, the Grundy production company released a video entitled *Scott and Charlene: A Love Story*. Kylie rightly considered that she might be type-cast as Charlene if this syrup was stuck on the shelves year after year. At PWL, they had already noticed that she was beginning to change naturally into a trendier young woman, wearing clothes that suited her more than the jeans-and-sweater Charlene look. Kylie decided to take her grievance to court, but was allocated a presiding judge who said he had never heard of Kylie Minogue before the case and that he had 'fast-forwarded his way through the video because he wasn't prepared to spend an hour-and-a-half watching it.' The judge found against Kylie, declaring that it was obviously the success of *Neighbours* that had directly launched her career.

To say Kylie was annoyed is an understatement and she certainly voiced her opinion on this issue: 'It's not even *Neighbours*. That's not what I was paid a measly fee of money for [Aus $2000 a week] . . . I have spent a lot of time getting away from Charlene. I know some people say, "*Neighbours* made you what you are." But it didn't. It's exploitation.'

Kylie was on a five-year contract with PWL and, after just one year she was a millionairess, her fortune carefully invested by her father Ron, who was very tough when dealing with the machinations of the pop world. When Waterman was in Australia recording 'Especially For You', he was cornered by Minogue Senior who demanded that Kylie see some of her hard-earned cash. A startled

Waterman had to write out a cheque to Kaydeebee on the spot, for a substantial amount. Part of that money was speedily put down as a deposit on an Aus $500,000 dollar house in Melbourne, even though Kylie knew she would scarcely live there, if at all.

More importantly, she was a very proud artist and, as she grew up, she became more aware of what she considered to be a lack of respect for her contribution. Kylie was growing in confidence. Her debut album became the biggest-selling album of all time by a female artist – enough to turn anyone's head. However, she did not suddenly think she could do better without Stock, Aitken and Waterman. It was a gradual process, over which she agonized, as Jason Donovan remembered: 'Kylie struggled very much with the whole Stock, Aitken Waterman thing. I always wondered, "Why are you doing it? Just get out, if you don't like it – get out."'

The Hit Factory was not a cosy air-kissing organization. Artists could either stay for the bumpy ride or, like Rick Astley, jump ship. This was conveyor-belt business and Kylie Minogue records were continually on the production line. Waterman had great respect for Kylie as a professional, but admitted he never got 'that close' to performers personally: 'We work with artists. We don't work with friends. I always think it is too dangerous to get too close to an artist. You'll always get let down because they will shit on you.' That strong view did not stop Waterman letting Kylie and her mother Carol live in his flat above the studio (he moved into a hotel), while Kylie was recording her first album. Nor did it stop Waterman inviting Kylie to stay at his country mansion, where she was able to indulge her love of horses. At the time, Kylie was being hounded about her new relationship with Michael Hutchence and needed a refuge. One Sunday morning, Kylie's horse shied at a milk lorry and bolted into the distance. Waterman, terrified that his leading artist was in peril, set off in pursuit on his large grey, only to realize that he had totally lost control of the animal in his furious gallop. Far from being the rescuer, he needed rescuing himself. He was thrown off, catching his foot in the stirrup. He was wearing a riding hat, so was fortunate that only his ego was bruised as he was carted along. Suddenly, Kylie appeared from nowhere and stopped his horse from dragging him any further up the road.

The one exception to the 'no mates' working philosophy of SAW was Jason Donovan. Waterman declared, 'He was a mate and he was treated like a mate. We had a genuine affection for the guy.' Jason shared Waterman's passion for cars, and the pair would dash off to Silverstone together to watch the motor racing. Jason was also the beneficiary of a genuine 'happy accident' chain of events. When Rick Astley abruptly left, he left behind a song which had already been prepared for him. The very next day, when Jason walked in, Waterman said he had found just the song for him, 'Too Many Broken Hearts'. The track became Jason's first solo number one.

As Kylie gained in confidence, her professional routine with The Hit Factory was no longer what she wanted it to be. She would turn up at the studio and they would play her the backing track, print out the lyrics, and then Mike Stock would go through it, showing her the cues. And she went straight in front of the microphone and did her vocal in one take, or perhaps two. Kylie was frustrated: 'I just wanted to be a bit more involved, and it reached the point where I was not happy any more at being told to go and "have a cup of tea till we call you".'

The problem for Kylie was how to break the chains binding her to PWL. Returning to the Hollywood analogy, Kylie's progression is reminiscent of the young Judy Garland (minus the drugs). The petite Garland was also trapped as a child star, controlled by factories, desperate to throw off the child/woman image which had brought her initial fame. She would also become an icon to a gay community magnetized by her mixture of camp and vulnerability. Kylie threw off the chains in rebellious, aggressive fashion. The blonde wig and micro-skirt of her 'Hutchence era' were a bold statement of intent. This was consolidated by her increased artistic involvement in her videos and the use of producers independent of Stock, Aitken and Waterman.

Kylie had gone to Pete Waterman and told him that she wanted to write with Matt Aitken and Mike Stock. He told her that would not be possible because the three of them worked as a unit. He said she would have to collaborate with someone else. Waterman acknowledged that Kylie was headstrong about her career but also described her as his 'star centre forward'. Perhaps The Hit Factory had underestimated just how strong and just how motivated Kylie actually is. These days, a more confident Kylie will happily admit that her career is the most important thing in her life. The pop business is not a game to her. She is not a little dolly bird passing the time until she gets married.

Mike Stock recognized as early as 1990 that Kylie, with the massive success she had enjoyed in the past two years, would not be satisfied with just coming in and singing. He predicted, 'She'll want to do it all very soon and we won't be involved anymore.' Kylie stayed with Stock, Aitken and Waterman until the end of her contract. When Jason left the stable in 1991, she was the only original remaining artist. Jason saw himself as a grungy Michael Hutchence-type rock star – guitar, tousled hair and jeans, an image a million miles away from the clean-cut pop star that SAW wanted. Jason ended up starring in an Andrew Lloyd Webber musical that had even less street cred than any Stock, Aitken and Waterman collaboration.

Kylie had twenty successive hits on the PWL label, including four number ones. Even so, for a while it seemed like daggers drawn between Kylie and her three mentors. Kylie felt she needed to distance herself from them. But now, she and Waterman are reconciled in a mutual admiration society. Kylie has confessed that she ran a million miles away from the PWL days in her ulti-mately successful quest to change the public perception of her. These days, she is in 'awe of that time', and the trio's ability to churn out hit after hit. She has even said that she would not rule out working with Pete Waterman again. Ironically, it was the triumvirate themselves who fell out. Stock and Aitken ended up on one side of a legal battle over Kylie's back catalogue and Waterman on the other.

'Now everyone says "Ooh, what great songs!"'

7

Media Relations

Kylie was openly crying in the street in Melbourne after some
boyfriend trouble when a man came up to her, bold as brass,
tapped her on the shoulder, shoved a scruffy piece of paper
under her nose and asked, 'Can I have your autograph?' Kylie
was so shocked she signed her name.

Younger Kylie fans will have no idea that the woman so
loved by the media these days was treated quite shame-
fully by the press in the early part of her career. The
legendary Fleet Street columnist Jean Rook of the *Daily
Express* was perhaps the chief culprit. Rook was the very
worst kind of bullying old dinosaur, coasting by on a reputation that sometimes bordered on parody. Not for
nothing was she the inspiration for the satirical Glenda
Slagg in *Private Eye* magazine. She targeted poor Kylie,
who was completely unprepared for the poison pen of
this wrinkly Rita Skeeter.

In March 1988, Kylie flew in to Heathrow to finish the
vocals for her first album and to do some publicity
because, after all, she was number one in the UK. To
begin with, she was exhausted thanks to a punishing
schedule. When she arrived, Kylie was shocked by the

microscopic scrutiny afforded every celebrity by the British press, and this was the start of a lifelong hate affair with the tabloids. To a certain extent, she was the target of innate racism by good old Brits against all things Antipodean. It's not something Australian visitors to the UK expect, but it is by no means reserved for the non-white population – because it is white on white, it is ignored and laughed off.

It was naïve, however, of Kylie and her management to think the latest pop sensation and soap star would in any way escape media attention. Kylie asked her manager what she could expect at the airport. Terry Blamey told her to relax and get some sleep, because nobody knew she was arriving on that flight. He had taken the precaution of booking the seats only a couple of hours before take-off. Unfortunately, it would have made no difference if he had booked them two minutes before departure – the telephone lines between Melbourne and London were buzzing, and Fleet Street's finest had plenty of time to trickle out along the M4 to wait for their prey. Kylie stepped off the plane in dark glasses, an old pair of scruffy sandals and a wraparound skirt.

It had not helped that Kylie was escorted by burly minders the size of Ayers Rock, who were not exactly the type you would want to invite home for tea with mother. Minders behaving badly has always been a sure-fire way to achieve newspaper coverage, as a list of other over-protected female stars from Madonna to Britney Spears illustrates. On this occasion, it just irritated everyone.

Jean Rook commented, 'Maybe getting off a plane looking as if you've just crawled out of a kangaroo's pouch is Australian style but Kylie Minogue's disappointing arrival at Heathrow was worse than just the sloppily-dressed girl-next-door. She looked like a slept-in Qantas blanket.' That was the kindest bit. She went on to describe Kylie as a 'filthy-mooded funnel-web spider' and suggested that Kylie could take lessons from a real high-flying star, like Joan Collins. Poor Kylie probably did not have a clue who Joan Collins was. Rook's assassination coincided with the publication of topless pictures of Kylie in the *Sun*. They had been taken when she was holidaying in Bali with Jason Donovan, some eighteen months earlier.

It was time for the shutters to come down. Terry Blamey decided, at least temporarily, that Kylie was receiving too much publicity, and that her audience was in danger of getting sick of her. Officially, she refused all interviews for a while, because she needed rest to recharge her batteries. The publicity bandwagon had been temporarily derailed, and even requests from Australian media were turned down. One of the few newspapers to achieve access was the *Melbourne Sun*, which had carried 150 stories about Kylie in one year. The editor Colin Duck explained that featuring Kylie meant they sold more papers. It was as simple as that, and very much the same formula that accounted for the enormous coverage the late Princess Diana always received.

'Kylie Minogue Limited' got together and decided that Kylie must never be caught out again by the media. It was very much a necessary evil which had to be controlled as much as possible. Instead of a wide eyed, enthusiastic young woman from Melbourne, Kylie was neatly packaged and always immaculate. It was the image of a new 'corporate' Kylie that was presented to the world. Behind the smiling face, Kylie may have been feeling the strain but, on the surface, she toed the company line of being the world's most normal girl – as if her star-spangled life had ever been normal. She never courted controversy. She would always say that she was 'tired', 'nervous' at this or that and always flash a big toothy smile. She was asked if she would like to live overseas and replied, 'I'll always call Australia home,' which did not answer the question. It would not be long before London was her permanent home.

Kylie is a far better actress than she is given credit for and she is a past master at giving nothing away. Former pop columnist Rick Sky placed her at number one in his list of worst interviewees, although he admitted her beauty was some compensation. 'She was incredibly unforthcoming,' he recalled. 'It made me wonder what a nineteen-year-old girl had to hide. She was quite po-faced and everything I asked her about came to a dead end.' In the beginning, Kylie was worried about spilling the beans about Jason, or that she would be questioned about rumours of anorexia. After a while, it just became second nature to give away nothing or, more precisely, exactly as much as she wanted to divulge.

She also had back-up. Andrew Watt, a local Melbourne music journalist, was commissioned by Mushroom to write Kylie's fanzine copy, the soft-focus biography that is oxygen for every star. He was also conveniently placed in press conferences to derail things, should any tough questions be asked about topless photos or weight loss. Watt would put up his hand and ask, most sincerely, 'So Kylie, what's it like working with Pete Waterman?' Soon, Kylie herself became adept at deflecting these questions without her 'plant'.

This did not stop her putting her foot in it every so

often. When she was in South Africa in late 1989, the year before Nelson Mandela's 'walk to freedom', she was asked what she thought about the situation in that country. She replied, 'I think they should stop killing the rhinos.' Once said, there was no retracting it, although Kylie denied the report when it appeared, claiming that the journalist obviously had a 'deep hatred for me'. The Kylie of the mid-nineties might have claimed that she was being ironic, but at this time it was not part of her image makeover to come across as a blonde airhead. Having been 'burned', as she herself put it, Kylie vowed never to be caught out in that fashion again.

It has led to some embarrassing exchanges, of which there is no better example than the time she shared an interview for *Select* magazine with Primal Scream front man, Bobby Gillespie. It was the night after the UK General Election in 1992, which the Tory party, under John Major, won.

Gillespie: 'What did you think about last night, Kylie? We were sickened, totally.

Kylie: I wouldn't wish to express my opinions. I've made that mistake before [rhinos?] and it was blown totally out of all proportion, so I vowed not to talk about it. Ever.

Interviewer: What happened then?

Kylie: I don't even want to get into it, it's like bringing it up again. I have interest in politics, but not involvement. My interest is in the environment. [rhinos?]

Gillespie: Well, we don't give a shit about the environment . . . we care about people.

Interviewer: Kylie, much has been made of your
   SexKylie makeover . . .

The control that Kylie herself, Terry Blamey and Ron
Minogue exercised over all things Kylie was edging
towards a stranglehold. From the outset, Blamey has
sought to maintain the public image and, consequently,
the public affection in which Kylie is held. Sometimes
the public let them down. On one occasion she went
with Pete Waterman to Peter Stringfellow's now defunct
Hippodrome nightclub off Leicester Square in London.
The story may have become exaggerated in the
retelling but one eye witness said that a drunken mob of
jealous girls started calling her names and jostling her.
One allegedly spat on Kylie, full in the face, as she was
sat down: 'She didn't say a word – just struggled out of
her seat and was ushered out.' Kylie learnt a valuable
lesson that night – nobody cool ever went to the
Hippodrome.

Having learnt their lesson over the mauling Kylie
received at the hands of the British press, 'Kylie Minogue
Limited' have taken steps to make sure it has never happened again. From those early days, Terry Blamey has
closely controlled her image and, more importantly, her
image changes. Kaydeebee has a stranglehold on the
copyright for all her pictures, her music and her mer-
chandise. In effect, Kylie owns all things Kylie. Her bank
account swells a little every time you see a picture of her
in a magazine. There is likely to be trouble if anybody
tries to take an unauthorized picture of Kylie.

After the final concert of her Australian tour in 1991,
there was a party at The Freezer nightclub in the

Darlinghurst district of Sydney. One freelance photographer was asked to leave his cameras at the door, but sneaked in a small Instamatic and started taking pictures of Kylie with an actor called Marcus Graham. When he left the club, he claimed he was pursued by one of Kylie's minders and a party guest who, he alleged, pinned him up against a wall, took five rolls of film from him and opened up every one of his cameras. It was just at the time Kylie and Michael Hutchence had been in the newspapers after having broken up, so maybe Kylie was particularly touchy about having her picture taken with another man. Terry Blamey, with masterful understatement, said of the incident, 'We didn't want to create a scene.'

One of the amusing side effects of the care with which Kylie and Terry Blamey have taken over media coverage is in her apparent fixation with food and diets over the years. It all started in the 1980s when she was still in *Neighbours* and plagued by rumours of anorexia nervosa. This really got under Kylie's skin.

Kylie has always been very thin and fragile and female celebrities have to deal with scrutiny of their physique and physical wellbeing. The front pages of the popular magazine, *heat*, are constantly noting thinnest or fattest 'celebs'. The fascination with Kylie's weight has continued year after year. She fluctuates between six and a half stone and seven stone (forty-four kilos). Her doctors, when she was in *Neighbours* were so worried about her inability to keep her weight up that they devised a special high-energy diet. The 'brown rice' regime was not something she enjoyed.

The whole food issue with Kylie and the press has the air of someone telling her twenty years ago to always eat something in interviews and she has religiously followed that instruction. If she really put away the amount of grub she apparently eats, her famous rear end would be dragging along the ground.

February 1988: Journalist Jane Oddy notes that Kylie was 'tucking into calorific profiteroles'. The same month, the *Melbourne Sun* breaks off from congratulating her on reaching number one in the UK, to note that she was 'nibbling on a sandwich after having complained of hunger while having her photograph taken'. She dismissed concern that she now weighed six stone (thirty-eight kilos): 'I'm skinny, that's all.'

February 1989: A year on and she is telling *Smash Hits* that she tries to eat healthily: 'I'm not a vegetarian,' she insists, 'but I try not to eat things with too much fat or sugar.' She then proceeds to pass on the recipe for 'yummy' banana cream pie, of which sugar is a principal ingredient. At the time, she is sipping a strawberry-flavoured soya milk shake.

May 1989: Kylie is filming *The Delinquents* in Thailand, and tells a magazine journalist on the phone, 'Oh my God, a tray of strawberry cakes has just arrived.'

October 1996: The *Daily Mail* is shocked at 'how painfully thin, even ill, Kylie looked as she toyed with a rocket salad.'

August 1997: Kylie meets David Thomas of the *Daily*

Telegraph at the trendy Soho House in London. She demolishes 'an oversized ravioli, prior to polishing off a plate of penne and a crème brulée.'

September 1997: In a private dining room at an exclusive Soho club Kylie is spotted by *MixMag* 'demolishing a plate of nouvelle cuisine noodles and sniggering over newspaper reports that she is anorexic.'

October 1997: She talks to *Esquire* magazine at Soho House. This time, 'She has a small portion of tagliatelle, eats half a dozen mouthfuls and pushes the plate aside.'

November 1997: Kylie, says *Cleo* magazine in Australia, is in the kitchen 'having a discreet nibble of pasta.'

June 1998: Kylie tells Swedish magazine *Solo* that she enjoys dinner at the fashionable London restaurant Nobu, where she always has yellowtail sashimi with jalapeno.

June 1999: An interview with both Kylie and Dannii for *Esquire* magazine. Kylie leaps from soup to chocolate cake. Dannii has cheese.

October 1999: Kylie tells *UK Style*, 'I'm cooking a family dinner tonight, so I've got to pick up some tuna steaks and wine.'

June 2000: *The Big Issue* magazine observes, 'She crams fruit salad into her mouth and pretends to talk through it.'

June 2000: The Australian magazine *Who Weekly* reports, 'Kylie is toying with her tomato and herb penne at Lunasa, a stylish bar in London's Fulham.'

July 2000: She tells Tony Romando of *Minx* that after seven years of being a vegetarian she has changed back to meat. 'I'm far healthier,' she confides.

September 2001: The *Daily Mirror* reveals, 'Despite her childlike physique, though, she has a mammoth appetite and has just finished a huge steak and chips.'

October 2001: Kylie recalls in *Time Out* that she had been camping eighteen months earlier and had spent the time cooking 'eggs and bacon on the fire'.

October 2001: She informs *Rolling Stone* that she enjoys working in Peter Gabriel's Bath studio because of the kitchen. She enthuses, 'There's really good food in there.'

December 2001: A comprehensive feature appears in *The Face*, chatting to Kylie over a couple days. Kylie starts off by munching an apple, she eats toast as her hair is done, she has chicken for lunch, she eats a bacon sandwich as her plane takes off for Germany, orders a rump steak in a Berlin restaurant, nibbles chicken pieces during a costume fitting to keep her energy levels up and, for good measure, confides that she loves bangers and mash.

Winter 2001: *Now* reveals that Kylie does not diet especially. 'I do eat junk food like chips and ice cream,' she confides.

December 2001: *TV Hits* magazine asks Kylie what she eats. 'I tend to eat little amounts all through the day but I've had occasions when I order a huge meal and people look at me at the end, absolutely shocked.'

February 2002: Kylie tells *heat* magazine that she is now following a diet called Eat Yourself Slim, in which you can eat as much as you want, as long as you don't eat certain foods.

February 2002: Kylie tells *heat* magazine, in another interview, that the previous night she ate a dark chocolate truffle cake: 'My main course wasn't very nice, so I moved straight on to dessert.'

January 2004: *heat* reports that Kylie has to hire staff to remind her to have her meals while on tour: 'My problem is that I forget to eat in stressful situations,' she revealed.

How on earth did Kylie fit in singing and performing, when so much time was taken up with eating? There is a serious side to this obsessive reportage of Kylie's eating habits. She does need to eat regularly, to stave off the old enemies of tiredness and exhaustion. In the past few years, of course, far more urgent health issues have dominated media coverage of Kylie. She did, however, admit on *Sky TV* in July 2006 that one thing she needed to do among all the things necessary to stay on top of her cancer battle: 'Eat', she said.

'I love my food, actually.'

PART TWO

THE WILD ROSE

8

The Sexual Revolution

Michael Hutchence was in typically worse-for-wear mode
when he first met Kylie at a club in Sydney's King Cross area.
She was standing self consciously against a wall surrounded
by minders when he lurched over and declared, 'I don't know
what we should do first – have lunch or f***.' Kylie was
completely tongue-tied.

Her association with Michael Hutchence had a cata-
clysmic effect on Kylie. The popular version of their
relationship is that Kylie was a virginal girl-next-door,
giving herself up to be sacrificed on the altar of perver-
sion by the demonic Hutchence. Lurid tales always
accompany the Hutchence name. Suggestions abound
that he liked three-in-a-bed sex, was more than intrigued
by sado-masochism and had a taste for heroin. He certainly confessed to his family that he tried heroin. As for
sexual shenanigans, he himself would tell the story of
how, once when he was on tour, he was presented with a
seventeen-year-old nymphet wearing nothing more than a
dog collar and lead. For the most part it is all hearsay and
innuendo, mainly third and fourth hand – the traditional
stuff of rock myths. Hardly any concrete evidence exists of

his debauchery. Newspaper articles and books about the dead star are not littered with kiss-and-tell tales supporting the popular view of his lifestyle.

And Kylie was no virgin – in fact, she was already quite an expert. She had enjoyed a full relationship with Jason Donovan and flings with other teenage boys. She was, perhaps, developing a taste for the dangerous side of sex, the thrill of getting caught. She was like a naughty schoolgirl, with a lollipop in her mouth and the Kama Sutra in her satchel. This is not to suggest a fascination with the Marquis de Sade, more a desire to seize the moment when passion presented an opportunity. Kylie's most revealing observation about her relationship with Hutchence remains, 'Michael was not as bad as everyone thought, and I was not as good. We met somewhere in the middle.'

Michael Hutchence was the classic leader of a rock band. He enjoyed taking his pick of girls and narcotics. He had the arrogance and exhibitionism of a born performer, but cloaked them in an almost childlike enthusiasm that made him fun to be with. He was twenty-seven when he met Kylie and the most famous rock star in Australia. Kylie would have been in awe of him regardless of his swaggering upfront suggestion of sex. She observed, 'I couldn't believe he would talk to me, and I couldn't believe what he'd just said. I was speechless.'

Kylie was still very suburban despite her rapid rise to pop fame. Her acting career had led to abnormal teenage years. Being a young actress, almost a child star, is like being a boy wonder at football – you don't live in the real world, but in a strange, timeless environment, where you are cosseted and protected. Kylie had the qualities of an ingénue. She had intrigued Hutchence. Before he crossed paths with her again, he mentioned her name in an interview in *Smash Hits* magazine: 'Kylie Minogue . . . hmmmm . . . she's got a horrible voice . . . actually I met her once and she was very sweet.'

While Kylie was growing up, protected in the Melbourne suburb of Camberwell, Michael Hutchence was already travelling the world, and had enjoyed a cosmopolitan and enlightened upbringing. He was born Michael Kelland John Hutchence, in Sydney on 22 January 1960. The name Kelland was after his father Kell, an international businessman who bore a passing resemblance to David Niven. His glamorous mother Patricia was a model, and also ran a modelling school in the city. When Michael was four, his father accepted a job as managing director of a firm importing whisky and champagne for restaurants in Hong Kong. It would mean a major upheaval for the family.

It was a very urbane ex-pat world in which Michael, his younger brother Rhett and teenage stepsister Tina found themselves. After a nine-hour flight from the January sun of Sydney to the bustling, humid, Far East metropolis, the family checked in to the Hong Kong Hilton. Michael Hutchence seemed to spend a good deal of his life in the impersonal environment of an expensive hotel room. The family settled in to a life of cocktail parties and afternoon tea. And soul music. Michael recalled, 'There were loads of parties and good music like James Brown and Aretha Franklin. Mine were hip parents.' His mother found work as a make-up artist on movies being shot in Hong Kong. The actress Nastassja Kinski was the same age as Michael and was a guest at his sixth birthday party, when her father Klaus was starring in a film called *Sumuru*. When the family moved in to their own apartment, they employed two servants, who would address young Michael as 'Master'.

He may not yet have been a 'man of the world', but Michael was certainly a 'boy of the world' by the time the family returned to Sydney in late 1972 when he was twelve. He was more an international citizen than an Australian. He explained in *Spin* magazine, 'I had a problem with Australia. In the first place, I hated it. I had all the same prejudices in my head that the English have about it – hats with corks dangling to keep the flies away and kangaroos. Once I got there I realized it was different, but I couldn't believe the people where I went to school. I just hated the place.' One saving grace was that his best friend at the school was Andrew Farriss, equally shy and even more serious, who would join Michael in finding fame with INXS. The pair would chat for hours, discussing poetry and music.

Michael, already a shy boy with a subtle lisp, retreated further into the world of books and, in particular, poetry, which remained a constant love in his life. He was soon to suffer another upheaval when his parents' marriage, which had been rocky in Hong Kong, collapsed completely with Patricia leaving for Los Angeles with Michael, now an impressionable fifteen, in tow. Michael took to life in LA like a duck to water, and began a lifelong enjoyment of girls and marijuana. But, at seventeen, Michael was back in Sydney and had decided a career in music was for him, especially when he discovered how easy it was to get girls, as the singer in the band. He played his first gig on 16 August 1977, the date Elvis Presley died. The band called themselves The Farriss Brothers, an uninspiring name, which would eventually be ditched in favour of INXS. As soon as he finished school later that year, Michael was off again, this time to Perth in Western Australia, with Andrew and the rest of the 'brothers'. Another year, another home.

By the time he reached the age of twenty, INXS had taken off, and were playing nightly gigs all across Australia. Michael was living with a girl called Vicky in Sydney. However, he had met another girl with whom he was to spend seven years. His relationship with Michele Bennett – tall, leggy and brunette – was arguably the most important of his life. They lived together in a two-bed-roomed terraced house Michael had bought in the Paddington area of Sydney. The relationship was very stable and loving, even though Michael was prone to infidelity. For all his reputation as a great womanizer and hellraiser, Michael had a surprising number of stable, important relationships throughout his short life. Michael's friends and family assumed that, one day, he and Michele would marry. Revealingly, his legendary status as a serial cheater on the road with INXS owed much to his fear of being alone. Even after their split, he would remain in constant touch with Michele – including the night he died – ringing her from all over the world, to seek reassurance and to help him get to sleep. His mother Patricia recalled that just hearing her voice would calm him down. She also described poignantly in her memoir to her son, *Just A Man*, how Michael had told her of their split: 'I watched him walking away, looking so lonely and, somehow, had a feeling that he and Michele would never,

ever break off their relationship. I was right, they never did. Until the day he died, Michael loved her.'

Intriguingly, in the light of his future break-up with Kylie, infidelity was only part of the problem with Michele. She wanted to pursue her career as a video and film producer, and he wanted someone to be with him, pandering to his every need, twenty-four hours a day. That person was not Michele Bennett and it certainly was not the ambitious Kylie Minogue. It may well have been his last love Paula Yates, but fate would cruelly intervene.

Hutchence was carrying a great deal of emotional baggage by the time he stumbled up to Kylie in that King's Cross club. This was no shallow Casanova. He was very well read, a pop philosopher, as well as a collector of fine art and beautiful things. Kylie Minogue was very collectable. The club where they met was hosting the party after the annual Countdown Music Awards ceremony, the Australian equivalent of the Grammys or the Brits. INXS had already collected a sackful of awards, but Kylie was a musical novice. She had won the TV Logie for Most Popular Actress in Australia for *Neighbours*, but had been invited to this event because 'The Loco-Motion', her first single in Australia, was the current number one. By contrast, INXS had produced one of the biggest albums worldwide in 1987, in their enduring rock masterpiece *Kick*, which sold eight million copies. Hutchence, never prone to public self-doubt, once boasted to a journalist, 'I am a f***ing great rock star.' And he was. No wonder Kylie was starstruck. But, amazingly, it was Kylie who made Michael Hutchence a 'celebrity'.

After that first unforgettable encounter, it would be another year before Kylie and Michael met again, this time in Melbourne. It was towards the end of 1988 and the mammoth INXS 'Kick' tour was coming to an end. Kylie and Jason had gone to the concert together and been invited to the end-of-tour party afterwards. Kylie's career had gone into overdrive during the past year, with her Stock, Aitken Waterman alliance in the UK triggering an enormous press interest. Her British debut single 'I Should Be So Lucky' was the biggest-selling record of the year in the British charts. Hutchence had not stood still either. The aptly named single, 'Need You Tonight', was a number one in the States and reached number two in the UK (only to be outsold a couple of weeks later by 'Especially For You' by Kylie and Jason). Kylie had even admitted in a pop profile that INXS was her favourite band. Kylie still was not at ease at celebrity functions, as if, in some way, she did not have a right to be mingling with so many famous people. The irony of her reticence was that she and Jason, the old married couple from *Neighbours*, would be the only guests recognized in every supermarket in the land – and probably most of the world.

During this second chance meeting, the conversation was more civilized. Hutchence apologized for his derogatory remarks about Kylie's music and proceeded to turn on the charm like a 200-watt bulb. He was not particularly handsome, with the thin frame of a rock star heavily involved in drugs. His intake had markedly increased during the tour, and he was seen literally knocking back a handful of ecstasy tablets before he went on stage. His face bore the residue pock marks of bad teenage acne and had led to him unkindly being called 'crater face'. He could not compete with the blond surfer-boy looks of Jason Donovan. But few women could resist his doleful eyes, or the feeling he gave them when he was talking to them that they were the centre of the universe.

Kylie has never been a heavy drinker and, while everyone else was over-indulging in the substances on offer, she allowed Hutchence to fetch her a Bailey's to sip. Kylie was not head-over-heels at this point. This was a rock party and she was not totally relaxed. Michael's mother Patricia recalled, 'Wholesome Jason and Kylie looked so out of place amidst the heavy rock and rollers.' Amusingly, she broke the habit of a lifetime to ask Jason and Kylie for an autograph and was deeply embarrassed to discover they were in the middle of an argument.

The romance so far had been such a slow starter that it resembled the desultory meetings of the film *When Harry Met Sally*. Kylie was actually asked by a teen magazine to comment on the INXS singer's new shorter haircut the following May: 'I think people really liked his long hair. I'm not really interested in Michael Hutchence, but I'm sure people will get used to it.'

When Michael next met Kylie, things began to move. It was late September 1989 and this time the city was Hong Kong. Intriguingly, Kylie had given an interview earlier in the month, in which she confided that she wanted to meet more pop stars because it would be interesting to talk to other people in the same business. But, she said, not about work: 'Talking about work is so boring!' She was about to get her chance. Michael's latest relationship with the svelte American model Jonnie had finished when he walked out, leaving her devastated in New York. He had a home in Hong Kong, a welcome haven where he could escape the glare of western fame, and indulge a passion for opium.

Out of the blue, he heard through a mutual friend that Kylie was coming to Hong Kong on her way to perform four concerts in Japan. He cleared his diary to make sure he was around when she visited. A dinner date was arranged and Kylie waited patiently in her hotel suite for the singer to pick her up. She waited and she waited. Hutchence had never been on time for anything and he was not about to start now. This did not go down well with 'Kylie Minogue Limited', who had formed their usual protective shield around her. When Hutchence eventually showed up, he was greeted by a gallery of angry faces – Kylie's mum Carol, manager Terry Blamey, a personal assistant and four dancers. The atmosphere failed to faze the rock star, who whisked Kylie off to a local restaurant and completely charmed her, despite the meal making her feel queasy. 'From that terrible start, we had a fantastic time,' she said. 'We talked and talked into the night until we literally had to be separated.'

Kylie was just twenty-one, famous but unworldly, and thus fascinated and overpowered by her companion's articulation and knowledge. Hutchence had a view or a witty comment on every subject, and Kylie was a blank canvas on which he could work. This time Kylie was completely hooked. But what was more surprising, so was Michael. He found her fun, fresh and genuine in a world full of fakes: 'She's a very underestimated person, she looks absolutely fabulous, she's very honest, she has no pretensions, she's unjaded. The amount of people in her position I've met and I wouldn't want to spend thirty seconds with. There is nothing worse than successful people who are miserable.'

After some sightseeing in Hong Kong, with Michael

as the perfect gentleman guide, the Kylie circus moved on to Japan for a gig at the Tokyo Dome in front of 38,000 fans. She was, and remains, an enormous star in Japan. After the show she was back in her hotel room, relaxing with her entourage, when Hutchence walked in. He had followed Kylie from Hong Kong, a clear indication of his intentions. Everyone decided to go out clubbing. Michael romantically kept trying to hold Kylie's hand like a lovestruck kid and Kylie kept slapping it playfully away. By the end of the evening, however, her resistance had melted. This night marked the start of a relationship which would blossom and flourish, making the year 1990 one of the happiest of Kylie's life. She fell deeply in love with her rock star. For his part, as his mother Patricia once wisely observed, 'Michael loved being "in love".'

Rumours that Michael and Kylie were an item quickly spread throughout the music world. Nobody could believe it. The public perception was that Michael was so cool and Kylie was so uncool. 'It was shocking for everyone,' she admitted, 'including me.' Even their respective families at first dismissed the rumours as pure gossip. By Christmas of that year, however, everyone knew. Already the famous couple had been playing a game of cat and mouse with the world's paparazzi, with photographs of them together being bought and sold for vast sums. Kylie was already accustomed to this daily intrusion, but it was new to Michael.

While Kylie's romance with Michael was blossoming, Jason Donovan was being portrayed as some sort of cuckolded fool. This is very unfair on Kylie, as her relationship with Jason had been drifting ever since their pop careers had exploded into life. Jason has admitted, 'I found it really hard to deal with her fame at the time. We broke up and she went out with Michael and it was splashed everywhere. I was the one that copped that. It was a hard time for me, having spent personal time with her and then her moving on to the guy that I wanted to be. That was pretty hard.' Kylie's friends are adamant that her relationship with Jason was over before her affair with Hutchence ignited. One explained, 'Kylie is quite moral.' Kylie did see Jason soon after she had fallen in love with Michael Hutchence. It was at the recording of Band Aid II's version of 'Do They Know It's Christmas?', destined to be the 1989 Christmas number one. An eyewitness observed that both Jason and Kylie were in tears: 'It was very awkward because they hadn't seen each other for some time. It was quite emotional.' Kylie and Jason had begun the year on top of the world with 'Especially For You', but ended it apart. Kylie was with Michael and a changed woman. It is a cruel irony that Jason enjoyed his first solo number one during the year – 'Too Many Broken Hearts'. Kylie, too, had a chart-topper with 'Hand on Your Heart', a plea to a lover to confess that their relationship is really over. Pop music, so often accused of being shallow, can sometimes provide a commentary on life and lives, as Kylie was soon to prove again with 'Better The Devil You Know', a song which appeared to encapsulate the image of Michael Hutchence.

Kylie was behaving like a teenager in love, even though she would soon be twenty-two. She had to fulfil commitments in the UK, including a short concert tour, but she was constantly on the phone to Michael, displaying a mixture of excitement and insecurity. In fairness, Michael did his share of calling her, and her entourage were getting used to his familiar greeting, 'Hi Babe', if one of them picked up the telephone when she was busy. When Kylie grabbed the phone, she would always leave the room so that she could talk privately. No one could fail to notice the immediate change that had come over Kylie. She described it as having had her blinkers taken off. During the next six months she would, under Michael's influence, start reshaping her life and taking control of her own destiny. It was this period, which so many perceived at the time as Kylie firmly going off the rails that actually sowed the seeds of survival. Back at PWL in London, they were noticing a complete personality change: 'After she met Michael, you could tell that she was stronger. Before, she might have said if she didn't think something was a good idea, but afterwards she just wouldn't do it.' The Hutchence philosophy was that she was a star, *the* star, and everyone around her was serving her, not the other way round. He described it as wearing an 'ego jacket' – whenever she messed up it was not her fault, it was the person in the jacket.

After her London commitments, Kylie was able to spend some quiet time with Michael in Hong Kong before they both flew on to his home in Sydney to prepare for Christmas. The romance was already public property, something denied her fans during her relationship with Jason Donovan. Kylie was used to the persistent press scrutiny and had managed it successfully during her time with *Neighbours*. Hutchence hated it. He was mortified when they were secretly photographed enjoying each other's company in Sydney's Centennial Park. The Australian magazine *Woman's Day* devoted three pages to a set of pictures showing the couple happy and embracing, with Kylie soaking up the sun in a bra top. They also appeared in the *News of the World*.

The cameras followed them everywhere – taking rides around the city on Michael's Harley-Davidson, going to the movies, or just hanging out in cafés, bars and clubs. Michael would recommend books for Kylie to read, or he would rent classic films like *Casablanca* and *Citizen Kane* for them to watch together in his minimally furnished apartment. Kylie revelled in Sydney's more cosmopolitan culture and, away from the camera shutters, she was having the time of her life. Such was her lover's influence that she broke her personal ban on taking drugs. It was not the sort of intake to persuade rehabilitation centres to put out a welcome mat. It amounted to no more than a little dope and the occasional ecstasy tablet, but it didn't stop the now notoriously false rumour spreading that Kylie was rushed to hospital to have her stomach pumped after her experimentation went wrong. She was most displeased, and only recently stated categorically, 'I was not even in the country at the time!'

Drugs have never played a major part in Kylie's life. She was not happy about Jason's consumption and, even under the influence of Hutchence, she never went through an opium-den phase. She did, however, appreciate her lover's point of view concerning freedom of choice. Drugs and, in particular, ecstasy were an essential ingredient of the rock-star lifestyle in the nineties and, in Sydney, Hutchence and his friends would indulge before hitting the clubs and staying out most of the night. It was exhausting and repetitive but, as Kylie explained to *Q* magazine, 'I've experimented, yes; some things you can only talk about if you've had experience of them – so I'm thankful for that experience. But I would condemn drugs now. I guess there's a drug for each decade and ecstasy is this decade's drug.'

Those who try to pin down Michael's influence on Kylie to one thing are missing the point. It was not just about popping a few pills or a more adventurous sex life. (That was part of it – not least when Kylie's luggage revealed a pair of handcuffs in an airport security check.) It was a life change. Kylie liked her new friends. Through Hutchence, for instance, she met Nick Cave, poet and Gothic Prince of Darkness, who was to have a huge creative influence on Kylie during the mid-nineties. This new 'circle' embraced Kylie. They did not treat her like a miniature Barbie doll or a trophy girlfriend for Michael. They found her bright, fun and a tonic for their jaded palates. As Tim Farriss, INXS guitarist and brother of Andrew, told music journalist Adrian Deevoy, 'Kylie's a lovely girl and Michael really loves her. So if you were thinking of writing anything smart arse about them, prepare to have your legs broken slowly and painfully.'

The rest of the world became aware of the change in Kylie at the Australian première of her first starring role in the feature film *The Delinquents*. Hutchence was there, looking every inch the dissolute rock star, complete with garishly patterned trousers, a waistcoat for a shirt and a pair of ill-fitting army boots. Next to him was a girl no one recognized, his latest conquest no doubt. She was petite, fit-looking with a tight 'suicide blonde' wig and a micro-dress with a pattern of noughts and crosses. The photographers took her picture in the weary way they reserved for nameless rock chicks, until the whisper went round. It was Kylie! Gone were the bubble haircut, the comfy denim teenage outfits and the self-effacing cheery smile. This was a sex bomb at a première, years before Liz Hurley and her ilk used such occasions to get noticed. It was a bold, rebellious statement, not just challenging the public perception of Kylie and that of her fans, but also making the powers that be at PWL sit up and splutter into their morning tea. It was a watershed moment in Kylie's career, and Hutchence gave her the courage to go through with it.

This was one of the few times in Kylie's career when her private and public life dovetailed neatly together. She wanted everyone to see her and to realize that she was now with Michael Hutchence: a new independent, grown-up Kylie. Soon, their respective careers would mean they would be apart more than they were together. Kylie was preparing for her first real tour, when she would be singing live with a full band instead of using backing tracks. She spent Christmas, as she always preferred to, with her family back in Melbourne and then plunged into rehearsals for her tour's first night at the Brisbane Entertainment Centre. She did, however, drop everything to fly into Sydney for Michael's thirtieth birthday party, which she helped organize in a large warehouse, a favoured venue for rock events. Her sister Dannii had helped her bake a special chocolate cake which, candles ablaze, Kylie brought into the room, followed by a bois-terous conga line of most of the 200 guests.

Kylie told Pete Waterman that she wanted some time off from recording in the early part of 1990. She stayed in Sydney, while Michael and INXS worked on a new album, which would eventually be entitled *X*. Kylie would spend most of the days hanging around the studio, grasping the opportunity to watch and learn, in a way she had never been allowed to in the studios of Stock, Aitken and Waterman. They took time off to travel back to Hong Kong and also took a holiday on Great Keppel Island on the idyllic north-eastern coast of Australia. Kylie travelled with Terry Blamey, but without Michael, to Los Angeles, to work with some American producers on tracks for a new album. She dedicated one of the songs called 'Count The Days' to the lover she was missing.

Kylie soon had to fly back to the UK for spring tour dates and the full extent of her 'change' was becoming apparent. In May, her new single 'Better The Devil You Know' was due for release and, for the first time, Kylie exercised control over her image. She presented Stock, Aitken and Waterman with the video for the song, which she had filmed in Melbourne, and they had little choice but to accept it. It was noticeable for the new, raunchy Kylie, dancing seductively in the arms of a muscular black dancer, and also for the large ring on her finger, a gift from Michael, which she seemed to be flashing for the camera at every opportunity. It was emblazoned with the letter M.

Michael joined her in London at the end of her tour. The relationship looked set to last, as the couple began a continental holiday by travelling on the romantic Orient Express. Kylie helped Michael choose a $500,000 villa to buy in the French village of Roquefort les Pins, on the Riviera between Nice and Cannes. It was a magnificent 400-year-old farmhouse, with five bedrooms. Kylie and Michael would speed up and down the coast on a motorbike. Back in London, they were in danger of becoming a familiar showbiz couple; Michael took Kylie to see John Malkovich in *Burn This,* a theatrical *tour de force* and one of the West End hits of the year. Eyewitnesses in the audience reported that he spent most of the performance twanging Kylie's bra strap. There was still time for another legendary story to emerge: this time it was that Michael and Kylie had joined the 'mile-high club' on a jumbo jet when the Australian Prime Minister Bob Hawke was seated a row in front. According to one of Michael's entourage, they had just a blanket to cover their modesty. Kylie is petite, but this is not something that should be attempted in economy seats. The whole incident was given a 'Carry On' flavour, with the suggestion that Mr Hawke had turned round and winked at them.

Kylie's life could not have been more perfect, or so it seemed. She now had control of her career for the first time. She was a multi-millionairess. And she was in love. The only cloud on the horizon was the fact that Michael was back on tour, promoting the new INXS album. It began in Europe but, over the coming months, would take him all over the world and keep them apart. Kylie could be forgiven for feeling insecure, considering his past reputation. The couple spent Christmas together at the farmhouse and Michael gave her a Gucci watch as a present. They were joined by fellow musician Chris Bailey and his wife Pearl, old friends from the time Michael was with Michele Bennett. Kylie cooked for everyone, and did her best to make it a happy, festive time, even though it was the first time she had spent the holiday season away from Melbourne and was missing her family.

What Kylie did not know was that the famous celebrity photographer Herb Ritts had introduced Michael to the breathtakingly beautiful Danish supermodel Helena Christensen, who was just nineteen. By the time he had crossed the Atlantic for January dates in Mexico and the States, he was spending almost as much time on the phone to Helena as he was to Kylie. Rumours of his womanizing – including with singer Belinda Carlisle – and pictures of him with glamorous companions were not helpful, but it is always one particular fixation which is the most dangerous for a relationship. Michael Hutchence loved being 'in love'. Kylie, promoting her new album *Rhythm of Love*, was more independent now than when she first met him. Did she still need him as much as she had done a year ago? Was Helena about to become his next 'work in progress'?

In New York, in February 1991, events took a complicated turn with both Helena and Kylie in town at the same time. Michael's mother Patricia recalled meeting Helena at the INXS concert at Meadowlands, the first time the model had seen the band. The next day, Patricia was expecting Michael to arrive for lunch with Miss Christensen and was stunned when he appeared with Kylie, for a distinctly frosty meal. She did not see Kylie again. Michael and Helena stayed together for four years, until Paula Yates arrived on the scene.

Kylie was inconsolable. Her friends offered as much support as they could, but she was heartbroken. Even those who were little more than work colleagues found themselves providing a shoulder to cry on. One who had never had a real conversation with the singer recalled, 'Kylie actually sobbed on my shoulder. It was very unusual for her because she wasn't that kind of person, but for me it was sort of a special moment that she was talking to me 'cause she didn't, she wasn't a natural, she would have her select people she'd talk to and I wasn't one of them, so she was obviously very down indeed for her to talk to me. It just started with "I'm feeling down" and went from there.'

'I would not have missed our relationship for anything.'

9

Coolification

On stage at the Royal Albert Hall, a white-haired old man with a long beard was reading poetry in Braille. In the wings, Kylie Minogue, scruffy as an unmade bed and wearing no make-up, was having second, third and fourth thoughts about taking her turn at the Poetry Olympics. She turned to Nick Cave, her creative Svengali, and whispered, 'Nick, God's on stage, how can we follow that?'

More than a year had passed since the demise of her relationship with Michael Hutchence before Kylie eventually split with Stock, Aitken and Waterman. Her final release for them was a *Greatest Hits* album which reached number one in September 1992, her third chart topping album on the PWL label. That was a good way to finish but musically, for the future, the writing was on the wall when her last single under that umbrella, 'Celebration', scraped into the charts at number twenty.

Professionally Kylie was faced with an uncertain future. Her parting from The Hit Factory was the final nail in Charlene's, the girl-next-door's coffin. Her relationship with Michael Hutchence, however, had not made her convincingly cool. He had given her the hint of sex appeal.

Her prestige had certainly risen when he described her as the best f*** he had enjoyed but she was still standing on the threshold of coolness.

Eventually, in February 1993, Kylie signed with deConstruction, an independent dance-orientated label which had cracked the mainstream market with the Manchester group M People. The group was led by Heather Small, a young singer who resembled a black Carmen Miranda and boasted a unique voice which launched a thousand karaoke impressions. Kylie was a fan, and M People actually produced and arranged 'Time Will Pass You By', the final track on *Kylie Minogue*, her first deConstruction album.

More significantly, part of the package involved the ultra-fashionable producers Steve Anderson and Dave Seaman, who worked under the name of Brothers In Rhythm. They fell over themselves to work with Kylie, and invited her to a studio session. This saw the birth of 'Confide In Me' and 'Dangerous Game', which would feature a smoother, more mature sound. Steve Anderson paid Kylie a tribute, one which she has been paid throughout her career – he declared her to be the most professional person he had ever worked with, and their mutual respect grew into a close friendship. He gave her confidence in her musical abilities, and she grew as an artist through this transitional period.

Brothers In Rhythm played their part in making Kylie cool. 'Confide In Me' was the first time people sat up and took notice of Kylie's lyrical contribution. When it was released as a single, the string-laden arrangement, the hint of Madonna, and the sophistication met with encouraging noises from the critics and the tills. It reached number two on the UK charts, kept off the top by the dire 'Saturday Night' by Whigfield, a one-hit wonder if ever there was one. Even 'The Loco-Motion Girl' would have turned her nose up at 'Saturday Night'. As a consolation, 'Confide In Me' made number one in Australia, New Zealand, Turkey, Croatia and Finland (as usual).

If 'Confide In Me' and the follow-up single 'Put Yourself In My Place' gave some impetus to Kylie's search for credibility then her alliance with Nick Cave gave her the means to push back the boundaries of public perception. The real Kylie loves to surprise and shock, something she achieved at the première for *The Delinquents* on Michael Hutchence's arm and also when she stripped for the video of 'Put Yourself In My Place'. She had always had a streak of exhibitionism but, until she fell under the influence of Nick Cave she had apparently accepted limitations which in reality did not exist. There were no limits for this new Kylie Minogue.

Nick Cave was a genuine original in the world of contemporary culture. A great friend of the late Michael Hutchence, Cave is a middle-class Australian, the son of a teacher. He went to school in Melbourne, where he founded a band which would later become The Boys Next Door. They released an album in Australia before changing their name to Birthday Party and moving to London in 1980. The band had a raw energy, while Cave had a brand of hip nonconformity which Hutchence, in particular, sought to emulate. Cave was dangerously cool. Intriguingly, it is this charismatic quality that Kylie finds so attractive in men.

When the band split up, Cave moved to West Berlin,

which in the eighties was at the forefront of experimental European culture. By 1984 a new line-up was formed, Nick Cave and The Bad Seeds, which may have been a reference to the gospel of St Matthew. Cave had been influenced by the Bible through his Anglican upbringing. Music author Spencer Bright observed, 'Cave is aptly named, inhabiting a twilight world somewhere between William Faulkner and William Burroughs. He is an intellectual with a grim take on life and death, filling his songs with apocalyptic characters and incidents. There's tons of murder and lust, revenge and retribution in his songs.'

Cave's lyrics were always poetic and, in 1989, he expanded his writing to a novel entitled *And The Ass Saw The Angel*. Of more significance in his appeal to a wider audience was the beautiful 1988 Wim Wenders film *Wings of Desire*, which featured two of Cave's songs. The movie, about an angel who falls in love on earth, remains a favourite of Kylie's since she was first persuaded to see it by Hutchence. A year later, Cave produced his own film *Ghosts . . . of the Civil Dead*, a prison movie starring Cave, written by him and featuring his own soundtrack.

The key ingredient that the gothic-looking Cave – the 'Prince of Darkness' – adds to his art is the challenging aspect, something that both Michael Hutchence and Kylie Minogue found appealing. Kylie has freely acknowledged that she is in awe of him: 'I think Nick Cave is wonderful,' she has simply said. She found him 'mild and gentle', making him sound more like a washing-up liquid than a cutting-edge talent.

Cave is also an example of something else that Kylie admires – he refuses to be pigeon-holed. His work is a total concept, not just singing or composing, but poetry and prose, photography and film. He, along with Hutchence and her next important boyfriend, Stephane Sednaoui, have helped Kylie stretch the boundaries she had set for herself.

Fate decreed that Kylie and Cave would connect. In the mid-nineties, when he moved back to London, he became one of Hutchence's closest friends. They formed an unlikely business alliance as partners in The Portobello Café, which was one of the most fashionable places to be seen. Kylie was often there and in other Notting Hill spots around this time, even though she still lived in Fulham. When Hutchence had a daughter with Paula Yates in 1996, he asked his mate Nick Cave to be godfather.

Cave first joined up with Kylie professionally when he asked her to sing on his 1995 album *Murder Ballads*, which featured songs dealing exclusively with murder. Kylie sang a duet, 'Where The Wild Roses Grow', which she has often said is her favourite among all her songs, a choice that might amaze her fans. The song is a haunting dialogue between a killer (Cave) and his victim (Kylie). He bludgeons her to death with a rock. Cave had always wanted to do a song with Kylie, finding her basic charm and lack of cynicism fascinating. While the rest of the world thought 'Better The Devil You Know' was a classic pop song, Cave discovered hidden poetic meaning in the combination of a dark lyric, describing a flawed, abusive love, and Kylie's own vocal innocence. He thought it a harrowing portrait of humanity, which could be likened to the Old Testament psalms.

Cave wrote 'Wild Roses' with Kylie specifically in mind, and acknowledged that it 'was a dangerous song for her

Little black number and red hair – almost unrecognizable at the première of
Muriel's Wedding in 1995

With Zane O'Donnell, one of several male models she has dated

With Lenny Kravitz at a *Vogue* party

Mercurial photographer Stephane Sednaoui was her first French connection, from 1995–1997

With legendary ladies-man
Tim Jefferies

Celebrity, as the
star of *Spooks*, was
six years away for
Rupert Penry-Jones
when he was Kylie's
boyfriend

'Marilyn' Minogue?

Kylie's sensational performance at the closing ceremony of the 2000 Olympic Games in Sydney

The famous gold hot pants – rear view

Live at the Hammersmith Apollo
in London, March 2001

At the *Smash Hits* Poll
Winners Party, 2001

Giving Robbie Williams a thrill at the MTV Europe Music Awards in Stockholm, November 2000

to sing'. It worked brilliantly, with Cave's Scott Walker-style baritone contrasting powerfully with Kylie's brittle vocal. In the video that accompanied the single, Kylie is seen in the pale repose of a dead Ophelia. To the surprise of many critics, the track reached number two in Australia and a very respectable eleven on the UK chart. It was actually Kylie's biggest UK hit in the five-year period between July 1995 and July 2000, when 'Spinning Around' announced that she was back.

Kylie would not have dared to show her face at the Poetry Olympics in July 1996 without the support of Nick Cave. She was unbilled which was a wise precaution as it kept cameras away from what might have been a humiliating experience. She stood in the wings, waif-like wearing green tracksuit pants and a clashing purple T-shirt. Eventually, it was her turn and Cave literally pushed his protégé on stage. Apprehensively, she stood in front of the microphone and began, 'In my imagination . . .'. It was the start of 'I Should Be So Lucky' and Kylie, with no musical accompaniment whatsoever, spoke the complete lyric to her biggest-selling record to that date. It was daring, courageous and took the audience's breath away. It was also a defining moment in Kylie's career because it allowed her to embrace her past, as well as giving her the confidence to push herself forward. Confidence has always been Kylie's drug of choice.

She admitted that she had done none of her normal preparation for a live performance that night; she did not put on the 'ego jacket' which Michael Hutchence had told her always to wear. Kylie remained unsure about the whole thing until she was actually out there, saying the words which she had sung a thousand times. Up until this night, she had distanced herself from her days at The Hit Factory, yet here she was, shouting to the world that this was part of her career and part of her. The extra ingredient of reciting the words in this fashion was that, without the bouncing melody, they took on ironic meaning.

It was a triumph. Afterwards, Kylie told *Cleo* magazine in Australia, 'People love to pigeon-hole you, no matter what you do. They place a box over you and you can't get out of it, but I have been able to stretch it a little, to lift up one side and peep out, to shuffle it here and there. I don't know how I've done it. I was supposed to be a one-hit wonder.'

The debt that Kylie owes to her unlikely alliance with Nick Cave is that he truly made her cool. The coolification of Kylie may or may not have begun with Michael Hutchence but, by the mid-nineties, there was an around-the-block queue of credible artists wanting to work with her. Kylie has always chosen collaborations carefully to enhance her image – even 'Especially For You' was timed to perfection. Kylie was ready to channel this new creative energy into her own music.

Cave had a profound influence on her next album, provisionally titled *Impossible Princess*, teaching her, as Kylie put it, to be totally truthful in her music, to unleash 'the core of myself'. The original concept for *Impossible Princess* was that it would be a collaboration between Kylie and Brothers In Rhythm. Anderson and Seaman were two of the most innovative producers in the music industry, so it is a tribute to Kylie that they scrapped their own ideas for her second deConstruction album, and allowed Kylie to supply the creative impetus. Anderson recalled, 'As soon as she started writing, it became clear that she was developing as an artist, so we scrapped our original plan and let most of the ideas come from her.'

The result is a darkly autobiographical lyric sheet, which reveals far more about Kylie than any interview in a glossy magazine or a newspaper. Her standard replies to the same old questions never rise above the mildly interesting. Here, though, there was no twee 'Your Arms Are In My Heart' candyfloss. They were complex, serious, introspective and challenging to the listener, none more so than 'Dreams', which chronicled the dreams of an impossible princess, wishing to 'taste every moment and try everything.'

Kylie was seeking a wider musical base and, so, decided on a number of other 'stoned cool' alliances in addition to Brothers In Rhythm. She enlisted Rob D, aka Clubbed To Death, Dave Ball, ex Soft Cell and now The Grid, and Rob Dougan of Mo' Wax. Some of the collaboration was rock-style spontaneity. 'I have a friend called Skinny who was playing Clubbed To Death around the house. I loved it and, out of the blue, he said he knew the guy . . .'

The stand-out track on *Impossible Princess* is by common consent 'Too Far', which features Kylie speed-whispering over an intense drum'n' bass beat. There was a loud lobby to release it as a single, owing to a huge club following for the Brothers In Rhythm unofficial remix. It was unofficial, in that deConstruction originally knew nothing about it, although Kylie, always up for something new, took time to re-sing vocals and add some ad libs. There is literally just a handful of promo copies, which would fetch a fortune if they ever came up for sale.

The best known collaboration on *Impossible Princess* was with the acclaimed Welsh band, Manic Street Preachers.

They had long been admirers of Kylie – bassist Nicky Wire once claimed to have been beaten up for wearing a Kylie T-shirt at school. She met vocalist James Dean Bradfield at an awards ceremony and discovered that in 1991 he had tried to reach her on several occasions to discuss working together. He had wanted her to sing on the vintage Manics' song 'Little Baby Nothing' – about a starlet used by men – but had eventually enlisted porn star Traci Lords when he could not get past the 'gates of PWL heaven'.

Kylie and Bradfield decided to meet for tea at his home, and Kylie took along some cherries. She also brought a bunch of lyrics, to try to persuade Bradfield to turn them into a real song for *Impossible Princess*. In the best traditions of songwriting, Bradfield strummed a bit and suggested she leave them with him. He played her a track, which she thought sounded like Tamla Motown, that he felt would suit her. She thought he was trying to discover what her own tastes were. 'It was a pop moment,' she recalled. This was the album that would unveil the truly creative Kylie. As soon as the outside world heard of the collaboration between Kylie and Bradfield, she was dubbed IndieKylie. The result of that first meeting was that Bradfield sent her a demo of 'I Don't Need Anyone', which Kylie loved, finding it refreshing and so different from what she had been working on before. Bradfield asked for some more lyrics and he then amalgamated two sets into one for 'Some Kind Of Bliss', a rocky pop classic. Both tracks were unmistakably Manics, guitars exploding like squibs around an anthemic melody.

'Some Kind Of Bliss' was released as a single in September 1997 and was a flop. Kylie had favoured releasing 'Limbo', a more overt dance cut with an incessant beat, which sounded a bit like Republica. It was her first release since the 'Wild Roses' collaboration two years earlier, so the results were very disappointing – not least for her record company deConstruction. Bradfield was apologetic, blaming himself: 'I loved her voice, got on with her and I am embarrassed that I failed her.' The track peaked at number twenty-two on the UK charts, the only consolation being that it reached a higher position than the re-issue the same month of 'Little Baby Nothing'. It fared even worse in Australia, where the heartland of Kylie's fan-base seemed to have deserted her – it only managed a pitiful number twenty-seven.

Some critics walloped 'Some Kind Of Bliss'. *NME* called it 'supremely irritating' and declared, 'Kylie belts out the lyrics like she's reading from an autocue. Any soul is lost in a slurry of bought-in brass and a ropey guitar solo that'd be more at home on a Shakin' Stevens record.' The difficulty for Kylie was that, despite the credibility she gained by her collaborations, she was still being perceived as the girl who launched a thousand tragic outfits. Or, even worse, as a girl-next-door which, in some unfair way, suggested IndieKylie was a fraud. It seemed like a return to the bad old days of Stock, Aitken and Waterman, when kicking Kylie was a national pastime.

With hindsight, releasing the Manics' track may have been a mistake because the publicity generated by this unlikely mixture tended to overshadow the rest of the album. Steve Anderson forthrightly believes that 'Some Kind Of Bliss' was a cop-out release to satisfy the demands of the media, who wanted it to be the single. He thought 'Too Far' and 'Jump' were more representative of the album.

For once, Kylie had no control over the tragic chain of events which scuppered the grand design for the *Impossible Princess* album. She had spent two years working on the project, a labour of love. The gestation period coincided with her relationship with photographer Stephane Sednaoui, which proved a fertile base for the most creative period of Kylie's life so far. The challenging aspect of her relationship triggered a challenging period in Kylie's career. The trash cans are littered with the careers of successful pop stars who suddenly think they can do it all, and inflict their dreadful songs and sentiments on a public which promptly goes off them. It was a brave career move for Kylie. The chasm between the Kylie of *Impossible Princess* and the Kylie of the Hit Factory is so wide, it is hard to believe they are the same person. It clearly showed that Kylie was prepared to take a chance on her own talent.

Both Kylie and her record company deConstruction – which was much more a dance label than an indie label – were dismayed at the poor sales of 'Some Kind Of Bliss'. By an unkind twist of fate, Princess Diana was killed the same week as its release and, despite extensive airplay, everyone was much more inclined to buy Elton John's tribute 'Candle In The Wind 1997', which accounted for 80 per cent of record sales that week. The whole marketing strategy was thrown – a hit single setting up the release of an album. Kylie took the bold step of agreeing to pull the plug – not least because an album entitled *Impossible Princess* did not seem tactful at this time. Kylie gamely said that it would have been insensitive to put the album out, so it was postponed for three months until after Christmas. 'There's no way you can prepare for something like the Princess of the country dying. It's thrown everybody,' she explained.

While it is very true that the death of Diana caused a thoroughly weird few weeks in the record industry – 'Candle In The Wind 1997' sold thirty-three million copies worldwide in three months – it still does not account for why 'Some Kind Of Bliss' failed to make the top twenty. There were still twenty-one better selling singles in the UK that week, and only one of them was a tribute to the Princess of Wales. The following week Kylie's single dropped out of the chart altogether, hardly a good advertisement for the album. The public did not buy into this new Kylie. Spencer Bright thought the record struck an attitude and a pose, rather than truly reflecting where Kylie was moving as an individual, and so was doomed to failure. He explained, 'The chemistry was not right. And most of the material was inferior to Stock, Aitken and Waterman.' Postponing the release of the album was an interesting commercial decision, as it meant no sales at Christmas, the time of the year when the most records are bought.

The new strategy was to release another single in the New Year when more exposure and a higher chart position could be achieved with lower sales. Alas, 'Did It Again' did little better than 'Some Kind Of Bliss', reaching number fourteen in the UK chart. The album was put back yet again, while a third single was put out. 'Breathe' had a more commercial, faster remix than the album version, but this too only reached number fourteen. Eventually, the album (now uninspiringly entitled *Kylie Minogue in Europe*), Kylie's pride and joy, found its way on to the shelves in March 1998, and tottered to number ten in the album charts, before sinking without trace. The whole sorry saga smacked of desperation on deConstruction's part. Kylie remained professionally polite about the whole thing, but it was profoundly disappointing.

Impossible Princess is, by some measure, the most challenging Kylie Minogue album. It remains the one where she had most personal input, especially in the lyrics, which reveal the vulnerable, melancholy and poetic Kylie, far removed from the glossy image of 'Kylie Minogue Limited'. Although the title can be considered an ironic nod to Kylie's reputation – 'the girl on the show pony at the circus' – it does, in fact, come from a book of poetry, *Impossible Poems to Break the Harts* (*sic*) *of Impossible Princesses*, which was given to her by the cult poet and children's author Billy Childish, another hip fan who found Kylie cool.

'I broke so many rules.'

10

Goodbye Yellow
Brick Road

Kylie seized her chance when she spotted a woman wearing
a T-shirt with KYLIE written across the front backstage at an
Awards ceremony. 'Nice to meet you', she told Madonna.

The release of 'Confide In Me', which boasted a super
sexy video, coincided with Kylie's first 'Hollywood' film, a
martial arts movie called *Street Fighter* starring Jean-Claude
Van Damme. Quite what Kylie thought she was doing
dressed up in battle fatigues, shooting a bazooka is a mystery. Years later her revealing comment on the film was,
'It seemed like a good idea at the time.' Kylie remains a
film star waiting to happen which is a pity because four
years earlier *The Delinquents* revealed the promise of better
things ahead.

Kylie is very different from the other female pop stars
who have tried to move their celebrity up a notch by
making a successful movie. She actually was an actress and
could reasonably have been expected to make some half
decent movies. Charlene Mitchell was still very fresh in the
mind when Kylie started filming *The Delinquents* in

Queensland in the spring of 1989. She was fitting it in between promoting her first million selling album and recording her second, *Enjoy Yourself*. Perhaps that has always been the problem for Kylie as a movie star – there are just not enough hours in the day to be a superstar at everything.

In *The Delinquents*, Kylie played a rebellious teenager called Lola Lovell, who was not the sort of girl likely to pitch up in Erinsborough. This was a rites-of-passage movie, set in a small, provincial town in the mid-1950s. The story centred on her love for a young drifter, Brownie Hansen, who was played by the American brat pack actor Charlie Schlatter, then one of a number of young Hollywood actors who appeared to be on the verge of major stardom, but who never quite achieved it. The film, based on a popular Australian novel, was generally thought to have suffered from the influence of its American financial backers (Warner), who diluted the homespun, ethnic feel of the original book.

In the film, Kylie had to remove her clothes on a number of occasions, thrash around in the sheets and, more controversially, be taken by her overbearing mother for an abortion when she was fifteen. Kylie was at pains to point out that the book was much more depressing and gritty than the film: 'If we had left it the way it was, it was so depressing you would have wanted to slash your wrists.' This was a totally different project for Kylie who, unlike her Stock, Aitken and Waterman incarnation, was allowed plenty of freedom to express her own ideas on set. It was a refreshing change to be taking part in something grown-up, at the same time as 'Hand On Your Heart' was topping the UK charts. Kylie was being introduced to a world where her opinion counted.

Perhaps inevitably, *The Delinquents* was condemned by the critics. The *Daily Mirror*, who, these days, loves all things Kylie, declared, 'Kylie has as much acting charisma as cold porridge', which was unnecessarily cruel. Although the film did well commercially in both the UK and Australia, it was a flop in the US which spoiled any prospects at this time of Kylie becoming a star there. Because of Kylie's involvement, the film remains a curio on the shelves of local video stores. Much more interesting than the film itself is the change it portrayed in Kylie's image. Lola Lovell was no 'girl-next-door' character. When the film premièred at the end of the year, Kylie was an item with Michael Hutchence, and that relationship garnered many more headlines than the film itself. Everyone was obsessed by Kylie's perceived change under the influence of the rock star, and *The Delinquents* became part and parcel of that. But Kylie filmed *The Delinquents* before she became involved with Hutchence. She was still with Jason Donovan, who would fly up to the location to visit her when his own schedule allowed. Kylie had taken the decision to distance herself from the public image of her as 'girl-next-door' Charlene, without Hutchence's influence.

One of the barriers to Kylie building on her starring role in *The Delinquents*, was the media obsession with focusing on her new 'rock chick' look, and her perceived corruption by Michael Hutchence, rather than on the film itself. In retrospect the film is beautifully shot with a great soundtrack and period feel. Kylie is far better in it than the original reviews suggested. In the context of the time, she was not yet a great media favourite and was not taken particularly seriously. Kylie herself thought the story 'beautiful and very touching.'

The Delinquents did not lead to movie stardom or even her next role. The director of *Street Fighter*, Steven De Souza, had seen Kylie on a magazine cover displaying 'The 30 Most Beautiful People In The World.' The film was based on a popular video game. Kylie played a character called Cammy, a British Intelligence officer, master of surveillance and lieutenant to Van Damme's Colonel Guile. It was a curious choice of film for Kylie, hardly a major role at a time when she was embarking on a period of much greater personal creativity. This was starlet stuff, although it did have the advantage of being filmed in Australia and Thailand. Kylie had to take martial arts lessons, in particular kick boxing, in order to make believable the notion of her petite frame as a lethal weapon. She also had to pump iron, resulting in a temporary inflation of her upper torso.

Kylie and Van Damme, who is not much taller than her, did not really spark in the film, although it did reasonably well at the box office, thanks to the actor's loyal fans. In the US, it took $70 million. One thing that Van Damme did do for Kylie was to teach her an exercise for maintaining a pert bottom, by squeezing the butt cheeks together. Kylie was very much in awe of the Belgian's backside, which she thought defied gravity – as her own quite obviously still does, even though Kylie always maintains that she does not work out.

After *Street Fighter*, Kylie went straight into her next movie, allegedly a comedy, *Bio Dome*, with Pauly Shore and Stephen Baldwin. Critic John Lavin, in *Movie Magazine International*, dismissed it as the 'biggest waste of celluloid space I have ever witnessed'. Kylie, who played a scientist, described it as *Bill & Ted* in an agricultural dome. She played one of the straight roles, while the two male leads played two 'goofy guys', who mistake a bio dome for a mall. And the fun starts there. By coincidence, the video for the single release 'Put Yourself In My Place' depicted Kylie in a weightless bubble, gradually shedding all her clothes, much more memorable than *Bio Dome*. During this period of the mid-nineties, Kylie's career was like a scatter gun, shooting her all over the place in the hope that some of the pellets might hit the target. Sadly, her movie choices did not even make the outer ring. At least Kylie realized it was time to take a break from a very bumpy Yellow Brick Road. She was disappointed and dis-illusioned with the way that in films women are shoved into tight, short skirts and paraded from one scene to another, with very little point to their existence. This might work successfully in a Kylie video, but becomes threadbare when stretched to an hour and a half. Kylie had wanted American exposure and, once again, had been left in the dark room. She also sat up and took notice when her normally phlegmatic father Ron said *Bio Dome* was 'diabolical'.

Instead of trying for a third 'nothing' part, Kylie accepted a role more in keeping with this creative mid-period of her career. At least this time she was the star. It was a short, strange, eleven-minute Australian film called *Hayride To Hell*, in which Kylie played 'The Girl', who begs a salesman named George Table to help her. One advan-tage for Kylie was that it involved a week's intensive filming in Sydney, and would allow her to take an extended three-month break in Australia at the begin-ning of 1995, spending time with her family and friends, as well as her then boyfriend Mark Gerber. In some ways,

Hayride To Hell was an extended video. Kylie Chameleon, darkly brunette, tells Table she is a diabetic and insists that he give her a lift to her apartment. She goes inside but faints in the elevator, where she is found by Table. She wakes up and hits him with a teddy bear, shouting, 'What the f*** have you done with my things?' It is challengingly arty, which was just the attraction for Kylie. The important thing is that it promoted a different Kylie at a time when she was diversifying. This was no starlet fodder. Kylie achieved a much greater sense of professional pride from this eleven-minute short than from both of her 'Hollywood' films combined.

In retrospect, the films *Street Fighter* and *Bio Dome* were the least cool projects Kylie became involved in during the nineties. A much more fruitful collaboration came about in 1997, when she appeared naked in a video for the contemporary artist and photographer Sam Taylor-Wood. Again, *Misfit* was a short art film, this time for the BBC and more an exhibit than a cinematographic concept. Taylor-Wood, who would be nominated for the Turner Prize the following year, was inspired by Kylie's beautiful androgyny. She portrayed Kylie as a street urchin, and teased the audience by having her sing, not with her own voice but that of a nineteenth-century castrato. Taylor-Wood was, and remains, very influential in the London art scene, not least because of her marriage in the same year to artists' agent Jay Jopling. Jopling owns the White Cube galleries, and represents a Who's Who of the most talked-about modern artists, including Taylor-Wood herself, Tracey Emin and Damien Hirst. It did Kylie no harm at all to be associated with so celebrated a circle.

Kylie's secret for attracting the most original artists of a generation to work with her is her ability to change, like the shape-shifter from *The X Files*. As such, she is a blank canvas, waiting to spring into colourful life at the touch of a paintbrush. That does not mean that Kylie brings nothing to the party – on the contrary, her own creative juices are encouraged by those around her. Taylor-Wood once described her as a 'multi-faceted chameleon woman'. Creative people give Kylie the confidence to be creative herself.

The death in 1997 of Princess Diana had cast a shadow over Kylie's album *Impossible Princess*. By an amazing and rather ghastly coincidence, that year she also completed a cameo role in a film *Diana & Me*, about an Australian tourist called Diana Spencer, who travels to London to meet her famous namesake. Kylie played herself, a celebrity hounded by a paparazzo – a plot line which, in the light of the controversy over Diana's pursuit by photographers, only made the whole thing ten times worse. The timing of the film was quite exquisite in its awfulness and, understandably, it never saw the light of day.

Kylie never gives up. Just as she still expects to break through in the American market, she still wants to attain credence as a movie actress. As with her music, Australia remains her starting point for regrouping. And so she made two films there for release in 2000, which reinforced her musical comeback. In the first, *Cut*, she doesn't last very long. Poor Kylie is a horror film director, who is butchered with a pair of gardening shears by a masked killer early in the action. It was really a cross between *Friday the 13th* and *Scream*. Kylie was doing a favour for *Hayride To Hell* director Kimble Rendall, who was making his first full-length feature, and to Mushroom Records boss Michael Gudinski, who was involved in his first major film project. The star of the film was former Hollywood brat packer Molly Ringwald, who had met Kylie over dinner in LA some six months before. Ringwald had been a teenage star just like Kylie, and had suffered some similar difficulties through not really being allowed to grow up. Although Kylie was only on set for a few days, Ringwald really liked her and tried to give her advice on how to 'crack' America.

Kylie also signed up for the lead in another Australian film. *Sample People* was a brash, low-budget, indie thriller, in which Kylie played a nightclub owner, who becomes entangled in various scams involving a lot of cash and drugs. The unknown director Clinton Smith had sent Kylie a script two years earlier and had been astonished to receive a call from Terry Blamey, saying that she had chosen to appear in his film. Kylie liked it because her character was quite cunning and resourceful, not a bit like Charlene from *Neighbours*. For the film, Kylie joined the Pet Shop Boys to sing a version of the pop classic 'The Real Thing', which many viewers thought the highlight of the movie.

Kylie's film career is distinctly weird. Perhaps she has suffered from being a big fish in a small pond as Charlene Mitchell. She may have won awards, but has never professed to have any confidence in her acting abilities. Kylie is always complaining about nerves, insecurities and lack of confidence but, unlike her music career, her movie path seems to lack any overall strategy or purpose. The original idea seems to have been to make her even more famous, and to turn the television star into an international movie star. But it did not work. Ironically, considering she was by far the biggest star of *Neighbours*, two other much more minor actors in the soap have gone on to make it big on the world stage – Russell Crowe and Guy Pearce.

Much was made at the time of Kylie's tiny cameo in the Oscar winning musical *Moulin Rouge* (2001). She played The Green Fairy, a sort of Tinkerbell complete with a scream provided by Ozzy Osbourne. We see Kylie twinkling in the night sky, and then she is gone. The director Baz Luhrmann, a fellow Australian, is a great fan of Kylie's and may well work with her again. Since *Moulin Rouge*, however, she has been heard and not seen – as the voice of Florence in the film of *The Magic Roundabout*. Being a pop superstar does not guarantee movie stardom. Mariah Carey, The Spice Girls and Britney Spears have all stalled at their first attempt. In modern times only Cher has a portfolio to be proud of, although Jennifer Lopez continues to grind out mediocre films. And then there is Madonna, the artist who Kylie has more in common with than any other. She has made some twenty films in twenty years, an astonishing number considering she is never considered a movie star. Like Kylie, she is by no means the worst actress in the world and some of her films, notably *Desperately Seeking Susan*, are bordering on the classic. Perhaps Madonna and Kylie share the same problem – they can never shake off their musical image to suspend the audience's belief, so essential for a movie. Madonna is always Madonna and Kylie is always Kylie. Perhaps they are simply too big to be movie stars.

Their relative movie disappointments are just one of many areas where Kylie and Madonna bear comparison.

Only in recent years has Kylie managed to shrug off the spectre of the most famous female pop star of all time. While she was still climbing into her mechanic's overalls for another Charlene scene in *Neighbours*, Madonna had chalked up five number ones and eighteen top ten hits in the UK. By a strange coincidence, the only year since 1984 in which Madonna did not have a top ten single was 1988, the year Kylie, under the Stock, Aitken and Waterman banner, had her first five. Unsurprisingly, Madonna was someone Kylie looked up to as a musical icon long before anybody thought of using the same word to describe her. Pete Waterman could never understand it: 'I found it amazing that she was outselling Madonna four to one, but still wanted to be her. Everyone wanted to be Kylie Minogue except Kylie Minogue, who wanted to be Madonna.'

In the early days, when Kylie tried to adopt a raunchier image during her time with Michael Hutchence, she lapped up the comparisons to Madonna, because of her aspirations to match her iconic image. By 1992, Kylie wished she had never heard of the Madonna comparisons, complaining that Madonna herself had borrowed the images of other stars, from Marilyn Monroe to Greta Garbo. 'I'm sick of people saying I am ripping off Madonna,' she moaned. The now defunct *Sky* magazine launched a withering attack on poor Kylie, undermining her sex appeal in the bitchiest of manners: 'When Kylie bares all, she shows us merely that she has nothing to show. Kylie is trying to follow Madonna – she bared all, thus Kylie must. But where Madonna understands the game, Kylie doesn't. Madonna's a tough egg, a control freak who manipulates her own image in order to manipulate us. Basically, Kylie isn't sex.' Just what twenty-six-year-old Kylie had done to provoke such unkind observations is a mystery, but post-1998 they would appear absolutely absurd.

Madonna had one important edge over Kylie for many years – a sense of irony. She once said, 'I love irony. I like the way things can be taken on different levels.' She was talking about one of her first hits, 'Like A Virgin', and the fact that it was considered provocative at the time. Kylie did not reach an understanding with irony until after her collaboration with Nick Cave in the mid-nineties. Irony was an essential part of her coolification. It is all about age and worldliness. 'I'm tough, I'm ambitious and I know exactly what I want.' That is a quote from Madonna, but it could just as easily have come from Kylie, who would show these qualities in abundance when making such a triumphant comeback in the late nineties.

Both women come from suburban, middle class backgrounds and were ambitious, precocious children. They are both Queens of Reinvention, gay icons and disco divas. While it is diverting to list the similarities of the two women, it is through their differences that they are more readily defined. Kylie is forever putting herself down; it is a self-deprecating style she has perfected over the years. She frequently declares herself to be nervous, and laughs at her various incarnations. Madonna would never do that. She considers herself to be an artist and not a commodity, like 'Kylie Minogue Limited'. She is also never afraid to have an opinion, or to shock. When she was advised not to swear when presenting the 2001 Turner Prize, it was like a red rag to a bull. She quite deliberately said 'motherf***er' and the moral majority of curtain twitchers promptly rang in to complain. One could not conceive of a situation when Kylie would say 'motherf***er' before the watershed on national television. Or after the watershed, for that matter. Her swearing is strictly behind closed doors.

Madonna is an object of desirability in a down and dirty way. A Madonna fantasy is what she might do to you. Kylie is desirable in a white, cotton knickers sort of way. A Kylie fantasy is what you might do to her. Irvine Welsh, the author of *Trainspotting*, wrote a short story *Where The Debris Meets The Sea*, about four celebrity women who lounge around in a Santa Monica beach-house and lust after unattainable Edinburgh manual workers ('schemies' as he called them). They are Kylie, Madonna, Victoria Principal and Kim Basinger. At one point, his Kylie fantasizes about replacing the beloved dog of a Scottish removal man, wishing that she was the animal wearing a collar, tied to his arm. Welsh, who is proud to reveal himself as one of Kylie's original fans, was more than impressed that she did not attempt to sue him.

The two great female icons of popular culture, Madonna and Kylie, will continue to draw comparisons. In October 2005, Madonna produced a video for her number one single, 'Hung Up' that focused determinedly on her rear, which is in very good shape for her age. For once she was following a trend which Kylie had begun during her great comeback. However, it is unlikely she will ever topple Kylie from her position of owner of the world's most famous derriere.

'It just makes me cringe when I think about it.'

11

A French Connection

While lunching at a fashionable Beverley Hills restaurant, Kylie was asked if she would like to join another table and meet plasticine-faced film star Jim Carrey. She agreed and the pair chatted and air kissed in the acknowledged way of good celebrity manners. It was the only time they met but Carrey instantly became the media's new man in Kylie's life.

A public fascination with her love life is something Kylie has always had to endure. The interest is almost prurient. We want to know who is having his wicked way with our little Kylie. She is closing in on thirty-nine and, despite thousands of words of speculation over the years, still single. If, as we now know, she was sexually experienced at sixteen, then that makes something like twenty-two years of being young, free and available.

It would be very sad indeed if she had been a nun for all that time. Fortunately, that is not the case, and Kylie has, as she likes to put it, 'a healthy appetite for most things'. She finds sex very enjoyable and once gave herself a performance mark of seven out of ten – eight on good occasions – so that there was always room for improvement. Kylie has never had a long term relationship, although by most celebrity standards two years is long enough to marry, divorce, have two kids and adopt another three. Despite his enormous importance in her life, Michael Hutchence was only romantically involved with Kylie for fifteen months. Jason Donovan was around for longer but, these days, Kylie appears faintly embarrassed by that, as if their romance was something she was involved in when she was just a kid, and before she became a woman. Perhaps it was Jason's own fault for blabbing a couple of years ago that he and Kylie had sex 'many times, four years' worth, actually.'

Even worse, Jason brought Michael Hutchence into the mix by declaring, 'He was my hero, the man I wanted to be. All I can say, and this is terrible, is that I was in there first. I can discover talent better than most.' Jason may have been 'in there' before Hutchence, but he was not the first. His remarks appear rather juvenile and boastful, and not exactly in keeping with his reputation as a good guy. When he had been asked previously about Michael and Kylie, he had answered more diplomatically, 'I wish them luck, any jealous thoughts don't even go through my mind,' a sentiment which he later contradicted. Rick Sky, who has interviewed Kylie and Jason on many occasions, always found him much the easier of the two to get along with: 'Jason's a lovely bloke, much softer than Kylie, and much more giving.' Perhaps Jason was, ultimately, too soft for Kylie. He has said that he prefers women to be difficult, dominant even: 'I'm a bit of a sucker for someone who gives me a hard time, maybe I'm a masochist. If someone's pulling you along by a string, you want it more, don't you?'

Kylie's own attitude to Jason these days is that of an

aunt who might see a nephew once in a while. They stay in touch, but their paths cross very rarely. She did not even know he was going to be a dad until she bumped into him by accident in the street.

Kylie's list of men who may have been 'in there', to use Jason's elegant phrase, includes model Zane O'Donnell (on-off, 1991–1993), singer Evan Dando (one-off, 1993), singer Lenny Kravitz (1993), actor/model Mark Gerber (1994), playboy Tim Jeffries (occasional, 1993/4, again in 1998), idiot comedian Pauly Shore (1995), photographer and video director Stephane Sednaoui (1995–7), music director Cassius Coleman (1998-9), actor Rupert Penry-Jones (1999), model James Gooding (2000–2002) and heart throb actor Olivier Martinez (2003–) Numerically, it's more than the Virgin Mary, but hardly a rampant number.

Just as entertaining is the list of men she has been linked to, but who are, in fact, a definite NO!: Jim Carrey, Chris Evans, Julian Lennon, Jay Kay, Roger Lloyd Pack and Prince. Disappointingly, it is also a negative for Kylie and Robbie Williams, a liaison which would have made them pop royalty and might have taken David and Victoria Beckham off the front pages.

And then there are the men we know nothing about, the secret admirers. Soon after she had split from Hutchence, she was seen leaving her Chelsea apartment with one of her dancers. The couple, scruffy and casual, had only managed a couple of steps down the street when a paparazzo was in their face taking pictures and a stat-uesque blonde reporter was firing questions. Kylie hared off in one direction, while the dancer bolted the other way. Running has never been one of Kylie's strengths and the journalist, despite wearing high heels, soon overtook her and pinned her up against a wall: 'Look,' said the reporter, 'I'm just going to ask you a couple of simple questions, so there's no point in either of us getting out of breath, right!' Poor Kylie had no choice other than to comply, and an article appeared in the *Daily Star*. It was a rare glimpse of the secret Kylie, someone who suffered from spots, and could not be bothered to do her hair when she was going out to grab the first coffee of the day. And why on earth should she be on show twenty-four hours a day? It was a similar situation to the one that she had found herself in at Heathrow Airport, when she had been mugged by Jean Rook and others. The secret Kylie, when discovered, is like a rabbit trapped in a car's headlamps. She does not mind divulging a little of her private life – but it is always on her own terms.

The men in her life seem to fall into two categories. Either they are drop-dead gorgeous, or they are larger than life. Kylie says the most important qualities she looks for in a man are charisma and humour, a rare combination: 'I'd like him to be artistic, too. I like to be swept off my feet.' There is one other credential shared by at least three of her lovers – they were more renowned for what was between their legs than between their ears.

Zane O'Donnell met Kylie on the video shoot for the single 'What Do I Have To Do?', a great gay favourite. O'Donnell was a strikingly handsome and well-built model from South Africa, who was blind in one eye, and who was best known for showing off his physique in a Levi Jeans ad. It is an amusing coincidence that several of Kylie's boyfriends grabbed her attention after they had removed most (or all) of their clothing in front of a camera. Even Kylie let the cat out of the bag about his attraction, when she admitted that they had 'discovered sex'. O'Donnell had a considerable reputation as a ladies' man. He had left his wife Lauren and their young son as his career began to take off. Lauren got something of her own back by declaring, 'The only way to stop him going off with other women is to castrate him.'

His relationship with Kylie was a stormy one, and they would split up and then get back together again, declaring undying love. They once separated on Valentine's Day in Paris, where Kylie was filming the video for 'Finer Feelings', her eighteenth UK single in just four years. A confidante observed, 'They spent a long time locked in deep conversations. I believe it was a mutual agreement, but Kylie was very down and almost tearful at times.'

Kylie, who too often for her own good can wear her heart on her sleeve when she is involved with someone, was also in floods of tears after they had a blazing row at a party given by fellow Australian and former Wimbledon champion Pat Cash, in Kingston upon Thames, near London. A friend of Kylie's confided how distraught she was, because she really wanted to make things work: 'She is still very fond of him, but the relationship is just not happening.'

That particular row was just before Kylie flew off for her annual Christmas break in Melbourne, at the end of 1992. It really was the death knell for their relationship. O'Donnell's career never amounted to much subsequently, and he only became newsworthy once more for discovering God and abandoning advertising jeans, in favour of a campaign to try to attract young people to church.

For someone so careful about her private life, sometimes Kylie can be astonishingly indiscreet. It is as if, every so often, she gets the devil in her, and hang the consequences. There was the sexual activity with Paul Marcolin in a passage next to a house where a party was in full swing; there was the full-blown sex with Michael Hutchence on a plane, in a seat within winking distance of the Australian premier and then there was Lemonheads singer Evan Dando, with whom she disappeared into a toilet at a party. This was an incident that soon achieved legendary status.

In 1993 Evan Dando had looked like he might follow the Michael Hutchence path to rock god. He was flavour-of-the-month after the release of the album *Come On Feel The Lemonheads* – and the classic rock ballad 'Into Your Arms' – and could be seen out and about with Johnny Depp and Courtney Love. Besides Kylie, he shared one other thing with Hutchence – a love of hard drugs. He once admitted that, during one binge, he had smoked so much crack that his voice was ruined for weeks. Dando was from Boston, but spent a good deal of the nineties in Australia. After an almost ten year period of relative obscurity, he finally released a solo album in 2003 and in 2006 put together a new line-up for The Lemonheads.

Kylie has admitted that there is some truth in the Evan Dando story, although they were never boyfriend and girlfriend. They were not really a one-night stand either – more a one-hour stand. The last time she was asked about it, she blushed and giggled: 'What can I say about it? There was some frivolity.'

Prince had been a childhood hero of Kylie Minogue. In all her early fanzine interviews, she answers the frequently asked

question: 'Who are your pop idols?' with an acknowledge-
ment of the influence of the petit purple one. He may have
been a hero with charisma to burn, but there is no evidence
that Kylie actually fancied him, although she once famously
described him as being 'sex on a stick'. In fairness, Kylie
never actually said that she thought he was a sexual lollipop.
What she actually said was: 'He's an interesting person and
the only person I really admire as a fan. He's so outrageous
and different. It's funny. He revolts some people but others
think he's sex on a stick.' As a small girl herself, Kylie tends to
prefer taller, well-built men – so Tom Cruise need not apply.

She met Prince backstage at one of his London concerts, after an introduction from a limousine driver they
shared in London. Kylie remained virtually unknown in
the US – 'The Loco-Motion Girl' – so Prince did not
wholly realize what a big star she was. 'I don't think he
knew much about me,' she confessed. At the time, Kylie
was looking for more artistic credibility, following her split
from Stock, Aitken and Waterman and her new alliance
with deConstruction Records, so it would not do any
harm at all to be placed next to Prince by the media. She
visited him at his London studios, where he playfully suggested she write some lyrics for him. Kylie may have been
seeking some working endorsement from Prince but, at
the end of the day, this was the same man who had taken
Sheena Easton under his wing.

Although Kylie has always protested there was never
anything between her and Prince, that did not stop her
fuelling the rumours herself with some typical celebrity
behaviour. They spent half an hour chatting at Tramp
nightclub in London's West End before leaving sepa-
rately. Prince set off for his hotel, the Conrad in Chelsea

Harbour, in the back of a huge chauffeur-driven limousine. A hundred yards or so down the road, the car pulled up and Kylie darted from out of the shadows and jumped in. They got out together at his hotel, although, to be fair to Kylie, it was only ten minutes from her home, should she have tired of massaging the man's ego.

She did visit his famous home, Paisley Park in Minneapolis, although she is adamant she was not another conquest. She assuredly did not want to be on that list. They did, however, enjoy a game of table tennis together, 'He's very good. I consider myself quite good at pool and table tennis, but he slaughtered me. I let myself down there. I remember doing one glorious flying leap and landing in the shagpile.'

Kylie did find the right moment to present Prince with the lyrics she had written to a song 'Baby Doll', which was pleasant enough without being Lennon and McCartney. Prince took it away and bashed out a melody to go with it, although it has yet to see the light of day on an album.

By coincidence, Kylie did have a minor fling with Lenny Kravitz, another talented and charismatic black artist but, once again, it did not produce any artistic sparks. He was enlisted to write a song for Kylie's first deConstruction album. The song never materialized but Kylie admitted, 'there was a little bit of truth' in the rumours that they had connected on a physical level. Coincidentally, Kravitz was a good friend of Michael Hutchence and a regular visitor to his French villa. Like all rock stars, Kravitz has a certain wild image to maintain, but he is one of the very few known to have taken his grandfather on tour with him.

Both Prince and Lenny Kravitz have enjoyed a great

reputation as rock Don Juans over the years, but even they must step aside for Tim Jeffries or 'Tim Who?', as he might be better described. 'Nice But Tim' ostensibly has nothing on his CV until it comes to the page detailing lovers and then he can fill in, among others, the names of Koo Stark, Elle Macpherson, Claudia Schiffer and Kylie. The reality is that Jeffries is amusing and congenial company, and works hard as a director of the London photographic gallery Hamiltons. He is a great friend of the couturier Valentino and moves easily in the world of fashion and photography, two of Kylie's great interests. He abhors the label 'playboy', but is stuck with it: 'A playboy is a relic of the 1950s, someone who was unbelievably rich, didn't work and who travelled the world in a private plane and that's not me. I am not a playboy – I am a hardworking art dealer.'

Jeffries has the priceless attribute, as far as his conquests are concerned, of being absolutely discreet, and has never blabbed about the beautiful women with whom he has been involved. In the mid-nineties, Kylie began to move away from the rock world to a more creative and fashion-based circle of friends – people who could satisfy her endless fascination with image. Jeffries was one of the friends who could open up that world for Kylie.

Kylie's next conquest was a former model-turned-actor called Mark Gerber, who bore a passing resemblance to Zane O'Donnell, and who had also revealed a prodigious endowment in the acclaimed Australian film *Sirens* in which he stripped off in his role as a stablehand. Coincidentally, the film also featured Tim Jeffries' ex, Elle Macpherson. Kylie rang Gerber after seeing the film, and discovered that he was visiting London. She suggested they go to the launch party of

fashion designer Donna Karan's shop in London, and they
hit it off. When Kylie went back to Australia for a visit, they got
together. The romance amounted to little more than a holiday dalliance. They were seen at various social events around
Sydney, including gigs of his band Flaming Boa at which Kylie
briefly took on the role of enthusiastic rock chick. But their
affair foundered when Kylie left Australia to fulfil career commitments. Rarely for her, Kylie commented on their
relationship: 'It's a long-distance romance and at the
moment my career is at the forefront of everything I do. Any
relationship is secondary.' These are thought-provoking
words indeed.

Pauly Shore was a case of 'from the sublime to the ridicu-
lous'. He was very much a product of nineties-style comedy in
the US – huge-grossing banana skins. He met Kylie on the set
of the film *Bio Dome*, which also starred Stephen Baldwin, and
which boasted the same production team as *Dumb and
Dumber*. Kylie played an Australian oceanographer called
Petra, a role Shore described as a 'baby scientist'. He also
referred to her as 'Barbie on the Shrimp'. Until he got
together with Kylie, his best-known girlfriend was a porn
queen called Savannah, who committed suicide. Kylie does
not make a habit of going out with people she works with,
but, in Pauly's case, they dated for about four months after
filming in the Bahamas had finished. Kylie described their
dating as 'hanging out', and ditched him when she fell under
the spell of a larger than life Parisian.

At last Kylie had met someone who took her breath
away, not because of his looks, but through the raw power
of his creative personality. Stephane Sednaoui was certainly not traditionally handsome. But, just as Michael
Hutchence had done, he made an instant impression on

Kylie by behaving outrageously. He did not make a risqué suggestion, but when they met at a party, he did lift Kylie up above his head and whirl her around, which certainly caught her attention. 'I'm attracted,' she said, 'but to what I don't know.' It was the middle of 1995 and Kylie was entering her most creative phase, encouraged by rock poet Nick Cave. Stephane became part of that phase and, with Cave, one of the two key mentors of Kylie's middle period.

Sednaoui was spontaneous and alarming. One newspaper suggested he favoured sexual encounters in public places. His most famous girlfriend before Kylie was the unpredictable and weird Icelandic star Björk who had said of him, 'He has an effect on people like a tidal wave.' Soon after they met, Kylie decided to drop everything and drive with him across America. Amusingly, her plane crossed mid Atlantic with one carrying Pauly Shore who was flying to London to see her. He got the message that their relationship was over.

Kylie and Stephane had been on just two dates, yet here she was emulating Jack Kerouac's *On The Road* journey with a man she hardly knew. They hired a Pontiac Trans-Am sportscar. Kylie loved every minute and told *Cosmopolitan* magazine, 'We were driving from town to town, desert to desert, staying in $20-a-night motel rooms. We had greasy breakfasts in roadside cafes and talked to truckers for hours about their lives. I was truly anonymous and free to be me.'

By the end of the trip, Kylie was enamoured: 'We were stuck in a car together for three weeks and we really bonded. We're in love.' On the trip Sednaoui took many pictures but one in particular, of Kylie gazing out from their silver convertible during a stop in North Carolina, encapsulated the vulnerable, natural look that she favoured during her time with Stephane. It was a naked look.

Stephane encouraged her to see things differently. He was an acclaimed stills photographer before moving into videography. One claim to fame was a series of pictures he took of the ill-fated Kurt Cobain laughing. When Kylie met him, his reputation as an experimental videographer was growing, boosted by his alliance with Madonna. Kylie had seen and been impressed with his video for Madonna's 1993 top ten hit 'Fever', and with his work on her short film *Justify My Love*. Sednaoui's company, Clip-Video, was one of the most sought-after in the nineties. He worked with the Red Hot Chili Peppers, The Smashing Pumpkins, Tricky, U2, Tina Turner, Alanis Morissette and, of course, Björk on her classic 'Big Time Sensuality'. He directed Kylie in her 1996 collaboration with Towa Tei entitled 'GBI' ('German Bold Italic') during her least commercial period.

With all due respect to the models she has been out with, the most important men in Kylie's life would not be seen dead modelling boxer shorts on a fashion runway – unless it was part of an ironic statement. Intriguingly, with both Michael Hutchence and Stephane Sednaoui there were fears that Kylie's health was suffering. Commentators noticed she was losing weight and looking dreadful. One picture prompted the *Daily Mail* to observe, 'It wasn't just the mousey hair – cut short and scrunched on top of her head – or the absence of make-up. What really shocked was how painfully thin, even ill, Kylie looked ...' In the picture, Sednaoui, wearing combat trousers, had tightened his hood close to his face to expose a single, staring eye. He laughed, 'It will be funny. People will think who is that crazy guy that Kylie's going out with?' He was right. They did think that – but they also wondered why.

The couple travelled extensively – to Australia, Hong Kong, Tokyo, Seoul, Los Angeles, and between their respective homes in Paris and London. It was a great adventure for Kylie. But they were also apart a good deal, and Kylie became devoted to her home computer, vainly trying to conduct a relationship via 'chat'. Kylie did take Stephane home to meet her parents in Melbourne, although we will never know what Ron Minogue made of the avant-garde Frenchman, then sporting an interesting mohican haircut.

The end for the couple, in late 1997, came quite suddenly. One moment there was speculation about marriage and babies and the next they were apart. In September, Kylie said, 'Stephane is extremely inspiring. I respect his artistry – he has his own style stamped on what he does.' In November, *Cleo* magazine declared, 'She doesn't want to talk about it, but suffice to say, there is much muttering about men behaving badly and Kylie isn't disagreeing.'

The official line is that the relationship just fizzled out and the couple have remained close friends – a familiar outcome where Kylie and past *amours* are concerned. Perhaps men like Hutchence and Sednaoui are just too exhausting for Kylie. Or perhaps her expectations are too high. Sednaoui remains in demand on the arty music scene and, in October 2001, did become a father when his girlfriend, cover girl Laetitia Casta, gave birth to a baby girl. The beautiful Laetitia, ten years younger than Kylie, is the face of L'Oréal, and has ambitions to be as famous as an actress as she is as a model.

A couple of years after she split with Stephane, Kylie posed for a portrait for her 1999 book of photographs. She has a mock tattoo on her arm with the names Jason, Michael and Stephane crossed out. It was a little joke but did reveal that Kylie sees herself as a one man at a time woman.

'I really need my own space and if I don't get it, I just take to my bath.'

12

Thirty Up

On stage, the zip holding up Kylie's cowgirl costume, was not properly fastened. Ever so slowly it came undone, gently lowering the costume to the floor. Underneath Kylie was 'stark bollock naked', so her mother Carol and creative director William Baker were in a state of high panic. Suddenly Kylie's PA Nathalie dashed forward and saved her modesty, much to the disappointment of the vast majority of the audience.

On a late November day in 1997, Kylie was awoken at 4 am by a telephone ringing persistently. Calls at that time in the morning are never good news. Michael Hutchence was dead, at the age of thirty-seven. He was the first person to die whom she had loved and, understandably, she was completely devastated. William Baker, her creative director, says in the book *Kylie La La La*, 'Kylie felt her world had crumbled under her feet.' She was at home in London and spent the whole day behind locked doors at home. She was to sing at G-A-Y that evening and everyone assumed she would cancel but she refused.

The strength of Kylie's show-must-go-on philosophy was never more tested but, as Baker recalls, 'Kylie was humbled by death. She felt to cancel a show in front of her ever-faithful gay audience was a cop-out.' Kylie was certain that she wanted to perform for a community which itself had experienced so much sadness and loss due to AIDS.

Michael Hutchence had been found naked, kneeling on the floor behind the door of his room at the fashionable Ritz Carlton Hotel in Double Bay, Sydney. His belt was around his neck, the buckle apparently having broken under his weight as he dangled from the hook on the back of the door. There was at the time, and remains to this day, intense speculation as to the reason for his death. The most controversial is that it was an act of auto-eroticism that went wrong.

The New South Wales Coroner Derek Hand decided a full inquest was not necessary. In his report, he stated, 'I am satisfied that the standard required to conclude that this death was a suicide has been reached.' Hutchence's blood contained a cocktail of cocaine, alcohol, Prozac and other prescription drugs. He was involved in a difficult custody wrangle with Bob Geldof over Paula Yates' children. One of the saddest aspects of the tragedy was that he had twice called his first serious love, Michele Bennett, but both times only connected to her answering phone. On hearing the messages and how upset he sounded, Michele rushed round to the hotel but could not raise him when she banged on his hotel door. Reluctantly, she left a message at reception and went home.

The untimely deaths of rock heroes seem to make time stand still: John Lennon, Kurt Cobain, Jim Morrison and Jimi Hendrix are just part of a list that will now for ever include Michael Hutchence. If his death was suicide, it is

even more distressing, because he had deserted his
eighteen-month-old baby with Paula Yates, Tiger Lily. Just
a short time before that fateful night, he had told journalist Sharon Klum that he 'would jump in front of a train
for his daughter'. Kylie was once asked what she thought
of the idea that Hutchence was just in search of an
orgasm – something which Prozac could sometimes
inhibit. She thought it made it more bearable to think
that he died for that reason, rather than killing himself
because he was in so much pain.

When you are a celebrity, you are never allowed to
forget a relationship. Not one. Kylie would never want to
forget Michael Hutchence, but for many years she
scarcely gave an interview, both before and after his
death, where his name has not been mentioned. The only
time they had reportedly got close since their break-up
was after an INXS concert in 1994 when, at the subse-
quent party, they were spotted disappearing into a toilet
cubicle for nearly an hour. It may have been a sexual
encounter, or Michael may have just wanted to chat to
Kylie while he got 'off his face' on one drug or another.
She was now firmly filed in his mind under 'f' for 'friend'.
In fact, they saw each other fairly regularly and remained
on good terms until his death. Kylie has always politely
explained that Michael was a great influence on her life,
and helped her to make the change from girl to woman.
Many tears have been shed, some in public and many in
private. But they are not bitter tears.

The most poignant memory came on New Year's Eve
1998, when she was celebrating with Stephane Sednaoui
in the town of Whistler in Canada. Out of the blue, an
INXS record came on the radio and she heard Michael's

voice once more. Out loud, she exclaimed, 'Of course, you turn up now!' She has sensed him with her on several occasions since his death. Hutchence remains a strong presence in her life, a little like a guardian angel, but more an intangible reassurance that life will continue to move forward if she takes control of her destiny. She told Kevin O'Sullivan of the *Daily Mirror*, 'I don't mind talking about Michael, but please don't say I cried.'

At Michael's funeral in Sydney, Kylie was quiet, dignified and did her best to support his grieving family. Nick Cave was there and, at the request of Paula Yates, sang The Lemonheads ballad 'Into My Arms'. It was a moving rendition, made truly bizarre by a man threatening to hurl himself off the balcony while he was singing.

With masterful timing, which would have tickled Hutchence, the heavens opened and a loud crack of thunder greeted the arrival of his coffin. Kylie even managed a smile at the celestial intervention. Michael Hutchence was most definitely not saintly, but nor was he the devil. His throwaway line that his hobby was 'corrupting Kylie' was nothing more than a soundbite. Kylie is demonstrably a stronger, more focused individual than he ever was. Ironically, her romance with Hutchence turned out to be a brilliant career move, something which hardly seemed the case at the time.

At the end of 1997 Kylie's career was in serious need of divine intervention. The ongoing saga of *Impossible Princess* was a nightmare. The second single 'Did It Again', a second collaboration with the Manic Street Preachers, reached a miserable number fourteen in the UK. And she was just as miserable in private. The demise of her relationship with Stephane and the death of Hutchence did not leave a lot to look forward to in 1998.

As it turned out Kylie already had her own personal angel, William Baker, on the payroll. He is her style guru and the man who converts her whims into reality. Baker, very camp and very gay, has seen Kylie's boyfriends come and go, but he is always there with a safety pin, some tit tape or a sequin. His close friends call him Joan, a tribute to his own personal icon Joan Collins. His official title in the Kylie world is 'creative director', but Kylie admits that they have such a close relationship that 'they are practically joined at the hip'. He is the kid sister Dannii was often too busy to be.

Baker met Kylie in 1993, when he was nineteen and working in the Vivienne Westwood store in Chelsea. Technically he was still at university in London studying theology, but he worked part-time as the 'Saturday boy' and dreamed of getting a break in the world of design. Kylie was already revered in the gay community. Baker had loved the video for the perennial gay favourite 'What Do I Have To Do?' in which Kylie does some ironing. He was thrilled at the image of a superstar doing domestic chores. On a whim, he rang Kylie's record label deConstruction, and asked if she needed a stylist, only to learn that she was abroad. He left his name, number and the name of the shop and never expected to hear anything more. Three weeks later Kylie calmly walked into the store. William could not believe it, but boldly seized his opportunity: 'I leapt from behind the counter and bombarded her with ideas, and somehow persuaded her to go for a coffee.' The pair adjourned to a café across the road and Kylie listened intently to William's ideas. 'She probably thought I was mad,' he told Kylie's website, *Limbo*. Fortunately, she thought no such thing. Kylie, though initially reserved, is very astute at sizing people up and knowing who might be useful to her, and the obviously bright, witty and enthusiastic Baker looked a promising addition to 'Kylie Minogue Limited' post Stock, Aitken and Waterman and she scribbled her number on a napkin, signing it 'Miss K'.

When he got back in touch, Kylie suggested Baker might want to meet her great friend Katerina Jebb, who was photographing Kylie at the time. Kat, as she is known to friends, has taken some of the most moving and erotic pictures of Kylie. She is one of the 'gurus' of the nineties who, along with Nick Cave and Stephane Sednaoui, developed Kylie's creativity and taste. They had met in Paris a few years earlier. Katerina tells the story of that first meeting at her apartment when Kylie and an assistant appeared on the doorstep bearing champagne, the singer's favourite drink. Soon after, Kylie arrived with a sleeping bag and moved in. It was a difficult time because Katerina suffered a serious car accident shortly afterwards and was hospitalized. Kylie was there to help when she was allowed to go home. She even managed to persuade Katerina to take her picture even though she could not hold the camera herself and had to have it placed on a stand. The two women are soul mates so it was a big deal for Kylie to introduce her to William Baker.

From that meeting came the idea of a shoot based around a Debbie Harry theme – the glamorous singer from Blondie whom Kylie had long admired and regularly watched on old videos. Baker dashed home and raided his boyfriend's old punk-era wardrobe for costumes for Kylie. He settled on a pair of ripped tights and a sleeveless Marilyn Monroe T-shirt which had once belonged to a girl who had worked at Andy Warhol's New York factory in the early seventies. Kylie loved the pictures, which were arty enough to fit into the overall strategy of her mid-nineties creativity, and they appeared in a small limited edition book that accompanied the release of the *Kylie Minogue* album.

Baker and Kylie became great friends and confidants. She likes to call him Willie. He is able to tune into her creative wavelength, as well as sharing her sense of campness. Kylie is *very* camp and always has been. She loves diamanté and dressing up. To reclaim her position at the top of the tree, indeed to climb even higher than before, Kylie's strategy involved winning back the two areas of her fan base which had made it all possible in the first place, Australia and the gay community. With Baker's help she was able to do both on her barnstorming 1998 'Intimate and Live' tour. It was goodbye to grunge and heroin chic and hello to high camp and ostrich feathers.

Kylie does not take herself as seriously as some observers believe. She takes her career much more seriously than she takes herself. The images that she and Baker have come up with over the years are often no more than hammy pastiches of a look they have picked up from watching an old episode of *Dynasty*, or even *Doctor Who*, on the television. They are style magpies with attitude – if it's funny or different, then why not try it? Baker has likened their approach to the tongue-in-cheek style of a Hollywood B–movie actress. For the concert celebrating twenty-five years of Mushroom Records in Melbourne,

Kylie was a geisha, emerging slowly from a pink glitter birthday cake, singing 'You will like my sense of style . . . You will like my sense of style.' It was camp of the highest order.

In addition to the sense of fun that Baker brings to the party, he is also fiercely protective of his friend and style collaborator. He was incandescent with rage at the creation of the sobriquet 'IndieKylie' as a label hung on Kylie during the *Impossible Princess* project. He echoed the views of Steve Anderson from Brothers In Rhythm, who believed the record company put too much emphasis on her Manic Street Preachers tracks, which were unrepresentative of the whole work. Kylie, diplomatically, has left it to these two friends and advisers to put across that particular point of view. Baker declared, 'Kylie has never been, and never will be, indie.'

One of the more popular and patronising ways of explaining 'Kylie chameleon' is that she is constantly being defined by her boyfriends. Hutchence and Sednaoui were able to influence her because she looked up to them. But Kylie has always been her own woman, absorbing ideas from others and putting her own spin on them. The sexy, rebellious look of the Hutchence era had already been brewing before they became a couple. The more curvaceous shape of her *Street Fighter* era was down to martial arts training. She went up three bra sizes, prompting the usual speculation that she had been cosmetically enhanced. Perhaps her least successful look was as a street waif when she was with Stephane. To a certain extent it was 'heroin chic' but everyone thought she was ill. At least it was different, and she did not look like Madonna.

By the time of the 1998 'Intimate and Live' tour, Kylie's image needed a kick up her very famous backside. The Kylie that she and William Baker proceeded to present to the world was a camp classic, her stage show was like a Las Vegas cabaret extravaganza, nothing like an average pop concert. The disappointingly received *Impossible Princess* album may have been the most interesting she had ever done, but it did not lend itself to visually exciting presentation. It was brooding and introspective, and not in the least Liza Minnelli. Kylie began the set by showcasing some of the album, opening with a moody rendition of 'Too Far', Kylie clad in black descending a silver staircase in impossibly high heels. But the style momentum clicked into gear when she appeared underneath a glittery pink 'K' and sang 'I Should Be So Lucky', wearing a tiny, spangly showgirl's dress that revealed her perfectly proportioned legs. But she did not just belt out 'Lucky' as she had a thousand times before. This was a new jazzy arrangement, a putting-on-a-show Broadway Ballad, and it was thrilling. It absolutely brought the house down at every concert on the tour, from the Palais Theatre, Melbourne, to the Shepherd's Bush Empire in west London. Not only was it fun and kitsch, but it was also brilliantly done and caught the attention of all the jaded reviewers. The *Independent on Sunday* purred, 'It was fantastic. An inspired arrangement and Kylie even sang it well. The helium she overdosed on in the late 1980s has worn off.' Kylie was reclaiming her audience, the fans that she has said 'grew up with her'. Her image and music had finally fused into one, and this is the crucial element in her rapid rise to style icon in the late nineties.

After 'Lucky', the show hurtled into Abba's 'Dancing

Queen', an honorary Australian anthem since it featured in the film *Muriel's Wedding*. Kylie was flanked by two male dancers, wearing little but a few peacock feathers and some lurid pink shorts that left nothing to the imagination. They were pure Baker who happened, at the time, to be the boyfriend of one of the well-toned, well-muscled boys – the Fabulous Baker Boys. Tongue-in-cheek renditions of 'Shocked' and 'Better The Devil You Know' pleased her devoted fan base before 'Confide In Me', arguably her strongest song to date, provided a sultry encore. The show was a triumph and proved that Kylie was back. It was a daring return to form and demonstrated that at the age of thirty Kylie had the maturity to carry off any design William Baker cared to throw at her.

And she had fun. Her mother Carol, who was on tour with her to help with the costumes, also adores William. During one performance, while Kylie was belting out a song Carol and William enjoyed a drink backstage. 'After all', recalled Baker, 'It was sponsored by Absolut vodka.' They decided it would be a hoot to dress up in wigs and costumes – Carol was Baby Spice and William was Boy George, who he used to follow about when he was younger. Kylie bounced off stage to be greeted by these two 'stars' acting up like a pair of old drag queens. She was laughing so much she literally had to be pushed back on for the encore.

The size of the venues in Australia gave Kylie enough space to exploit her own and Baker's ideas to the full. They had wanted to depict all the different images, or incarnations, that Kylie had brought to life over the years – rock slut, show pony, stripper and even cowgirl for the track 'Cowboy Style', well before Madonna adopted this look in 2000. Baker himself had painstakingly covered all the hats in sequins and silver glitter. He remembered giving some away to the Kylie fans in Australia, who went to every single show and stood at the front cheering their heroine. Even Cliff Richard fans are not this devoted.

The 'Intimate and Live' tour was of enormous importance to Kylie's career and the public's perception of her, because it allowed her to reposition herself in the market place. It was her first major tour for seven years, and she was able to deliver the present without deserting the past. Formerly, she had been embarrassed by her previous incarnations, but now she gloried in them. She had the confidence not to reject 'I Should Be So Lucky', although she drew the line, on this occasion, at 'The Loco-Motion'. Steve Anderson, who produced the show, was determined that there would be no song involving moving your arms like a train, and threatened to stay behind in the UK if there was.

'I am a big girl now.'

13

Gay Old Times

Wearing a pink tutu, and surrounded by a thirty-strong legion of admiring, similarly-dressed drag queens, Kylie performed 'What Do I Have To Do?' for her 20,000 strong gay audience. She had wanted to sing 'Better The Devil You Know', but that number had already been commandeered by some forty other 'Kylies'.

One important, maybe the most important, concert in the Kylie revival year of 1998 when, incidentally, she had no new record releases, was her appearance at Sydney's famous gay Mardi Gras in February. Her sister Dannii had already appeared in the afternoon, but in the evening Kylie was on stage. This time she did get to perform 'Better The Devil You Know' – BTDYK, as it is known at gay events – and she brought the house down with fireworks and dancers. The crowd went ballistic. The reception endorsed the view that Kylie would always be the pre-eminent gay icon of her generation.

From the very beginnings, with 'The Loco-Motion' and 'I Should Be So Lucky', Kylie was adopted by the gay culture of Melbourne and, particularly, Sydney. 'Kylie Nights', where drag queens would dress up and perform as Kylie, became hugely popular. The first she says she knew about these events was on a trip back to Australia, when she was driving past The Albury, the most famous gay club in Sydney. It was a Sunday night and one of her friends mentioned that it was 'Kylie Night'. She had absolutely no idea that such a thing existed, and was all for going in and amazing everyone: 'I was almost the last to know about it.' Kylie had this fantasy picture of herself leaping on to the bar and doing a routine from *South Pacific.* Unfortunately, she was not allowed in that night, because the club would have needed special security measures to handle the pandemonium that would certainly have ensued.

Kylie did get to see a 'Kylie Show' at The Three Faces club in Melbourne, on her Christmas visit home in 1993. It was the first time Kylie had seen anyone impersonating her. She loved two performers in particular – one who wore ostrich-feather pink hot pants, like those she had worn in the video for 'Shocked' and another who donned the noughts and crosses dress, with which she had amazed her fans at *The Delinquents* première. Kylie was not an innocent where gay culture was concerned. She had been an actress since the age of eleven and inevitably came across the usual blend of luvvies and camp thespians that make up the profession. Kylie once mentioned that on *Neighbours,* for instance, both her make-up artist and hairdresser were gay, so homosexuality was hardly a shock. It might have been a shock to an innocent girl-next-door – but then Kylie was never that innocent.

It was not just gay men in Australia who adopted Kylie. She became a downtrodden heroine for the gay community throughout the world. She herself cited 1989 as the crucial year when a gay audience started supporting her and reacting against the accusations that she was both 'popular and uncool'. These attacks made her appear a victim, a key ingredient in becoming a gay icon. In most cases, there must be tragedy in the diva's life. Madonna, for instance, lost her mother at the age of five and was brought up by her father, Silvio. Kylie noted this anomaly in her status when she proclaimed, 'I am not a traditional gay icon. There's been no tragedy in my life, just my tragic outfits.'

Kylie has achieved her status more through her battle to find a true identity and her own voice in a pop world determined not to take seriously a suburban girl from Melbourne, than through any tragic history. Paul Watson explored this in his 1999 paper about gay icons in pop. He explained, 'Gay men embrace those who represent embodied conflicts similar to their own and whose oppression explodes into a torrent of sensuality that is sublimated through their sound.' As Kylie herself has said, she changed her image because it was the only thing she had control over. Gay men could identify with her various incarnations and her search for a true self, especially as she was an appealing mixture of vulnerability and fragility. Watson believed Kylie became such a powerful image for gay men because she, like them, had fled to the city to escape 'blind suburbia'. Kylie's career has been a personal voyage of discovery, from soap star, to servile singer of Stock, Aitken and Waterman songs, to raunchier Kylie, and on to IndieKylie and beyond. The struggle for self-awareness, the willingness to reinvent herself and break the chains of pop subservience are all aspects of

Performing at the 2002 Brit Awards in Earls Court, London

With her 'scruff from Essex', model James Gooding at the Royal première of *Charlie's Angels*, in November 2000

With Gooding again, this time at the NRJ music awards in January 2002

Arriving at the 2002 Brits where she picked up awards for Best International Female and Best International Album

Presenting the Outstanding Contribution to Music Award to Sting

A rare picture with her long-standing manager Terry Blamey (far left), at an EMI event in February 2004

Justin Timberlake made all the right moves to ensure that he and Kylie stole the show – and the headlines – at the 2003 Brit Awards

At the November 2003 launch for her album *Body Language*

On stage at a BBC Radio 1 and *Top of the Pops* concert in December 2004

Going public with her 'rock' Olivier Martinez. Kylie's relationship with the French actor
has been her longest yet, four years next February

At the 2005 *Elle* Style Awards where she picked up the award for Lifetime Achievement

With William Baker and Marianne Faithfull at a Chanel Catwalk Show in January 2005. Baker, who is Kylie's Creative Director, has been an integral part of the team since 1993

A surprise appearance on stage with Dannii at G-A-Y in June 2006. This was Kylie's first public appearance since being diagnosed with breast cancer

With Jake Shears at Elton John's 2006 White Tie and Tiara Ball. Since working together in 2003, the Scissor Sisters and Kylie have become the best of friends

With a young fan at a signing for her new children's book, *The Showgirl Princess*, in September 2006

A radiant Kylie steals the show as she introduces the Scissor Sisters on stage at their free 'Red' concert in Trafalgar Square, September 2006

Kylie's career that are attractive to gay society. Watson argued, 'The narrative of Minogue's life could have been an adaptation from the diaries of dejection of a gay man, who felt instant empathy with her plight of pop subordination.'

Unintentionally, and much to Pete Waterman's surprise, the music he was producing in the late 1980s hit exactly the right note with the gay market. He now acknowledges that he was making money out of the 'pink pound', but just did not realize it at the time. From their earliest number one in 1985, 'You Spin Me Round' by Dead Or Alive, Stock, Aitken and Waterman employed a formula of incessantly catchy melodies and very good-looking singers, which was manna from heaven to the gay clubs of the time. Waterman told *BBC Radio 1*, 'Kylie is a strange amalgam of pop and gay. We wrote songs about normal feelings – "I still love you, I don't know why". Of course she became a gay icon. She was saying things that, if you are emotionally sensitive, you feel every day of your life.'

Paul Watson elaborated on this theory by recognizing that her gay audience could empathise with Kylie as they 'shared and reflected on the betrayal and indignation that they collectively experienced by men'. This could not be better illustrated than by the sentiments of 'Better The Devil You Know', arguably the all-time gay favourite among Kylie's songs. Her performances in the nineties at the Gay and Lesbian Mardi Gras cemented her position of favour.

Kylie's persona as a *survivor* in the pop world has been absolutely vital in her maintaining the loyalty of her gay audience. Paradoxically, she has needed that audience to survive, but those fans have stuck with her because of their admiration for her perseverance. Not for nothing is Gloria Gaynor's 'I Will Survive' an all-time classic song for both gay men and gay women. Kylie is slightly bemused by her appeal to a gay audience of both sexes. When she was asked by *Boyz* magazine if she got 'hit on by girls', she replied ambiguously, 'Not really, no.'

She is really chuffed to be a gay icon. She confessed, 'They are incredibly loyal. I'm flattered that they pretty much adopted me before I even knew about it.' At a charity show at the Royal Albert Hall in 1995, she reprised her duet of 'Sisters Are Doing It For Themselves'. Her partner on this occasion was not her sister Dannii, but a man dressed up as Donatella Versace. The man was Elton John at his most flamboyant.

'Better The Devil You Know' featured again in 2000, when she showcased numbers from her comeback album, *Light Years,* at G-A-Y at the London Astoria. She only did seven songs, but changed costumes four times, including the ever-popular red, spangly dress and a pair of devil's horns. Her gay fans have always appreciated Kylie's outfits, and William Baker seldom disappoints them. The designer Patrick Cox observed, 'She's a living Barbie doll. All gay men want to play with her, dress her up and comb her hair.' One of the more amusing reviews of a Kylie concert pointed out that the majority of men there were more interested in the embroidered stitching on her hot pants than what lies beneath. They are not interested in learning anything about the real woman behind their image of her as a cute little sister. Theirs is unconditional adoration and anything that upsets this is liable to be labelled filth or sacrilege. They

want to take Kylie home and keep her in a box in the
bedroom. To a certain extent, that is what all Kylie fans
want to do: men who lust after her would want to take
her out and re-enact the sexual experiences of Michael
Hutchence, while young girls would want to swap clothes
and compare lipsticks with her.

Crucially, Kylie has never shunned or alienated her
gay audience. Ironically, that was exactly the mistake
that Jason Donovan made, and his career has been in
decline ever since. In the Stock, Aitken and Waterman
days, Jason, too, was adopted by a gay audience. He was
a good-looking, muscular blond, who sang prettily of his
broken heart. He was also the number one teen idol. It
was the spring of 1992 and Jason was appearing in the
Lloyd Webber musical *Joseph and the Amazing Technicolor
Dreamcoat* when posters of him started appearing outside the Palladium Theatre in London with the logo,
'Queer as F***'. As fast as they could be pulled down,
another would be put up. There was absolutely no evidence to support the assertion. Jason was the victim of a
whispering campaign that was trying to force gay
celebrities out into the open and admit their true
sexuality.

The Face magazine which, at the time, was seriously
cool – Kylie aspired to feature in its pages – wrote about
the campaign. They acknowledged that Jason was not gay,
but reprinted the poster and also called him 'bleached-
blond'. Jason decided to sue for defamation and
immediately put himself in an absolutely 'no win' situation; sure enough, he won the case but was, ultimately, the
loser. If he had ignored the magazine with its relatively
small readership (relative to national newspapers), he

might have sailed on with nothing more to face than the sort of whispers which affect a number of artists. Mel C and Ricky Martin are just two modern stars who ignore repeated innuendo. But, by fighting the case, Jason made the original poster headline national news. His gay audience ostracized him because he seemed to be disowning them, as if to be called gay was positively the worst thing that could happen to a man. And his heterosexual audience thought there could be no smoke without fire. Even today, when he has a steady girlfriend and two young children, mention of his name is still likely to provoke a debate on whether he is actually gay or not.

Jason Donovan has not had a top ten record in the UK since *The Face* débâcle. After the court case, he sunk deeper into drugs. *The Face* extended his agony by starting a fighting fund to raise money to pay his damages, even though he agreed to waive most of them. He admitted that he was 'going crazy with drugs', and the newspapers took great delight in stories of Jason falling over in clubs and generally behaving badly. The lowest point came in January 1995 – his drug problems became public knowledge when he was found slumped on the pavement outside the fashionable Viper Room in Los Angeles, and had to be rushed to hospital. Even his father Terry Donovan made public his concerns over Jason's welfare and drug use. Jason revealed, 'The drugs thing started getting big for me after the court case. I had wanted to make the move from *Smash Hits* to *The Face* but I couldn't move there. I was snookered and I couldn't come to terms with that.' He could not reinvent himself.

Kylie made the transition that eluded Jason, although he did have some cause for optimism in 2002. On the night that Kylie received two Brit awards, a now drug-free

Jason was revealed to be playing a small venue in Grimsby for £2,000. His boyish looks may have gone, but he is still a good-natured, good-humoured interviewee. The *Sun* newspaper even launched a campaign entitled 'Let's Get Donovan On Again' which revived interest and had Jason dreaming that he, too, might one day win a Brit.

'We went pink and proud.'

PART THREE
SHOWGIRL

14

Small, Beautiful and Portable

Despite all the rumours and reports Kylie and Dannii have only sung one duet in public since the days of *Young Talent Time*. It was Dannii's wedding day and Kylie was chief bridesmaid. At the reception, the bride and her bridesmaid, still wearing their wedding outfits, linked arms and belted out, 'We Are Family'.

Brit awards were still just pipe dreams for Kylie Minogue as her hugely successful 'Intimate and Live' tour came to a close in 1998. Her alliance with deConstruction limped to an inevitable conclusion with the announcement in the summer that she had parted company with them after the release of a new mixes greatest hits album, *Hits +*. She had released only two albums of new material in five years, so could hardly have been said to be a money-spinner for the label. DeConstruction is now defunct so Kylie jumped ship at the right time. Officially, the split was completely amicable. Kylie was a very rich woman so there was absolutely no need for her to rush into another deal.

The two most popular numbers on the tour, by a

considerable measure, were 'Better the Devil You Know' and 'Dancing Queen'. They may have been camp classics but, crucially, they were also numbers that were completely familiar. The audience would expect them, anticipating the moment when they could sing along. The psychology of touring changed dramatically in the nineties, an approach pioneered by The Rolling Stones, arguably the most successful touring band of all time. It is very simple. Put on a show full of your fans' favourite numbers like 'Honky Tonk Women' and 'Start Me Up' and throw in the occasional new song. Paul McCartney, U2, The Eagles, Brian Wilson, Duran Duran and many others jumped on what is almost a nostalgia bandwagon. Even Robbie Williams, the most successful British solo artist of recent years peppers his show with Robster standards – his classic 'Angels' is instant nostalgia.

The two key ingredients to cash in on the public mood were indestructible fan loyalty and an extensive back catalogue. Kylie did have both but she still needed to progress as an artist or she would have been stuck in a rut as a pink curio, trotting out the same show every year. Kylie and William Baker are well aware that the strongest card in her hand is image. In effect the songs could stay the same as long as the image changed. Kylie became a style icon for the new millennium while her new music, when it finally materialised, was a throw-back to the sound that had made her so popular in the first place – a deadly combination.

Kylie has often said that she changed her look so often, especially in the early days of Stock, Aitken and Waterman because it was the only thing she had control over. Kylie's first stylist in London was Kelly Cooper Barr who looked after the Stock, Aitken and Waterman stable – never the most stylish bunch. Cooper Barr was presented with a well-scrubbed girl with unruly hair, who looked about twelve. She was instructed to 'turn her into the next Olivia Newton-John'. Kylie would have been delighted to emulate the star of *Grease*, a childhood heroine, but the willowy Newton-John and the diminutive Kylie were poles apart. 'I remember looking at Kylie,' said Cooper Barr, 'and thinking it was never going to happen. She was a soap star and I could never imagine her being as big as Newton-John.' But she had her instructions, and Cooper Barr was determined to do her best, although it never occurred to her to try and make anything sexy of Kylie: 'I despaired of turning this childlike figure into anything approaching a star.' Kylie was so small – sometimes a size six would fall off her – that they struggled to find outfits for her, most of the time resorting to figure-hugging Lycra, topped off with huge platform shoes and knee socks. Kylie can laugh about it now, but at the time she looked a sight.

Kylie has probably suffered more barbs – and allegedly funny allusions – to her size than any other star. She has had to bear every conceivable description of her lack of stature: 'pint-sized chartbuster', 'diminutive diva', 'pop pixie', 'perfectly tiny', 'pop trinket', 'wee Kylie', 'miniature Madonna', and, unsurprisingly, the well-worn remark that she is always the last to know it's raining. Sometimes Kylie can be quite coy about her actual height, stating enigmatically that 'it varies'. She is actually 152 centimetres high, just a hair above five feet, a height she shares with her mother Carol. Sister Dannii is also petite. Kylie used to hate being small, especially as she was easy to spot in school photos: 'I was usually the one holding that darn board in front.' Kylie is by no means the only pop star who is on the small side, but she is the one who has had her height alluded to in almost every newspaper article from the time of 'I Should Be So Lucky' to the present day.

Kylie did, however, have one ally who didn't care whether she was short or tall, voluptuous or slim – the camera. No one can tell how tall you are if you are the only person in front of the camera and, eventually, Kylie realized that being small actually made her stand out in the crowd. There are so many pictures of Kylie in existence she could probably start a new currency – 'that will be six Kylie photos please'.

The camera has always loved Kylie. It was something Jan Russ, the casting director for *Neighbours*, had specifically noticed at her first audition. The plain, mousy girl was totally transformed by the time her image appeared on a television monitor. Kylie has always had the gift of being able to flirt with the camera. It was the same when she came to London. One stylist recalled, 'Put Kylie in front of a camera and she becomes alive. She makes love to the camera. She is fantastic at posing, as if it is the most natural thing in the world. Not having any inhibitions about your body helps.'

In those early days Kylie longed to be a cover girl. She was once smuggled into Raymond's Revue Bar, home of the famous Soho sex show, for a photo shoot. She was not exactly hiding under a blanket, but it would have ruined the surprise if the newspapers had been tipped off that she was seen going in. Kylie was very excited about it because it was her first fashion shoot for *Vogue* and she was desperate for it to be a success. The front cover of *Vogue* would be a credible style statement at last. The exposure would have also helped her gain international recognition.

The idea of photographing Kylie in a slightly seedy setting was an enterprising one, and she threw herself into a series of poses, wearing an alarming array of feathers. Everybody was waiting excitedly to see the finished result when the magazine hit the news-stands, especially the choice of picture they had decided to use on the cover. Disappointingly, the magazine arrived and the cover picture was of a standard, glossy model. Poor Kylie had been dumped inside, admittedly over eight pages. One of her entourage recalled, 'She could not understand why. But the magazine seemed to have the attitude that "we take the pictures and if there isn't an appropriate one for the cover, then we will use something else." Kylie was disappointed. We all believed when she did the shoot that it was for the front cover.'

Now, it seems an incredible decision to demote Kylie to 'inside'. But it would be many years before an image of Kylie on the front cover of a magazine would increase sales in the UK. She did learn from the experience, exerting more control over her image and gaining a greater understanding of the medium through her alliances with, among others, Stephane Sednaoui and Katerina Jebb. She realised it was not enough to smile cheesily at the lens.

The transformation of Kylie, from Charlene Mitchell to the most desirable woman on the planet, did not happen overnight, despite the claims of a pair of gold hot pants. The reality is that Kylie had been striving to be considered sexy for more than a decade, but nobody would take her seriously. In the early days, no red-blooded male would have voted Kylie as the number one doll with whom they would want to spend the night. She might have won a poll for which celebrity would be your preferred babysitter. It was a case of 'look at Charlene flaunting those long eyelashes – what does she think she's doing?' They even stuck a label on this incarnation – SexKylie – just as she became IndieKylie during her collaboration with the Manic Street Preachers and ArtyKylie when she performed with Nick Cave. SexKylie was considered fraudulent. The implication was that all the hair lacquer and bare flesh in the world was not going to transform this middle-class, suburban Miss Nice into a sex symbol.

In 1988, one magazine even featured Kim Wilde versus Kylie Minogue and gave the British singer eight out of ten for looks, while assessing Kylie as a six, claiming she was a 'bit on the skinny side'. Kim also won the style stakes, scoring another eight for her 'natural grace', whereas Kylie looked like 'she should be modelling digital watches', and was allotted a feeble four. It has been a huge effort, but today Kylie would assuredly score ten out of ten in both sections. Kim is now an old married lady with children, happily participating in eighties revival concerts when not designing gardens. Kylie is winning prestigious awards and is unlikely ever to be seen fronting a Stock, Aitken and Waterman tribute tour.

At the end of the 'Intimate and Live' tour Kylie and Baker produced a masterstroke – not a new record but a book. It would give Kylie absolute credibility as a woman of substance and style. It would consolidate the good work of the tour – namely that Kylie was now a much-loved institution like Ovaltine and *Coronation Street,* a star entirely at ease with all her previous images. The book, *Kylie* – titles have never been her strong point – was a study in reinvention, with images from throughout her life and career, and featured close-ups of most parts of her body, many life-size, including arm, foot, ears and bottom. The final product revealed that Kylie was reconciled with her past. In many of the previously unseen photographs, quite a few of which were taken by Baker, Sednaoui and Jebb, Kylie looks absolutely fabulous. She observed that she had to 'learn' how to have a photograph taken in the early days of her career. She also knows her best angle, such an important consideration for celebrities: 'Years of experience have taught me that angles do exist – everyone has one. Sometimes I'll get photographers trying to do things and I'll be like "I don't want to be rude but take my picture from the front and a little to the side and that's it." People say I do this arched eyebrow thing but they just take over.' Kylie's own favourites among her pictures are the ones in which she is laughing.

In the book, one of the photographs, taken in 1994, has Kylie dressed as a schoolgirl, five years before Britney Spears copied the look. Another photo has Kylie dressed as a nun on a rocking horse. William Baker's own photo of Kylie from 1997 depicts her naked, kneeling on a velvet sofa, a naughty, yet innocently happy grin on her face, and her curvaceous bottom much in evidence.

The project was a little egotistical but did contain some fascinating text – eulogistic vignettes from friends and admirers, like Baz Luhrmann, Nick Cave, Julie Burchill and Katerina Jebb. The violinist Nigel Kennedy revealed that he called his violin 'Kylie' because it was 'small, beautiful and portable'. Baker was fulsome in his praise of Kylie, asserting that her image changes were not cleverly orchestrated publicity stunts. More pertinently, he recognized that fashion had moved on, and that what was considered banal in the nineties was now thought to be fabulous, which is exactly what happened to Kylie herself in the latter part of the decade. *Kylie* was all about image and a life lived in the public eye. Kylie admirers might have welcomed more of an insight into the private Kylie but that has never been her style.

The best explanation as to why promoting Kylie as a style icon of a generation succeeded in 1999 while being laughable ten years earlier is proffered by Kelly Cooper Barr. Kelly and Kylie used to go to clubs together in the late eighties and it was always the make-up artist who would get chatted up, because the wolves on the dance floor would invariably assume that she was the famous pop star. Nobody recognized Kylie. The difference more than a decade later was age. Kelly explained, 'Most women don't smoulder until they get to their early thirties and reach sexual maturity.' In other words, sex appeal has given Kylie style. And style has given Kylie sex appeal.

Doing the unexpected might be another ingredient. In March 1999, Kylie could be found on the beautiful island of Barbados – not relaxing, as she was fully entitled to do, but acting on stage. It was a long way from *Neighbours*. Once again Kylie was challenging herself – as well as getting off with a fit looking member of the cast. She had been persuaded by Johnny Kidd, father of model Jodie Kidd, to appear in a production of *The Tempest*, at a cultural festival he organized annually in the hibiscus and palm tree-lined gardens of his plantation estate. It was a musical version of the play – loosely called *The Caribbean Tempest* – but it was still Shakespeare; and not too many of the Bard's verses involved the Aussie pastimes of partaking of a 'smoothie' or behaving like a 'dag'. The mastermind behind the extravaganza was Kit Hesketh-Harvey, best known for his UK fringe-act Kit and the Widow. He adapted the Shakespearean verse to use as lyrics for fifteen new songs. His only disappointment was that Kylie, who played Miranda, refused to sing. She was determined to play the role completely straight and not turn it into a kitsch classic. Hesketh-Harvey observed that she was a model cast member, and even helped carry the props.

In the play Kylie was surrounded by Shakespearean actors, like David Calder and Rupert Penry-Jones. After Kylie, the best-known face, at the time, belonged to Roger Lloyd Pack, familiar on British television in *Only Fools and Horses* and *The Vicar of Dibley*. Kylie's reward for her dedication to the role was an honourable, if slightly patronising, mention in a review in *The Times*: 'The casting of Kylie Minogue as Miranda may have raised the odd knowing smile in anticipation, but she conducted herself more than adequately.' The production eventually made its way to Sydney, sadly without Kylie who, by this time, was hard at work on her comeback album.

Barbados was the perfect setting for a new romance. Kylie had been dating various men since Stephane Sednaoui but no one too serious. One liaison, with musical director Cassius Coleman, lasted on and off for six months but, as usual, her career came first. Cassius certainly made the effort, and flew out to Barbados to visit Kylie. Unfortunately for him, Kylie had already fallen for her leading man, Rupert Penry-Jones. He had all the credentials for being a heart throb, as well as a spark of creativity – a good combination for Kylie.

Like the other blond hunk in her life, Jason Donovan, Rupert came from a showbusiness background. His mother, Angela Thorne, was an actress in the British TV series *To the Manor Born* with Penelope Keith, and his father, Peter Penry-Jones, acted in the popular television drama *Colditz*, as well as the more recent *Longitude*. Rupert was privately educated at Dulwich College in London, and disappointed his parents a little by choosing the same acting profession, mainly because they knew only too well the times of financial strife that might result. Fortunately Rupert, over six feet tall, blond with piercing blue eyes, started with a bang by being spotted by model agency Storm when he was just seventeen, and being whisked off to the Milan catwalk. He therefore had experience of the fashion world of which Kylie is so enamoured. He also revealed an impressive physique in the film *Virtual Sexuality*, which contained so many sex scenes that he had to spend an entire week naked to get them all shot.

Penry-Jones has serious acting ambitions. He achieved his first step when he was understudy to Ralph Fiennes in a production of *Hamlet* in the mid-nineties. His Caribbean odyssey helped pave the way for a lead role with the RSC, as the eponymous hero in Schiller's *Don Carlos*. Kylie did her bit by going up from London to Stratford-upon-Avon to support him. She could be seen perched daintily on the back of his motorbike, something she had a lot of practice of when she rode pillion on Michael Hutchence's Harley. The only difference was the English weather. On

Rupert's bike Kylie would wear socks on her hands to keep out the cold.

Rupert was smitten with Kylie and found it very difficult to follow the familiar path of secrecy: 'We're very good friends,' he declared, unconvincingly. 'We're not going out with each other. But if I was going out with someone, it would be her.' In reality, they went out for close on ten months, but he never admitted it, although he told journalist Chrissy Iley: 'Part of me wanted to scream it from the roof tops!' He did take Kylie home to meet his parents, and they liked her. They had Sunday lunch and Kylie chatted away. Her ability to mix easily, even though she is so famous, is something that Michael Hutchence's mother noticed when her son first introduced her to Kylie.

In the end, it was the familiar story of work killing their relationship. He was in Stratford, and she would be in Los Angeles or Melbourne or London. To his credit, Penry-Jones is enthusiastically complimentary about his famous ex-girlfriend: 'I thought I was one of the luckiest men in the world and, to be honest, I can't believe it lasted more than a week.' He also revealed Kylie to be a free spirit: 'I don't think she's ever going to belong to anybody.'

For a while it seemed that Rupert Penry-Jones would be just another conquest who would remain most famous for being one of Kylie's exes. That changed in 2004 when he became the star of the successful BBC series *Spooks*. His acting career had been progressing with great promise but he hit the jackpot with his role as intelligence officer Adam Carter. In 2007 he will play the lead role of Captain Wentworth in a new television production of *Persuasion* by Jane Austen.

*

Dannii was doing no better in the relationship stakes although she did have the distinction, if that's the right word, of beating Kylie to the altar. Her wedding in 1994 was a glittering affair with the pictures sold to *Hello!* In Australian terms it was showbiz royalty. The groom was Julian McMahon, her co-star in *Home and Away* and the son of former Australian prime minister, Sir William McMahon. Kylie was a bridesmaid and played the role of the unattached spinster sister. She was alleged to have designed Dannii's wedding dress, which was a bit of a surprise to the New York couturier who supplied it.

The marriage to McMahon lasted no more than fifteen months before collapsing acrimoniously amid rumours that he was playing less at home and more away. McMahon, now a big TV star in the US thanks to his role in *Nip Tuck*, was portrayed as a cad, especially as he had professed undying devotion to Dannii on their wedding day. 'She is my world,' he cried. After the break-up, Kylie was a considerable comfort to her sister, a divorcee at twenty-three, who found herself now back living in London. In the early days, the sisters had lived together but, latterly, Dannii has preferred her independence. However, they talk almost daily on the telephone, particularly if they want to moan about the men in their lives – which is most days. They are rarely seen together in public, preferring to catch up and have a gossip with a take-away pizza, a bottle of wine and something good on the telly.

Dannii found love again two years later, in a whirlwind romance with ex-Formula One World Champion Jacques Villeneuve. They met at the 1999 Spanish Grand Prix, became engaged, and Dannii moved away from London and the shadow of her elder sister to share Villeneuve's £2 million penthouse apartment in Monaco. Up until now, Kylie has not made any ostensible sacrifices for love; that is not the case with Dannii, who immediately dropped out of sight to be with her millionaire. Alas, the engagement did not last and, after eighteen months in Monaco, Dannii returned to London once more to focus on her career. Neither girl, it seemed then, would ever crack the two-year barrier and either one of the sisters could have made the following statement: 'I don't regard them [past relationships] as failures. You aren't going to find Mr Right by sitting at home. You have got to go out and try a few.' It was, in fact, Kylie speaking.

When Dannii split up with Jacques, she had her hair cut short for her part as Esmerelda in the West End musical *Notre Dame de Paris*. She was thrilled to be at last doing something that Kylie had never done. There is a suspicion that Dannii's eagerness to plunge into marriage and engagements is because they, too, are something Kylie has never done.

Dannii continues to be disarmingly frank about herself in interviews: 'I was the most crap singer and crap dancer and crap everything, but I worked my bollocks off, because that's what I wanted to do.' At least she has the consolation – if it is one – of being the Minogue sister preferred by X Factor judge Simon Cowell, who called Kylie a 'one-trick pony'. In Cowell's defence, Dannii was often considered to be the prettier of the two sisters until the past five years or so, during which Kylie has really blossomed.

Poor Dannii got a rotten press for years, portrayed as the pushier, less talented sister. Dannii was the one whose changing body shape, to a more voluptuous 'Baywatch' physique, derailed any suggestion that Kylie too might have quietly gone up a bra size. It is considered vulgar when Dannii takes her clothes off for *Australian Playboy*, but tasteful or arty when Kylie does the same thing for *Sky* or *GQ* magazine. Dannii's perceived shortcomings have helped to define Kylie's good qualities.

Friends of both women believe Dannii to be the warmer, more compassionate sister, ruled more by her heart than her head. She was always thought to be the more feisty, but, in fact, is probably more maternal and likely to be the first to send flowers if a friend has a baby. She is also a compulsive shopaholic, who spends money like it is going out of fashion, does not understand the meaning of the phrase 'clothes budget' and has always needed her father to keep a firm eye on her finances.

The majority of Kylie's relationships seem to end just before the turn of the year, as if she is putting her house in order before she returns home for her usual month-long break with her family and prepares for the next stage of her career. After Rupert, however, she did not head straight back to Melbourne. Instead she went to entertain the Australian troops in East Timor, Indonesia, where they had been sent to keep the peace after a bloody civil war. Kylie was the forces' pin up but more Marilyn Monroe than Vera Lynn. Kylie, in a tight-fitting, wet-through white shirt, skin-tight olive pants and boots, handed out Christmas cards which she had specially signed for the boys. She flew by helicopter to areas of mud, monsoon rains and mosquitoes – hardly the King's Road – to try to cheer up the men who would not be travelling back home for Christmas, which was five days away.

Kylie was profoundly affected by what she witnessed, especially when those not lucky enough to be singing Christmas carols with Kylie found a mass grave of butchered civilians, just a few miles away. She declared simply, 'I am fiercely proud of being Australian and to be part of all this is among the most rewarding things I have done.'

'Style is your own interpretation of what you are and what you project to others.'

15

Gold Hot Pants

Robbie Williams had no idea what Kylie would be wearing when she joined him on stage in Manchester to sing their hit duet 'Kids'. It turned out to be a silver slip of a costume which left nothing to the imagination and left Robbie sweating. 'For a second he lost it and I loved it', said Kylie.

A minuscule pair of gold bondage hot pants slid teasingly up and down a pole, while their wearer sang a modern disco classic. 'Spinning Around' was the track which took Kylie back to the top of the UK charts for the first time since 1990. It had been ten long years. The video for 'Spinning Around' was even more important than the song itself. It provocatively displayed the allure of a woman who had reached her sexual peak and was not afraid of shouting it to the world. Even Kylie was in awe of those hot pants, asserting that they had 'a mind of their own'. They plucked the strings of sexual fantasy for the millions of men who could not believe that they were being worn by the girl with the bubble haircut and the anaemic eighties hit list. More importantly, it brought this new sexy image to a younger audience, which had no pre-conceptions as to the kind of artist Kylie was.

The video also launched Kylie's bottom on an unsuspecting world – as if that part of her body had not really existed before. In reality, her bottom was nothing new to the readers of lads' mags. It had notoriously been revealed on the front cover of *GQ* magazine, as a re-enactment of the famous Athena poster. Under the banner 'Kylie at your Service', she was pictured dressed in white tennis clothing and wearing no knickers. Afterwards, Kylie insisted her G-string had been air-brushed out, which is neither here nor there. Celebrities are forever bleating about magazines using technology to change photographs, usually protesting that they were not actually naked. Kylie and her management, however, have always maintained a stranglehold on photo shoots, anxious to protect and project the exact image they want at any given time.

Not everybody was impressed. Charlotte Raven in the *Guardian*, perceptively wrote, 'This is not a stolen moment but the product of the model's wish to show the world her butt.' In other words, this was Kylie manipulating her public image in a calculating and, ultimately, very successful manner. In her defence, Kylie took a very light-hearted approach to the whole thing: 'I thought it would be fun to show a bit of cheek,' she said. The only truly bogus thing was Kylie pretending to play tennis – as if she would! Kylie is not a great fan of outdoor sports.

The video for 'Spinning Around' was just as pointless. It was not the first time Kylie had squeezed into a pair of hot pants for a video. For 'Some Kind of Bliss', she wore a skimpy denim pair, which gave her the germ of the idea that this might be something to exploit in the future. When she asked Johnny Douglas, one of her producers, why he liked that particular video, he confided that it all came down to those hot pants. Kylie filed away that information for use on the next available occasion. The famous gold hot pants were actually passed on to Kylie by William Baker, who found them on a market stall for 50 pence. Who on earth other than Kylie could ever wear them? – there is hardly enough material to cover an oyster shell.

Baker had worked out that Kylie's bottom was her best feature, and would give her an edge whenever she showed it off. They were also the perfect symbol for her reincarnation as a disco diva. 'Spinning Around' was the first release from a new album *Light Years* and provided Kylie with her fifth number one but, more significantly, her first since 1990. It reached the top spot in July 2000 and, just a month later, Kylie was back on *Top of the Pops* for a performance that turned out to be a very smart career move. She sang a duet with Robbie Williams, a rousing track which would feature on both their new albums.

Robbie had a big crush on Kylie. He may have been the biggest solo star in Britain, but this was Kylie Minogue and he had been just an ordinary fourteen year-old, football-obsessed boy from Stoke-on-Trent when she had taken the charts by storm with 'I Should Be So Lucky'. Kylie, the older woman, knew exactly how to play it with Robbie. A record company insider observed, 'He would follow her around and she was like, "Robbie, you stink", but I think she ended up quite liking him really.' Robbie himself admitted he was slightly nervous of Kylie. There was never any romance, despite attempts by the media to link the two of them together. It would have been a wonderful story if they had become an item, but, at the time, Kylie had a steady boyfriend and Robbie adopted his usual, outrageous, naughty-boy persona, asking publicly, 'Do you reckon she'd shag me?'

Kylie may have got her own back a little in Manchester but it's fair to say she had always had a soft spot for Robbie, nominating him on more than one occasion as her favourite member of Take That. She is not a fan of boy bands, but thought Robbie stood out: 'I always knew he was going to be a star. He's such a natural.' Robbie and Kylie were put together by their management teams. Robbie was on Chrysalis which, like Kylie's new record label Parlophone, is a subsidiary of EMI. They were keen to reposition Kylie in the mainstream after her few years in the independent wilderness. Robbie jumped at the chance to write some songs for *Light Years*. He told her she had everything going for her but just needed a good song to turn things around – just as 'Angels' had for him a couple of years before. With his songwriting partner Guy Chambers, he contributed three songs: the mellow lounge-track 'Loveboat', the high camp 'Your Disco Needs You' and the anthemic 'Kids'. Kylie shared the songwriting credit on the first two. She actually asked Robbie for a song called 'Loveboat' because she liked it as a title. It was Robbie who thought up the phrase 'Your Disco Needs You'. He also wrote the lyrics to 'Kids', which were quite mischievous, to say the least, with their tongue-in-cheek references to anal sex. Only Robbie could rhyme 'sodomy' with 'Billy Connolly'. 'Kids' was a superb dance track, although Robbie seemed to be struggling with a high-pitched falsetto for most of the song. Surprisingly the dream couple were kept off the number one spot by U2's 'Beautiful Day'.

Robbie and Kylie were perfect musical partners. They made each other appear sexy and naughty at the same time. Although Kylie might prefer to disagree, Robbie also made her appear hip at a vital time. 'Spinning Around' went straight to number one on a wave of support from Kylie's gay fan base, but that achievement would have been wasted if her comeback had begun and ended there. An alliance with Robbie was guaranteed to cement her position in the mainstream marketplace. Not only would the great man not alienate her gay fans, he would introduce Kylie to a whole new generation of young girls, who would see her next to Robbie and want to be just like her. He had just had a big selling number one with 'Rock DJ', so between them Kylie and Robbie monopolized the charts for a few months. The other reason why Robbie was such a perfect musical partner for Kylie is that he augmented her camp image. Robbie may not yet be a gay icon of Kylie's stature – although Take That found popularity appearing live in gay clubs before they became chart stars – but he is a showman *par excellence,* who can move effortlessly between brooding sexuality and naughtiness, just a step away from being a drag queen. His 'Rock DJ' became a great favourite among the transvestite ladyboys of Bangkok when Robbie toured the Far East. They loved it when Robbie bared his bottom and simulated sex with a cardboard cut-out of Kylie.

Kylie showcased 'Your Disco Needs You' when she appeared at Privilege in Ibiza, which billed itself as the largest nightclub in the world. The fact that Kylie was chosen as the inaugural live act at the venue was testimony to the fact that it was now officially OK to be a fan.

The 'K' from the 'Intimate And Live' tour had been replaced by 'Kylie' in neon bulbs, very seventies disco. Her dancers, clad in black, made robotic moves close to the swimming pool at the front of the stage. And there was Kylie at the top of the stairs – Tinkerbell herself – dressed in a pink vinyl jacket, pink micro-skirt with a slit up the back and little pink boots, giving the crowd a big, cheesy 'Lucky' grin. How times had changed. Or had they? In 1990, almost exactly ten years earlier, Kylie was asked what her latest fashion buy had been – it was a pair of pink ostrich feather hot pants. Perhaps Kylie was just not cool enough for them in those days.

The last time there had been live music on the Mediterranean DJ Mecca of Ibiza was in 1988, and you can bet nobody would have been seen dead turning up to watch Kylie Minogue perform her Stock, Aitken and Waterman fodder. This island prides itself on a reputation for hedonism and Kylie was at that time too naff for that – not any more. 'Your Disco Needs You' outcamped the Village People for slightly sleazy fun. The dancers removed their tops to reveal oiled pecs (men) and powdered breasts decorated with black tassels (women). Kylie, meanwhile, had changed into a gold bikini top and frilly hot pants. There was the decadent air of *Cabaret*, with none of the threatening overtones. One reviewer noted, 'No one really dances during Kylie's set – they're too busy leering.'

As an album *Light Years* lightened the mood. Any lingering feeling of 'down' from her more mature sound of the mid nineties was swept away. Kylie told *Rolling Stone* magazine that she only had one instruction for the various songwriters: 'I said "These are my keywords:

poolside, beach, cocktails and disco". I wanted to indulge the over-the-top side of my character and I think we did it.'

Over-the-top is the only way to describe Kylie's spectacular performance of a lifetime at the closing ceremony of the Sydney Olympics in October 2000. More than 3.7 billion people in 185 countries watched the event – a few more even than watched Charlene marry Scott. What an entrance Kylie made! A bevy of muscled Bondi Beach life savers carried her on a surf board to the centre of the main stadium, where a live audience of 100,000 people had gathered, all in party mood. She was dressed in the identical costume worn by Nikki Webster, the child who had starred in the opening ceremony. It was some sort of slightly tortuous symbolism, typical of the Olympics, of a girl maturing to a woman – rather ironic considering it was Kylie, the most famous of all child-women that Nikki had matured into.

The beach boys hoisted Kylie on to the stage where her dancers, a vision in pink, obscured her while they began their athletic movements to the strains of Abba's 'Dancing Queen'. Suddenly, the announcer's voice rang out above the audience: 'Mesdames et Messieurs . . . Miss (the music pauses for a split second and the dancers are frozen in time) Kylie Minogue.' And there she was, miraculously changed into the costume of a Busby Berkeley showgirl, complete with a magnificent head-dress. She performed 'Dancing Queen', the alternative national anthem of Australia, and her own 'On A Night Like This' and was, by common consent, magnificent. As if to crown her status as the world's number one gay icon, she was encircled by an enormous representation of Sydney's drag queens in all their finery, their devotion to Kylie absolutely constant and unaffected through the years. Her performance was the ultimate in camp and, as such, is unlikely to be topped. Many of Australia's most popular figures performed or appeared at either the opening or closing ceremonies, but it was Kylie not Greg Norman, nor even Olivia Newton-John, Kylie's own childhood heroine, who stole the show. Hers was the performance that stuck in the memory.

The Olympic Games did more than confirm Kylie's position as the number one gay icon, it established her as the world's all-Australian heroine. Even though she had deserted her homeland for London a decade earlier, hers would be the first name inked in during a game of 'list five famous Australians'. To use an old cliché – you can take Kylie out of Australia but you cannot take Australia out of Kylie. She once admitted, 'In my heart I am so Australian. I am so ridiculously patriotic.'

At the end of the Olympic closing ceremony, Kylie returned to the stage to sing along to the Australian favourite 'Waltzing Matilda'. Poignantly, the surviving members of INXS were among those on stage with her. Kylie's position as a performer of fame and stature was assured throughout the world. Or nearly. One place remained unconquered: the United States of America. Kylie's very first hit, 'The Loco-Motion' remained her biggest success there and the unwanted sobriquet 'The Loco-Motion Girl' lingered on. The famous and much-lauded Australian film *Priscilla Queen of the Desert*, about drag queens crossing Australia in a battered old bus, was originally going to be about acts from the 'Kylie Show'. This would have been colossal international exposure for

Kylie. Alas, it was decided that Kylie's name would not sell the film to the US public, so the plot was changed to make them Abba impersonators. The promoters obviously felt that 'The Loco-Motion Girl' was not going to sell ten tickets to a barn dance. It was little better for Kylie to be described as the Australian Madonna, which suggested something parochial and imitative. Kylie was not an absolute unknown in the US because her American gay fans still adored her, but she could walk down Rodeo Drive in Los Angeles and be taken for a boutique assistant, rather than one of the world's biggest superstars. The only places in the US where Kylie is likely to be recognized are in traditionally gay areas, like the Chelsea district of Manhattan: 'It can get a little manic there. The boys start to go wild.'

What Kylie needed to go back into battle in the US was a universally acclaimed, big-selling record. *Light Years*, 'Spinning Around' and 'Kids' had re-established her in the UK and other strong Kylie markets, but the follow-up would be crucial. She was with The Beatles' old record label Parlophone, who had a commercial tie-up in the States with Capitol records, so the framework would be in place just so long as there was a half-decent record to promote. *Light Years* was a very pink album. The next release needed to be more mainstream. Kylie herself was heavily involved in producing and writing the new album, to be called *Fever*, but one song was destined to change the perception of Kylie worldwide. Finally, despite all the hits in between, she would have a record bigger than 'I Should Be So Lucky'.

When the demo for 'Can't Get You Out Of My Head' arrived at the offices of Parlophone in West London, it was almost perfect. The voice sounded familiar. It was former dance music darling Cathy Dennis, who had five top ten records in the 1990s, and a much-copied bob haircut, but was a bigger name in Europe and the US than in the UK. Her biggest solo hits were '(Touch Me) All Night Long' and a version of The Kinks' classic 'Waterloo Sunset'. The melody for 'Better the Devil You Know' was actually inspired by 'Come On And Get My Love' by D Mob on which Cathy sang the vocal in 1989. Cathy has a similar self-deprecatory style to Kylie: 'It never even crossed my mind that I could be a pop star, because I came from Norwich. Pop stars don't come from Norwich.' She has a healthy contempt for many singers, Kylie excepted, of course: 'They're celebrities, not pop artists – if you asked them about music they wouldn't have a Scooby-doo.'

Ironically, Cathy was probably a bigger name Stateside than Kylie but, by the end of the nineties, she had tired of performing and had become a full-time writer for other artists. She has written most of the S Club 7 hits. Her collaborator on the song with the most infectious hook of 2001 was Rob Davis, guitarist with the seventies chart act Mud and one of the campest figures of the glam rock age. Davis was also responsible for the catchiest dance record of 2000, Spiller's 'Groovejet', which featured Sophie Ellis-Bextor on vocals. Cathy was not convinced that 'Can't Get You Out Of My Head' was number one material. But when Kylie first heard the demo, she leaped around, saying, 'When can I do it?'

The song was an obvious choice for first single from the new album. It had all the ingredients of a Stock, Aitken and Waterman hit, but in a more sophisticated package. The first line sounded eerily similar to Dead or Alive's chorus: 'You Spin Me Right Round'.

To whip up some publicity, and thus increase record sales, there were stories of great rivalry between Kylie and Victoria Beckham. This was a cynical marketing trick to try to persuade more people to buy the record they preferred – thereby increasing sales of both tracks. The media generally colluded with this mock battle. The outcome was complete victory for Kylie, when her record went straight in at number one in the UK charts on 23 September 2001. Kylie sold 306,000 copies in the first week of release, compared with 35,000 of Victoria's 'Not Such An Innocent Girl', which only made number six. As a recording artist 'Posh Spice' is just not taken seriously by the media or the public, a state of affairs which Kylie knows all about from her own career. Victoria Beckham is also disadvantaged because she is happily married, with three children she adores. Kylie is single, available and can be a little dangerous. There's nothing dangerous about sitting around in your mansion watching television with your hubby. The public is not that stupid. Kylie's single proceeded to top the charts in twenty countries worldwide. Ironically in Finland, which has traditionally adored Kylie, it only reached number two. To make up for that Finnish disappointment, the single topped the chart in both the United Arab Emirates and Israel. Kylie unites the world!

In the months that followed scarcely a day went by without Kylie featuring on a newspaper front page, a magazine cover, on television or radio. Suddenly, Kylie became a British national institution, like *Dad's Army* or *Del Boy*, a position she holds to this day. Yes, she is a sexy and stylish survivor making the best music of her career, but she is also a reassuring presence, especially after the shock of 11 September. In 2001, Bryan Appleyard, of the *Sunday Times* no less, observed, 'God's in his heaven, Kylie's at number one, surely nothing really bad can happen now.'

Not all the news was welcome. A few weeks after the release of the single, a suspect package arrived at the EMI offices. It allegedly contained soil and a note warning the record company that owns Parlophone to drop Kylie, or else staff would be infected with anthrax. The perpetrator apparently loathed *Neighbours*. On a jollier note, Kylie featured in *An Audience with Kylie Minogue*. Brendan and Dannii were there and her brother grinned uncomfortably when the spotlight settled on them. Dannii has always basked in it but, for the most part, Brendan has managed to keep well away. He has had to suffer some embarrassments over the years particularly when Kylie revealed he was once a fan of eighties rock group Kiss and used to borrow his mother's high-heeled boots and paint stars around his eyes in homage to his heroes. Mostly, however, it has worked out well for him – the reflected adulation of having famous sisters with none of the aggravation of being a star. When Kylie became well known, Brendan, a good-looking, dark-haired boy would accompany her to parties, and generally have the girls swooning in his direction. One admirer from the *Neighbours* days recalled wistfully, 'He was gorgeous, quiet and just a really nice guy.'

Kylie remains protective of Brendan, who is very much part of her private world. Keeping away from public scrutiny allowed him to take time out to backpack around the world before settling in Sydney where he now earns his living as a cameraman.

Pete Waterman was also on show at *An Audience*, looking every inch the proud father watching his daughter in a school nativity play. A tremor of expectation filtered through the audience when the band played the opening bars of 'Especially For You'. Kylie and Jason together again? Poor Jason – he had been replaced by Kermit the Frog, who said to Kylie, 'If you kiss me, I might turn into Jason Donovan.' Kylie replied, 'I like you just the way you are.' Everyone had a good laugh at Jason's expense.

When *Fever* was released in October 2001, it debuted at number one in the UK album charts. Awards began to pile up from all over the world. In Germany, Kylie won the 'Bambi' award for best comeback of the year. Tickets for four UK dates in 2002 sold out within one hour. Already, plans were well advanced to promote Kylie as a star in the US. The single was released and Kylie was promoting it everywhere, including on the *Tonight Show* with Jay Leno. She reached number one in the dance charts and climbed into the top twenty of the Billboard Hot 100 chart. *Fever* was released in the US just after it won best international album at the 2002 Brit awards at the end of February. The reviews were good, although the description of Kylie as a pop vixen was cringe-making. *Billboard* said, '*Fever* harks back to a more innocent time when sex and dance floors merged to create one carefree nation under a groove.' The album entered the charts at number three, a wonderful result. The same week the single finally made the top ten.

Meanwhile, Kylie's spectacularly pert behind was showing absolutely no desire to head south as she crept past her mid-thirties. It is a remarkable achievement in a woman of her age to have the world's most photographed and applauded rear. There has never been such a fixation on a bottom. In anyone other than Kylie it might be considered 'pervy' but, somehow, in Kylie's case, it is considered good clean, family fun – a latter day equivalent of Barbara Windsor's boobs. Kylie herself has likened her sexuality to a *Carry On* film, which is not exactly accurate. The fascination with her fanny, as Americans would call it, *is* rather pervy if you consider part of the sexual allure to be her persona of a child-woman.

The pinnacle for Kylie's rear end, to date, occurred in the aftermath of the 2001 MTV Music Awards, when her immaculate behind was the runaway winner of a Best Arse competition, voted for by the public on MTV's interactive service. Entire photo galleries on the web are now devoted to pictures of her bottom. Brian Appleyard described it as a 'wonder of nature'. As the MTV site eulogized, 'We believe that, if used properly, it [Kylie's arse] could help the world come together in peace and harmony, rebuild cities and probably crack a nut the size of a continent.'

Kylie can be a little touchy about her bottom. She has even had people asking her to turn around so they can get a closer look. When one interviewer asked if he could talk about her arse, she replied firmly, 'I've put it away for a while now.' Inevitably there was a backlash over Kylie's bottom, with newspaper suggestions after a breathtaking Brits performance that all was not as natural as it seemed. It was described as a 'bumlash'. Kylie was mortified by the stories, especially as they undermined her perfectly natural image. A rearguard action in friendly magazines and newspapers strongly refuted the very idea of cosmetic enhancement. Having used her bottom as a pertinent weapon in her re-emergence, it was time for Kylie to play down this particular feature in case it had a counter-productive effect.

'I'm like safe sex.'

16

Kylie's Wrecked My Life

Kylie and her friends were having dinner one evening when the conversation turned to winning the National Lottery and what they would all do if they had the money. Half-way through the conversation Kylie suddenly realized, 'But I *have* got the money.'

The whole world, it seemed was waiting for some happy news. Kylie only had to walk down the street smiling and a frenzy of media speculation would follow. 'Friends' seemed to be quoted everywhere saying that the couple were planning a wedding very soon. 'Friends' also said Kylie was taking time off in the hope of starting a family. Yet within months former male model James Gooding had sold his story to the *News of the World* under the sensational front page headline: 'Kylie's Wrecked My Life.'

Kylie had met Gooding at a pool party in Los Angeles at the beginning of 2000. She had flown to California to put the finishing touches to *Light Years*. Her relationship with Rupert Penry-Jones was over and she, as usual, was throwing herself into work. Gooding was a model with dark, brooding looks, just the sort of man usually favoured by Kylie. When they were introduced she went weak at the knees. The party was a bit boring so James, who at the time was living in LA, suggested they should go and get something to eat. But they did not rush into a full-blown passionate affair at once, instead going for a series of getting-to-know-you dates, which was a refreshing change for Kylie. He, endearingly, recalled, 'She was just this little, funny, geeky girl who I thought was really cute.' He took her bowling which is something she has always enjoyed. She called him her 'delightful scruff from Essex'.

Kylie managed to keep her new romance secret for an outstanding length of time, considering her fame. She confessed that there was someone special, but did not name him, although she said she was 'enjoying the romance'. Gooding moved back to London, but did not move into Kylie's millionaire home. Kylie's cautious approach may have had something to do with his age. He was seven years younger than her, but had been in the world of fashion since he was eighteen, his photogenic looks so much in demand that he had earned the unwanted sobriquet of 'supermodel'. There is something of a role reversal with Kylie and certain of her men. Zane, Mark, Rupert, James – they are trophy boyfriends, great-looking adornments to hang off your arm.

One of the qualities Kylie liked in James Gooding was his domesticity. Long-term, Kylie has not reacted well to the energy sapping relationships she endured with Hutchence and Sednaoui. Gooding was not hard work. One of his favourite pursuits is making little cardboard boxes. He takes a blank piece of card and then makes a little box from it, into which he puts a gift. He once made a 'really cool box' for Kylie. He likes cooking and the two of them would curl up on the sofa together and watch *Pop*

Idol or they would sip drinks on the balcony of her Chelsea home. Somehow he never seemed exciting enough for Kylie, who described their friendship as a 'nice, simple romance.'

Gooding painted a picture of their relationship in the *News of the World* that made them resemble Darby and Joan. After coffee and croissants at his flat in Shoreditch, they would wander round Brick Lane market buying old records and bunches of flowers. Then they would go home where James would cook a Sunday roast. Kylie's favourite apparently was a 'nice leg of lamb, broccoli and roast spuds.' They would then settle down on the sofa and watch television or a *Bridget Jones* video. Cor blimey Missus, the only detail missing from this scene of domestic bliss was a slice of Battenburg cake and *Last of the Summer Wine*.

Kylie went to stay with Gooding's mother Jenny Young, who lives in a modest terraced house in the quaintly named Kirby-le-Soken in Essex, near the seaside resort of Walton-on-the-Naze. James split his time as a child between Essex and Scotland where his father David lived and where he originally went to a boarding school in Rannoch. Jenny and Kylie got on well together, as all mums do with her, and then had to run the gauntlet of everyone asking her if Kylie and her son were going to get married. Intriguingly, when Kylie went for her Christmas holiday to Melbourne James did not accompany her.

They did, however, enjoy a break in early November 2001 at Puerto Banus, on Spain's Costa Del Sol. They were seen looking in the window of a jewellery store, which prompted a frenzy of engagement speculation. They reportedly lingered over a £50,000 engagement ring. The romantic interlude even made the front cover of *OK!* magazine. It was all very cosy and Kylie was quoted as saying, 'James treats me like a princess – I think all women should be.'

In one interview, Kylie exclusively revealed to Dominic Mohan of the *Sun* that she had enjoyed 'a wonderful weekend with the man she loves.'

But just as they passed the important two-year barrier together the cracks were beginning to appear. There were whispers that he had a roving eye and pictures appeared of him enjoying the company of other glamorous women like Sophie Dahl and Beverly Bloom. Kylie was also seen storming out of a restaurant in tears, after apparently having words with him.

As with most break-ups, it was probably a combination of factors that led to the final parting. Perhaps Gooding never properly accepted the role that Kylie's career played in her life. Later, perhaps bitter after the relationship had finished, he described Kylie as a 'washed-up eighties star' when they met. Gooding also did not appreciate the game that Kylie was happy to play suggesting in the media that she and Robbie fancied each other and might become an item. Kylie was such an experienced tease in these matters, a deft touch that she had practised with Jason Donovan many years before.

Gooding later said that he was angry over the stunt and the way Kylie was happy to fuel the rumours, as if denying his existence. He told the *News of the World* that he asked her to issue a public statement denying that she and Robbie were an item but she refused. 'It was the first time I saw how Kylie's ambition was the most important thing in her life.'

James escorted Kylie to the Brits in March 2002 when

she won Best International Female and kissed her before she went up on stage to get the award from Russell Crowe – she also won Best International Album for *Fever*. This was the professional Kylie, a totally different person to the one nibbling roast lamb and carrots in Shoreditch. She slipped into a white mini dress that scarcely covered her bottom and a pair of knee high thigh boots and sang 'Can't Get You Out of My Head' and the New Order classic 'Blue Monday'.

Two months later their split was 'official' despite an apparently romantic break in Bali. Kylie had just begun a sell-out world tour showcasing *Fever*. It put a bit of a dampener on her most ambitious tour to date. Her sister Dannii revealed that Kylie was 'very upset about splitting up as they had been together a long time'. It had been a very volatile relationship and a combination of the split and the physical demands of the tour took its toll on Kylie's fragile frame during a year in which she should have been basking in one triumph after another. Dannii added that the split had been 'one of her downs'.

It soon became apparent that Kylie had in fact been battling the twin threats of stress and exhaustion throughout her entire time in show business. In a particularly candid moment, she had eventually admitted that she had suffered a little bit of a breakdown as long ago as 1988. In fact the first time her fragility was noticed had been even earlier, during her time on *The Henderson Kids*. Kylie is clearly not the all-round tough cookie some might think. Her doctors were so worried about the physical stress on her small frame when she was in *Neighbours* that they put her on a special high energy diet.

In February 1988, when her first UK single 'I Should

Be So Lucky' was number one, British music journalist, Jane Oddy, travelled over to Melbourne to have lunch with seventeen-year-old Kylie, during a break from her gruelling schedule on *Neighbours*. Jane was astonished at how exhausted Kylie looked: 'She was tired out and so thin.' Kylie told Jane about the effect her punishing schedule was having on her. 'I don't have any friends any more because I am just too tired to chat and I never have the time to go out and socialize. I have to cut out anything that's unnecessary, and that means most things apart from eating.' Kylie's parting words to Jane were particularly poignant in a seventeen-year-old girl: 'One day I'd like to lead a normal life and not be nagged by people about losing weight.'

Jane's anxieties were not misplaced and the situation got worse until Kylie finally cracked under the strain. She was quite literally working herself into the ground. In London her life at Stock, Aitken and Waterman's Hit Factory was a never-ending round of recording sessions, photo shoots, television appearances and the treadmill that accompanies any drive for fame. And it was not just in the UK. Kylie's popularity had exploded in Europe, and she was having to dart backwards and forwards across to the Continent, to fulfil constant demands on her time. She was heading for a nervous breakdown in the fast lane. A company insider explained, 'Kylie was young and very fragile because she was quite a small little thing so it was taking its toll. I don't think she'd say we flogged her to death but, in retrospect, we could maybe have cut down a bit. She was very tired and stressed out and would be like "Do I *have* to do all this?"' She was homesick and lonely, and trying to deal with the gradual disintegration of her relationship with Jason Donovan. Her sister Dannii revealed that Kylie would ring home every day, seeking solace from her family. Kylie herself admitted she could not eat or sleep, and was constantly crying.

It had all become too much for her and it was time for Terry Blamey to step in. From the very beginning he has been there for her. He understood that Kylie had had enough and, after consultation with Pete Waterman, whisked her on to a plane back to Melbourne to spend two months recovering at her parents' home. She did absolutely nothing, except for enjoying long lie-ins, taking her dog, Gabby, for walks, shopping in Chapel Street and meeting old girlfriends for coffee in St Kilda. Pete Waterman, who has always had the greatest respect for Kylie's talent, observed, 'She was a tiny girl and obviously had a huge workload, so she'd be exhausted half the time.'

Skip nearly fourteen years, and Kylie is back at the top of the tree and enjoying a greater popularity than ever. *The Face* magazine observed, 'She can't sleep, can't remember what day it is, gets up and cries in the night.' The writer Chris Heath reported that Kylie was running on empty, over-busy and a little ill. She had, in fact, spent much of 2001, arguably her most successful year since 1988, battling many of the same problems of physical exhaustion as she did back then. She spent some time in hospital laid low by a virus when exhaustion had left her too weak to fight it. The incredible thing is that nothing much seems to have changed. She punishes herself, so that she can continue to drink the elixir of fame.

Her 2002 World Tour also left its mark on her brittle

constitution. When it finished in August the gruelling schedule combined with the emotional fall-out from her break-up with boyfriend James Gooding found Kylie again seeking comfort and rest in the bosom of her family. This time she and her mother Carol headed off to a retreat in the Western Australian outback. Once more Kylie had reached breaking point. Some things remain totally constant in her life and the support of her mother and father is the principal one. When in the mid nineties she was struggling with stress and tiredness she phoned them up and asked if they could come over and visit her. They dropped everything and flew straight over to England to spend two weeks cheering her up.

At the end of 2001, everybody had a scare when Ron, at sixty, had to have an operation for prostate cancer. He has always been the power behind the Minogue family, so it came as a shock to Kylie, stuck 12,000 miles away while her father was in hospital. For once, her manager Terry Blamey was positively garrulous: 'Thankfully the news is good,' he said. 'Kylie was very concerned, but the operation was 100 per cent successful and Ron has been cleared by the doctors. He is fully recovered and is resting at home with his family.'

When Kylie went back to visit, she promptly bought her parents a new home in Canterbury with a heated swimming pool and tennis court. Although in need of a little refurbishment, the two-storey house is in one of the most prestigious residential streets in the whole of Melbourne. Kylie bought the house at auction for Aus $2.43 million, which is the equivalent of about £890,000 – a very expensive property by Australian standards. Their old single-storey family home in Alexandra Avenue was sold at auction on 23 February 2002 and made Aus $1,300,000. A few days earlier, at the Brit awards, Kylie paid tribute to her father: 'He will be so proud of me. He'll be the first person I call when I come off stage.'

The happiness Kylie felt at those awards in 2002 contrasted sharply with the ghastly night a year later, on February 23 when she and James Gooding had their final bust-up – they had remained close despite splitting up. The catalyst for their last row was Justin Timberlake, then heart throb of the moment, just as Robbie had been a couple of years earlier. It was a publicist's dream. Justin and Kylie appeared on stage together to perform the old Blondie hit 'Rapture' and gained all the media coverage going with the master stroke of Justin fondling Kylie's bottom. The reports that he 'grabbed' her bum were a little over the top as the number was thoroughly rehearsed. Kylie looked sensational in a little black mini dress and Justin, in black and white silver hip hop gear seemed to linger over his public grope.

Justin, a consummate professional, said all the right things afterwards: 'She's got the hottest ass I've ever seen. On a scale of one to ten it was a fifty eight.' Gooding was in the audience and according to his account in the Sunday papers enjoyed the show, but was less happy afterwards when he found Kylie sitting with Justin. She apparently frostily refused his offer of a drink and the two proceeded to have a very public and frank exchange of views.

Eventually Gooding followed Kylie outside to continue their conversation only for a bouncer to block his way, leaving Kylie to step into her limo without him. He probably did not realise that Kylie was still on her 'date' with Justin. She and Dannii joined Justin for a cosy dinner 'a

douze' – the three stars with assorted minders and hang-
ers-on – at the Montpeliano restaurant in Knightsbridge.
Then they moved on to an EMI reception at the
Sanderson hotel just off Oxford Street where they were
joined by Janet Jackson. Dannii left the party with Justin
and they drove back to Knightsbridge, to the Mandarin
Oriental Hotel, where the singer had a suite for his stay in
London. This was the starting point for speculation that
Dannii spent the night in his room – not true. Dannii
later confessed that she was just catching a ride in Justin's
car and never went to the hotel room at all: 'It was the
best one night stand I never had', she laughed.

While Dannii returned to her Battersea home Kylie
slipped in to the Mandarin Oriental, entirely unnoticed
except by a tabloid journalist who gleefully reported a
night of passion between her and Justin. Hardly – Kylie
clocked in at 3.53 am and clocked out of the back
entrance at 6 am. It was practically a carbon copy of the
ruse Robbie Williams had perpetrated with Nicole
Kidman – another non-romance. All Justin would say is
that he had phoned Kylie and invited her over for a drink:
that was probably all there was to it. Justin categorically
does not have a reputation as a 'player'.

After the Brits, it was time for the Grammys and, perhaps, the master plan became clearer. Kylie flew to New
York, to present an award on stage to Justin, who quipped
'Can I grab your ass again?' She had provided him with
publicity gold in the UK and now he was returning the
favour in the US. It was clearly a case of 'You scratch my
bum and I'll scratch yours.'

This all passed James Gooding by when he was spotted
banging on the door of Kylie's Chelsea home while she

was at the Mandarin Oriental. According to his account he spent the rest of the evening drinking champagne, taking coke and munching on sleeping pills. Not surprisingly it wasn't long before he was booked into rehab at the Farm Place clinic in Surrey. He stayed ten days and sold his story shortly after leaving.

For such a high profile star, Kylie has been fortunate to have escaped kiss and tell stories until Gooding but it must have been a total shock to see the intensity of his feelings about her. He complained, 'She turned into a self-obsessed, virtually friendless control freak, desperate to pursue her own ambitions.' And that was only week one!

Week two of his story was more familiar tabloid territory with Gooding recalling the night 'Kylie was intent on lust in the forest.' It was all good knockabout sex-in-a-tent fun and to add the interest Gooding also disclosed that he'd had romances with Martine McCutcheon and former *Hollyoaks* star Davinia Taylor. He also revealed that the rumours about his fling with Sophie Dahl were all true despite the initial denials. The affair with Sophie had been while Kylie was on tour in 2001 and had spelt the beginning of the end when he confessed all to the singer. Their relationship was distinctly on-off after that. Following his newspaper revelations it was permanently in the off position.

Kylie reacted to the revelations in a dignified and surprisingly tolerant way. She suggested that James should move on. 'We had a great time', she said. 'But it's run its course even though I remain fond of him.' It would have been very easy for Kylie to lambaste Gooding for disloyalty but she quickly put it behind her. Her reaction was made considerably easier by the fact that she had fallen in love with France's answer to Brad Pitt.

For his part Gooding has managed to turn his life round from this low point. He gave up drugs and moved back to LA to continue his ambition to be a professional photographer. Intriguing, at least for all amateur psychologists, was an interview he gave to the *Sunday Times* in which he revealed the trauma he had felt when his parents split up when he was six and how he had been put into foster care because of his resentment of his step father. 'Someone I loved leaving me would be my mother's [perceived] abandonment all over again.' he said.

His first exhibition entitled 'Game On' was launched at the Barbican in the summer of 2002 and moved on to Edinburgh in October. As well as shots of video games' players the exhibition featured one picture of Kylie naked in the bath. Subsequently in 2005, he held another exhibition, called 'State' at the Florence Gallery in the West End. He is no longer described as Kylie's boyfriend in the press – a soubriquet he loathed. He is now described as Kylie's ex-boyfriend.

'It's a nice simple romance which is great.'

17

French Connection II

Guests at the pre-wedding banquet of Vanisha Mittal and Amit Bhatia in Paris were thrilled when Kylie took to the specially erected stage and sang a medley of hits for half an hour including her number ones, 'Spinning Around' and 'Slow'. Why did Kylie do it? Well, she was paid £200,000 . . .

The French Brad Pitt was actor Olivier Martinez. He and Kylie bumped into each other in a hotel lobby the same night Kylie had appeared at the Grammys. She liked what she saw. With an easy charm, he suggested they might dine together the next time she was in Los Angeles, which, it just so happened would be almost immediately. Their first 'date' was a trip to the very fashionable restaurant, The Ivy, in Beverly Hills. Being seen at such a well known celebrity-spotting haunt signified that Kylie was not going to bother to keep this new man under wraps. It also meant that she could move seamlessly into a new romance as far as the media was concerned, thereby consigning her relationship with James Gooding to yesterday's news.

Shortly afterwards, Olivier and Kylie were photographed hand in hand arriving at the Café de Flore in his home town of Paris. It was 5 March 2003, just four days before the notorious Gooding revelations in the *News of the World*. The occasion was the 50th birthday party for the fashion house, Chloé. Kylie looked graceful and smiling. Olivier oozed Gallic charisma in a black leather biker coat and patterned red neckerchief. He looked raffish and handsome. Allowing herself to be photographed by paparazzi and general hoi polloi had never been Kylie's style so it was interesting that she decided on this approach with such a new friendship. These early pictures with Olivier leading Kylie by the hand suggested that here was a confident, self assured man. Kylie sang four love songs and observers suggested she seemed to be singing them for Olivier.

Although little known in the UK, Martinez, two years older than Kylie, had been acting since 1990 but had only started to reach a large international audience the year before he met Kylie, when he made his Hollywood break-through in *Unfaithful* alongside Richard Gere and Diane Lane. In the film he played a handsome stranger with whom Diane Lane has an adulterous affair. She was nominated for an Oscar for her performance and took most of the attention but, nevertheless, it represented good progress in the US for Olivier. For his role as the New York book seller, he needed to reveal a smouldering, sensual side in order to make it believable that Diane Lane would cheat on Richard Gere. The love scenes were steamy and quite explicit. Vince Passaro in *Interview* magazine noted, 'He plays the books dealer with just the right mix of callousness and caring that a decent but essentially immature man would feel toward an older, married woman who really, really likes to drop by and have sex with him. A lot.' Rather winningly, Olivier confessed that he had been raised in a very traditional way and was not particularly comfortable with such erotic love scenes. He pointed out that it was very rare in French films for actors to appear naked.

The director, Adrian Lyne, who also made *Fatal Attraction* and *Basic Instinct*, paid Olivier the compliment: 'He's very beguiling, doing even ordinary things.'

Before his Hollywood breakthrough, Olivier was already very well known in his own country. If he were British, we would be describing him as a working-class hero. He describes himself as a 'real Parisian', although he is in fact half-Spanish. As a young man he looked set to go into the family firm, which in his case was not a business but a proud tradition of boxing. His father Robert, a Spanish Moroccan, was a champion welter-weight in his native North Africa. 'He was very good' explained Olivier, simply but proudly. Olivier left school, as Kylie did, early and had a number of jobs like selling jeans and waiting tables before trying his luck in the boxing ring. He boxed professionally, also as a welter-weight, for three years although, unlike many of his cousins who also box, he was never particularly serious about it. A near-fatal motorbike accident ended any ambitions he had in the ring. He spent months immo-bilised and, for a while, it was touch and go if he would survive. After the accident he observed, 'It puts every-thing into perspective, the money and fame . . .'

These days he has a good sense of humour about his former trade: 'If you compare me to an actor, I'm proba-bly one of the best boxers in the profession. But if you compare me as a boxer, I'm probably one of the best actors.'

After quitting the ring his father worked as a mechanic while his mother, Rosemarie, was a secretary. They were never poor, something Olivier thought important in defining his future career. He grew up in a community of open-minded people where he never felt obliged to follow in his father's footsteps. Instead of training to become a mechanic when he finished his obligatory military service, he was persuaded by friends to train to be an actor. On little more than a whim he auditioned for the Conservatoire National Supérieur d'Art Dramatique in Paris and, to his surprise, was accepted. He observed, 'It was a kind of miracle. By chance I had this opportunity and I took it and my life changed.'

After a couple of television parts, he was cast opposite the great Yves Montand in *IP5: L'île aux Pachyderms*. Encouragingly he was nominated as Most Promising Actor for a Cesar, the French equivalent of the Oscars, for his role as a young robber on his way to the Pyrenees who picks up an old man (Montand). Essentially it was an elegiac road movie and, poignantly, proved to be Montand's last. The doyen of French cinema, one of Olivier's idols, died of a heart attack shortly after completing the film.

He may not have won the Cesar at his first attempt but he made no mistake in his second feature, *Un, Deux, Trois, Soleil,* where he played alongside another of his heroes, Marcello Mastroianni. Again he was nominated as Most Promising Newcomer for his role as a thief. This time he had to parade his seduction techniques on a young girl from a Marseilles slum. 'I'm going to change your destiny', he whispered as he unhooked her bra. *Filmcritic.com* thought his performance 'wonderful'. By any standards

Martinez's introduction to the movies was sensational. Here was an actor of substance and promise and by no means a slice of Gallic beefcake.

Olivier became accustomed to dealing with a voracious media when he starred opposite the beautiful Juliet Binoche in the acclaimed film *The Horseman on the Roof* (*Le Hussard sur le Toit*) which at the time was the most expensive French movie ever made. The gossip soon began that the two were dating. The rumours proved to be entirely true even though the couple threatened to sue a magazine for incorrectly suggesting Binoche was pregnant. This time Binoche won the Cesar, although Olivier received many plaudits for his romantic portrayal of a young Italian officer helping a woman search for her husband in cholera-ravaged Provence. It was during the American promotional tour for the film that Martinez was first described as the French Brad Pitt. Ironically, he could authentically have starred in the film *Fight Club* but the comparison did register Olivier on the Hollywood radar. In the end he lived with Binoche for three years. They split in 1997 and he saw in the new Millenium in Los Angeles making English language films in a not very convincing accent. He spoke very little English when he met Juliette Binoche and had to take lessons to prepare for Hollywood.

Martinez is very ambitious, not to be the world's biggest movie star but to be considered a great actor. He may have been respected in France but his native movie business was frustrating him. He admitted that the whole process of film-making in France did not move fast enough for him. The move to the US was like beginning his career all over again. 'My goal', he revealed, 'is to get some interesting parts and make enough money to live free.'

One of the first things Olivier did when he moved to LA was to start dating the actress Mira Sorvino. She is best known to British audiences for her role as the ditzy prostitute in Woody Allen's *Mighty Aphrodite*, for which she won an Oscar for best supporting actress. In real life Sorvino is renowned as one of the most intelligent and articulate women in Hollywood. She speaks fluent French which was helpful for Olivier. She is cultured, well read and studied Chinese at Harvard. She spent a year in Beijing researching a prize-winning thesis on racism in China and is also fluent in Mandarin Chinese.

Olivier's relationship with Sorvino would not have lasted a minute if he had only brought looks and charm to the table. Martinez is considered and thoughtful and far from being a trophy companion. Crucially for Kylie, more than any man she had ever been linked with, Martinez was accomplished in dealing with the everyday problems of being a star. He may not have particularly enjoyed the constant attention but he was able to handle it. Alain Grasset, a well known columnist for *Le Parisien* newspaper, described the Frenchman as 'well-grounded' and a man who could be Mr Right for Kylie, if she craved stability in her life. Olivier told *Interview* magazine, 'I see my friends, my family, my cousins work all day long for very little money and if I have this problem of not being able to walk on the streets, it's not a big deal.'

Three days after being photographed with Kylie in Paris, the couple headed south, turning up at a football match in Marseilles before moving on to St Tropez. It was a part of France that Kylie had enjoyed so much with

Michael Hutchence and here she was again, looking up old haunts on the back of a motorbike. Olivier has a passion for them and owns two. After the Cote D'Azur it was on to London where they were pictured strolling down the Fulham Road, enjoying a coffee before catching an open-topped tourist bus where they were seen kissing and cuddling in the back.

Their spring idyll continued through to May when they were photographed sailing in the romantic surroundings of Portofino in Italy. Two weeks later they had reached Monte Carlo where they again appeared very relaxed in public, arriving for the Laureus World Sports Awards. They were beginning to look like one of the world's most glamorous couples. Kylie looked fabulous in a bright red gown while Olivier, who obviously had forgotten to pack his razor for their sailing trip, looked cool and sophisticated in head to toe black.

The effect of so many public sightings was to take the mystery out of Kylie's new romance. There was absolutely no point in a paparazzo jumping out of the bushes and exclaiming 'Aha. Caught You!' The world knew that all the rumours were true. Even Dannii Minogue enthusiastically endorsed the romance saying that Martinez was 'gorgeous and really nice' and that Kylie wanted kids soon. Dannii is always delightfully open with the press but even she would have been more guarded if Kylie had insisted. Clearly Kylie wanted the world to know she was with an eligible French film star. Olivier may have been brought up amid the sweat of the boxing ring and the grease of the garage but he was now a mature, urbane man of the world who loved jazz and French movies. Kylie likes to feel stretched by the important men in her life.

She called him Olly and he called her Honey. Kylie speaks French but does not pretend to be fluent. She has many French-based friends and went out with Stephane Sednaoui for two years so she was considerably better than the average tourist. She probably spoke French as well as Olivier spoke English. Of course it did not take long before the glossy magazines were suggesting that Olivier was following in the best Kylie traditions of being famously well endowed.

After their holiday it was time to face the reality of their careers once more. Olivier had spent much of the previous year filming the action blockbuster *S.W.A.T.* alongside Colin Farrell and Samuel L Jackson. He was not yet the star but it was more than helpful to his career when the movie took over $37 million on its opening weekend. Almost inevitably, because he is handsome and French, Martinez quickly gained a reputation in Hollywood as a lady-killer. It may or may not have been justified but Kylie was soon plagued by the same old doubts that separation brings in the world of music and movies. While Kylie remained in London putting the finishing touches to her next album, Olivier could be found making a movie, *Taking Lives*, in the Quebec and Montreal areas of Canada with, of all people, Angelina Jolie. Angelina played an FBI agent on the trail of a serial killer while Olivier was a local cop. Angelina's mother, Marcheline Bertrand, is from Paris and Jolie, of course, means pretty in French. It took about ten seconds for the tabloid press to suggest that Angelina and Olivier were getting close. Poor Kylie, was the implication, she's picked a bad 'un again.

Infidelity has been a common thread running through Kylie's troubled dating over the years so, understandably, she is more than a little touchy. The rumours reached her back in London and were followed up by the alleged proof – pictures of Olivier and Angelina at a baseball game with her adopted son Maddox. Olivier insisted that Angelina was merely a friend but Kylie acted decisively by hopping on a jet to Canada to find out for herself what was going on. Kylie reportedly left Heathrow with a 'thunderous expression' on her face. The official line put about by 'sources' was that Olivier and Angelina were just friends and that there was nothing going on. It did not help that Mira Sorvino's mother was quoted as saying, 'If it's commitment she's after, she's dating the wrong man.'

The no-smoke without fire aficionados were congratulating themselves when pictures appeared of Kylie and Olivier looking glum on set. Kylie arrived when Olivier and Angelina were filming scenes together which was not the best timing and, according to eyewitness sources things were 'tense'. One said, 'Kylie arrived early and went straight to Olivier's trailer. There were no raised voices but they did not look too happy.' Kylie has kept her own counsel over whether she believed the rumours but her trip certainly seemed like making a drama out of a crisis. A week later Olivier appeared on American television and said that Kylie was 'cute, nice and interesting' which all seemed very gentlemanly.

For her part, Angelina Jolie said she was 'amazed' at all the gossip: 'Olivier and I were said to be together because we were at a ball game, but everybody else was there also. Basically I'm single. I worked with a bunch of men on a film recently, so I was tagged to all of them.'

That was pretty much it for the Angelina and Olivier rumours and there's always a great deal of hype to filter whenever a film needs to place itself in the public consciousness. From Kylie's point of view one could appreciate that Angelina Jolie is the worst nightmare for a woman trying to make a relationship work. She is voracious, Amazonian and beautiful. By a curious twist of fate, having been linked to the French Brad Pitt, she was subject to yet more rumours when she started filming *Mr and Mrs Smith* with the real thing the following year. This time it all turned out to be true.

At this stage Kylie's adoring public were undecided about Olivier Martinez's commitment to their favourite. Both Juliet Binoche and Mira Sorvino were over thirty when they became involved with him and both actresses subsequently had children in their late thirties.

Meanwhile Kylie was gearing up for her next album release, *Body Language* and the sultry first single from the album, 'Slow'. Jordan Paramour in *heat* magazine described the album as heralding the era of 'electro-pop Kylie' and described it as 'unashamedly sexy.'

What was immediately apparent about *Body Language* was that Kylie had already moved on from *Fever*. This was no *Fever II*. The feel was more contemporary than camp and certainly not disco. One of the minor drawbacks of the album was that 'Slow', the outstanding song was the first track. It went straight in to number one fuelled by another very suggestive video, which showed Kylie writhing around in a little dress on a beach towel surrounded by a host of well toned writhing bodies, also on towels. Kylie was the only one not wearing her swimwear. It was unambiguously all about sex and making love, slowly.

Kylie's improved status in the US thanks to *Fever* and

'Can't Get You Out Of My Head' led to the album being extensively reviewed there. *New York* magazine were suitably enthusiastic: 'You can't help but get lost in Minogue's music.' The reviewer, Ethan Brown, also thought 'Slow' was a 'template for pop singers who fancy themselves aesthetes'. Looking at Kylie's work as a whole 'Slow' was more an extension of 'Confide In Me' than 'Can't Get You Out Of My Head.'

Metro Weekly, the gay and lesbian Washington magazine identified the main problem with *Body Language* in that there was no obvious stand-out track: 'With its alluring minimalist rhythms and lyrical eroticism, the album works best when taken as a whole.' Perhaps inevitably the album performed disappointingly when compared with what had gone before. In the UK, it reached only number six and both follow-up singles, 'Red Blooded Woman' and 'Chocolate' failed to reach the top spot. Some better news was around the corner, however, when Kylie won her first Grammy with 'Come Into My World' which won Best Dance Recording. The only slight drawback was that the track was from *Fever* and not *Body Language.*

'I adore Paris.'

Langoustines in Portofino

Kylie was insistent that she had to get back to work and that her flight to Sydney left in two hours. Eventually her father Ron had heard enough and told her firmly to 'just sit down'.

Quietly, Kylie made a surprising announcement in April 2005. She was splitting from her Willie. A statement on her website said that William Baker was 'stepping down' from his position as creative director. They had been working closely together for eleven years. 'It was always our intention to finish our creative partnership with the *Greatest Hits* album and 'Showgirl' tour. Both feel it is the time to move on.' Kylie assured her fans that she and Baker were still the 'best of friends'.

The timing raised more than a few eyebrows. Baker was always there for Kylie with a spare sequin or ostrich feather and he seemed an immovable object. During her difficult times with James Gooding, it was Baker who she was happy to be seen out with – a buddy for all seasons. In this case when the going got tough, the tough went to Paris fashion shows. *Heat* magazine noted he was by her side through 'thick and thin'. None of the reports suggested the pair had suffered a major falling-out or even a tiff, but the timing of his departure, halfway through such a grand tour was food and drink to the rumour mill. Some reports jettisoned decorum and said that Kylie had dumped him.

Kylie's 'Showgirl' tour was a £5 million extravaganza. Fifteen trucks were needed to ferry the show including a £1 million art deco inspired set, thought to be the biggest ever built for an arena tour. One person's job was to carefully transport Kylie's array of feathers from venue to venue. She needed to come back with a bang after the relative disappointment of *Body Language*. After the outstanding success of the album *Fever* and the tour of that name there was bound to be a little anticlimax. She had taken it pretty easy in the last six months of 2004 – spending some time recording a couple of new tracks for a greatest hits compilation which would form the musical excuse for her tour. She revealed that the *Showgirl* set had taken a year to build and design. 'It has been a lifetime in the making', she added which was a neat sound bite. When the tickets went on sale they sold out in two hours.

Kylie's *Greatest Hits* packages are quite ubiquitous. Her first was as long ago as 1992 when the collection of her Stock, Aitken and Waterman material reached number one. Waterman released another compilation ten years later which still managed to hit the top twenty. Less successful was the *Hits* + compilation of 2000 from the deConstruction years. One thing was for sure, the new release could not be called *Greatest Hits*. Instead, *Ultimate Kylie* was released in November 2004 and the new track, 'I Believe In You', was only kept off the top spot by Band Aid II. It became an enormous worldwide hit.

She had not been feeling her best in the run-up to the

'Showgirl' tour, complaining that she was so tired and suggesting that, finally, she was getting a bit old for it all. Kylie
had always struggled with stress and exhaustion so, at the
time, her health was not a preoccupation. It did not help
that just a week before the tour was due to start, the
media was aquiver with excitement that Kylie might be
pregnant. She was pictured apparently showing the first
signs of a little baby bump. The green tunic dress she was
wearing when she stepped out of her London apartment
seemed a little too snug. That, of course, is all the evidence required these days for an orgy of speculation. The
articles, for instance, wondering whether Britney Spars
was pregnant with her first child seemed to go on for an
interminable time, suggesting she had the gestation
period of an elephant.

Others thought that the 'Showgirl' tour was yet again
proof that she was putting her 'all-consuming' career
before her relationships.

The tour opened in Glasgow and, as now seemed *de
rigueur* for Kylie performances, there was more talk of costume than music. Kylie would not have been out of place
in a Busby Berkeley musical. It was more of a fashion
night than a music event with commentators noting that
the style set list included specially designed outfits by Karl
Lagerfeld, John Galliano and Julien McDonald. For the
opening number, 'Better The Devil You Know' she wore a
jewel-encrusted corset by Galliano which took four
months to painstakingly put together, each jewel sewn by
hand. The body-hugger turned out to be a minuscule sixteen inches around the waist which guaranteed maximum
press coverage of the tour.

The ensemble was topped off by a plumed head dress

and a tail and Kylie was carried aloft by her customary near-naked male dancers wearing eight foot feather wings. Dave Simpson in the *Guardian* sardonically thought that it would be the 'first pop tour to prompt the interest of the Royal Society for the Protection of Birds.'

Part of the fun was anticipating how Kylie would make her entrance on stage following each of the six costume changes. For 'Love At First Sight' she was lounging decorously on a vaulting horse. Kylie was definitely encouraging nostalgia and she achieved the right response with the enthusiastic sing-along to 'Especially For You'. Kylie has now accepted the song for what it is, a pretty melody that her fans love. It was either the high spot or the low spot depending on how you were feeling. Less successful was a crooning, smokey version of 'The Loco-Motion'. This was definitely a song which existed solely to dance to. The overwhelming impression was that Kylie could do a greatest hits show every year. Alternatively, she could take the whole set to Vegas.

Olivier, meanwhile, was still shrugging off persistent rumours of him with other actresses including the exotic Mexican, Salma Hayek, with whom he was seen out in the evening in LA on four different occasions. He was also photographed kissing his *S.W.A.T.* co-star Michelle Rodriguez. Olivier, however, was far more concerned with the cold sweats Kylie was getting. And when she started being sick, practically all the time, he decided enough was enough and that it could not all be put down to the infamously narrow corset. He strongly encouraged her to have a medical check-up. Her doctors ran some tests and said they would get back to Kylie in due course with any findings.

During the break between the British leg and the Australian segment of the tour Kylie and Olivier flew to Melbourne to spend some time with her family. Just four days before the first date at the Sydney Superdome, her doctor came to see her at her parents' home. Olivier, father Ron, mother Carol and brother Brendan were all with her. The physician told her that she had early stage breast cancer. 'The moment my doctor told me, I went silent. My mum and dad were with me, then we all went to pieces.' At the time Kylie had started packing to fly to Sydney and had to be persuaded to sit back down by her father.

Kylie would later reveal all the emotions and feelings she felt in an interview with the presenter Cat Deeley for Rupert Murdoch's Sky Television. It made for riveting viewing and gave everybody a rare insight into the true despair of such an awful thing happening two weeks before your 37th birthday. Her ordeal lasted fourteen months – no performances, no records, no Kylie except for the dribble of news of how things were going for her.

She had a whole day to prepare herself before millions of fans all over the world needed to be told. How on earth do you prepare yourself? Kylie went for a walk along the beach with Olivier and Brendan. The next day her private despair would be front page news.

Kylie's own statement was rather dry but what could she say in the circumstances? Ever the professional, she said, 'I was so looking forward to bringing the *Showgirl* tour to Australian audiences and am sorry to have to disappoint my fans. Nevertheless, hopefully all will work out and I'll be back with you all soon.' At this stage, nobody was in the least bit interested in the fate of the tour.

Her tour promoter Michael Gudinski, a fixture in Kylie's camp from the beginning said all the right, reassuring things: 'It has come as a shock to her, the world and to her family but she is very fit. She is a fighter and hopes to be back doing what she loves sooner rather than later.'

Her sister Dannii, who, as always, would be such a trooper over the coming months, caught the first plane back to Melbourne. She echoed what everybody thought, 'The news is very upsetting', she said simply. Elton John, when he heard the news, shouted 'Oh my God the poor girl', and got straight on the phone.

The good news, if there was any, was that her family were with her, she was home in Melbourne and Olivier was there. Here was a man who had faced death himself. 'This is *our* fight. I'm not going anywhere. I'm here for you now and nothing else matters. Just get well.' Olivier would be true to that sentiment.

Three days after the official announcement Kylie was quietly admitted to the St Francis Xavier Cabrini hospital in Melbourne where a tumour was removed from her left breast in a partial mastectomy. That was just the beginning of a painful process of chemotherapy and uncertainty. She stayed at home with her parents for the first couple of months, literally under siege from photographers anxious to get a picture of 'brave' Kylie. She was too preoccupied with her own plight to worry about media but she felt bad for her family around her.

Kylie had the anxious wait while tests were completed to ascertain the strength and spread of the disease. Then she stunned everyone by deciding that she wanted to go back to Paris for her chemotherapy. 'I wanted a life with

my boyfriend in Paris', she admitted. It was not easy
breaking the news to Ron and Carol, who, naturally, were
so worried about her but, in the end, a compromise was
reached and her mother went with her.

These were the darkest days when Kylie was sometimes
too ill to even get up. She would feel a sense of achievement if she made it as far as the corner shop. She would
go into her bedroom for twenty minutes to contemplate
her life in quiet and solitude. She told Cat Deeley, 'I had
moments when I didn't want to look in the mirror.'

She voraciously read everything she could find on the
net about her condition. The stark facts were that breast
cancer affects one in nine women. One of her greatest
concerns was the effect chemotherapy might have on her
future chances of conceiving. Kylie opted for additional
treatment aimed at improving her chances of becoming
pregnant at a later date. The reality of the situation is that
Kylie will have to be entirely free of cancer for two or
three years before any procedure using this method of
conception could be attempted. It is a revolutionary
method in which her ovary tissue is transplanted back
into her body.

Surprisingly Kylie was relatively unfazed by losing her
hair, the inevitable consequence of chemotherapy. First of
all she cut it short and then, with a deep breath 'buzz-cut'
the whole thing. She also became extremely adept at tying
her headscarf so that there would never be a picture of
her without her head covered.

She was so used to changing her look as an actress and
performer that she took that in her stride. Dannii, who
she says was 'fabulous' during it all, would travel over on
Eurostar from London to cheer her up. Always a ball of

energy she would try and get Kylie up and moving about, or singing along to some cheesy old favourites, just as they had when they were kids.

Kylie kept a chemotherapy diary because she realised she was forgetting everything and her whole life had to revolve around her medical calendar of treatments at the Institut Gustave-Roussy and medication. She called this dreadful time 'chemo-brain'. She was desperately ill and by October 2005 her weight had dropped to six stone. She was also too poorly to contemplate any visit back to Australia for Christmas, something she always loved to do.

She had her final session of chemo just before Christmas 2005 and then had an anxious wait for the results of more tests. Eventually, she was given the all clear after the New Year and was well enough to travel to Melbourne for the back-up radiation treatment. She needed ten minute sessions five times a week. Fortunately, Olivier was there and she was able to properly enjoy her new £400,000 home on French Island, off the Melbourne coast. The news was promising. Dannii let slip that 'my best news to start the year is that my sister is in full remission' on her web site, although it may have been on purpose to let the world know what was happening. Olivier's mother Rosemarie revealed his family, who got on very well with Kylie, were delighted : 'All we want is for her to be happy,' she said graciously.

Kylie stayed in Australia until after the birth of her first nephew in April. Her brother Brendan's girlfriend had a baby boy, Charles, a first grandchild for Ron and Carol after forty years of marriage. Aunt Kylie spent her time making plans and writing lyrics about her ordeal. It was cathartic even if they never find their way on to an album.

She also made a list of things she wanted to do, simple things that made living worthwhile. They included going back to a favourite restaurant in Portofino to eat langoustine with Olivier – something she has now done. Throughout her ordeal Olivier was her rock. Kylie called him a very solid and strong character. He surprised a media who had decided he was a shallow film star and from day one was determined to prove that to be the case. At least now there were no pictures of him with alluring actresses. Instead, when Kylie felt well enough she would cling on to his back and he would whisk her through the streets of Paris on his motorcycle. With their helmets on they could not be recognised.

As she began to feel so much better Kylie would draw inspiration from the wonderful city of Paris. While it would never be home to her in the way that Melbourne and London are she loved the city, enjoying brunch in the Café des Flore in St Germain or lunch at her favourite Italian restaurant. On one memorable evening she was in a back store room at her home and through a small window could see the lights of the Eiffel Tower. 'They were twinkling for me', she told Cat Deeley.

Her hair was growing back including her eyebrows and eye lashes, allaying her fears that she would be the one person for whom this did not happen. She took pictures of Olivier's dog Sheba for a children's book she was preparing called *The Showgirl Princess*. Already there were projects on the go, not least her desire to finish off her tour.

The world saw a new, happy Kylie for the first time in April when pictures of her taken by Olivier were posted on her website and subsequently published throughout the world. Olivier has never taken photographs professionally but he managed to capture Kylie positively glowing with happiness – and with very short brown hair – when they were visiting Portofino.

In June 2006 there wasn't a dry eye in the house when completely unannounced she crept onto the stage at G-A-Y in London with a bunch of flowers for her sister Dannii who was performing that night. It may have been a surprise but there were pictures in all the papers the next day. It was very touching that she should make a 'come-back' with a lovely gesture to her sister. More public sightings followed – strolling in Paris with Olivier, in the front row at a Chanel fashion show, dancing salsa onstage at the Assembly Rooms in Edinburgh and attending a first night at Sadler's Wells. Kylie was gently moving back into the limelight.

Her 'rehabilitation' became a matter of frenzy when she announced she would be restarting her Australian tour in November 2006 followed by a week at Wembley in London in January 2007. She joked that instead of six quick changes there would be six slow changes and she might even use a chair. The concerts sold out in the blink of an eye. Another piece of good news was that William Baker would be back in the Kylie fold. He had not been standing still in the past year with a bunch of new projects including helping to style Victoria Beckham. Clearly Kylie has a special place in his affections, whatever the reasons for their temporary parting of the ways.

And then she appeared on television in the Cat Deeley interview and the world could see for itself how well she looked, full of smiles and sparkle. One of the most interesting things she talked about was the 'Kylie Effect' where women had sat up and taken notice of what had happened to her and were monitoring their own health more closely – a greater awareness of the risks of breast cancer would inevitably lead to more lives being saved.

Olivier Martinez, who has not had a film released since *Taking Lives,* summed up Kylie's ordeal: 'What doesn't kill you makes you stronger. When life tests you, you have to do your best. I'm there for her.'

Obviously it remains to be seen how Kylie is affected by her comeback concerts. Many years ago she described herself as a 'show pony' to a journalist and clearly she still loves performing. She is due to close the 'Showgirl' tours – as was originally intended – as the headline act at the 2007 Glastonbury Festival, proof if any more was needed that she is now a credible artist. It's officially OK to love Kylie.

'Obviously someone up there likes me. Thank Heavens!'

Heard and Seen

Singles

Release Date	Title	Highest UK Chart Position
December 1987	*I Should Be So Lucky*	1
May 1988	*Got To Be Certain*	2
July 1988	*The Loco-motion*	2
October 1988	*Je Ne Sais Pas Pourquoi*	2
November 1988	*Especially For You* (with Jason Donovan)	1
March 1989	*Hand On Your Heart*	1
July 1989	*Wouldn't Change A Thing*	2
October 1989	*Never Too Late*	4
January 1990	*Tears On My Pillow*	1
March 1990	*Better The Devil You Know*	2
October 1990	*Step Back In Time*	4
January 1991	*What Do I Have To Do*	6
May 1991	*Shocked*	6
August 1991	*Word Is Out*	16
October 1991	*If You Were With Me Now* (with Keith Washington)	4
November 1991	*Keep On Pumpin' It*	49
January 1992	*Give Me Just A Little More Time*	2
April 1992	*Finer Feelings*	11
August 1992	*What Kind Of Fool*	14
November 1992	*Celebration*	20
August 1994	*Confide In Me*	2
November 1994	*Put Yourself In My Place*	11
July 1995	*Where Is The Feeling*	16

Release Date	Title	Highest UK Chart Position
October 1995	*Where The Wild Roses Grow* (with Nick Cave)	11
September 1997	*Some Kind Of Bliss*	22
October 1997	*Did It Again*	14
March 1998	*Breathe*	14
October 1998	*GBI* (with Towa Tei)	68
June 2000	*Spinning Around*	1
September 2000	*On A Night Like This*	2
October 2000	*Kids* (with Robbie Williams)	2
December 2000	*Please Stay*	10
September 2001	*Can't Get You Out Of My Head*	1
February 2002	*In Your Eyes*	3
June 2002	*Love At First Sight*	2
October 2002	*Come Into My World*	8
November 2003	*Slow*	1
March 2004	*Red Blooded Woman*	5
June 2004	*Chocolate*	6
December 2004	*I Believe In You*	2
March 2005	*Giving You Up*	6

Albums

Release Date	Title (track listings in parentheses)	Highest UK Chart Position
July 1988	*Kylie* (I Should Be So Lucky; The Loco-Motion; Je Ne Sais Pas Pourquoi; It's No Secret; Got To Be Certain; Turn It Into Love; I Miss You; I'll Still Be Loving You; Look My Way; Love At First Sight)	1
October 1989	*Enjoy Yourself* (Hand On Your Heart; Wouldn't Change A Thing; Never Too Late; Nothing To Lose;	1

Release Date	Title (track listings in parentheses)	Highest UK Chart Position
	Tell Tale Signs; My Secret Heart; I'm Over Dreaming [Over You]; Tears On My Pillow; Heaven And Earth; Enjoy Yourself)	
November 1990	*Rhythm Of Love* (Better The Devil You Know; Step Back In Time; What Do I Have To Do; Secrets; Always Find The Time; The World Still Turns; Shocked; One Boy Girl; Things Can Only Get Better; Count The Days; Rhythm Of Love)	9
October 1991	*Let's Get To It* (Word Is Out; Give Me Just A Little More Time; Too Much Of A Good Thing; Finer Feelings; If You Were With Me Now [with Keith Washington]; Let's Get To It; Right Here, Right Now; Live And Learn; No World Without You; I Guess I Like It Like That)	15
August 1992	*Greatest Hits* (I Should Be So Lucky; Got To Be Certain; The Loco-Motion; Je Ne Sais Pas Pourquoi; Especially For You [with Jason Donovan]; Turn It Into Love; It's No Secret; Hand On Your Heart; Wouldn't Change A Thing; Never Too Late; Tears On My Pillow; Better The Devil You Know; Step Back In Time; What Do I Have To Do;	1

Release Date	Title (track listings in parentheses)	Highest UK Chart Position
	Shocked [DNA Mix]; Word Is Out [UK Remix]; If You Were With Me Now [with Keith Washington]; Give Me Just A Little More Time; Finer Feelings; What Kind Of Fool [Heard All That Before]; Where In The World; Celebration)	
September 1994	*Kylie Minogue* (Confide In Me; Surrender; If I Was Your Lover; Where Is The Feeling; Put Yourself In My Place; Dangerous Game; Automatic Love; Where Has The Love Gone; Falling; Time Will Pass You By)	4
March 1998	*Impossible Princess/Kylie Minogue in Europe* (Too Far; Cowboy Style; Some Kind Of Bliss; Did It Again; Breathe; Say Hey; Drunk; I Don't Need Anyone; Jump; Limbo; Through The Years; Dreams)	10
August 1998	*Mixes* Too Far [Brothers In Rhythm Mix]; Too Far [Junior Vasquez Remix]; Some Kind Of Bliss [Quivver Mix]; Breathe [Tee's Free Mix]; Breathe [Sash! Clab Mix]; Breathe [Nalin & Kane Mix]; Did It Again [T E's Goddess Of Contortion Mix]; Did It Again [Razor-n-Go Mix]; Too Far [Brothers In Rhythm Dub])	63

Release Date	Title (track listings in parentheses)	Highest UK Chart Position
September 2000	*Light Years* (Spinning Around; On A Night Like This; So Now Goodbye; Disco Down; Loveboat; Kookachoo; Your Disco Needs You; Please Stay; Bittersweet Goodbye; Butterfly; Under The Influence Of Love; I'm So High; Kids [with Robbie Williams]; Light Years; Password [hidden track])	2
October 2000	*Hits +* (Confide In Me; Put Yourself In My Place; Where Is The Feeling?; Some Kind Of Bliss; Did It Again; Breathe; Where The Wild Roses Grow[with Nick Cave]; If You Don't Love Me; Tears; Gotta Move On; Difficult By Design; Stay This Way; This Girl; Automatic Love [Acoustic Version]; Where Has The Love Gone; Take Me With You)	2
October 2001	*Fever* (More More More; Love At First Sight; Can't Get You Out Of My Head; Fever; Give It To Me; Fragile; Come Into My World; In Your Eyes; Dancefloor; Love Affair; Your Love; Burning Up)	1
November 2002	*Greatest Hits: CD 1* (I Should Be So Lucky; The Loco-Motion [7" Mix]; Hand On Your Heart; Got To Be Certain; , Better The Devil You Know; Wouldn't Change A Thing;	1

Release Date	**Title**	**Highest UK Chart**
	(track listings in parentheses)	**Position**

Celebration; Never Too Late;
What Do I Have To Do [7" Mix];
Je Ne Sais Pas Pourquoi;
Where In The World; Step Back In Time;
Especially For You [with Jason Donovan];
Say The Word – I'll Be There;
Shocked [D.N.A. Mix];
Word Is Out; Made In Heaven;
What Kind Of Fool [Heard All That Before];
Give Me Just A Little More Time;
Finer Feelings [Brothers In Rhythm 7" Mix];
If You Were With Me Now
[with Keith Washington];
Tears On My Pillow)
CD 2
(Hand On Your Heart [W.I.P. 2002 Mix];
I Should Be So Lucky [Extended Mix];
The Loco-Motion [Oz Tour Mix];
Made In Heaven [Heaven Scent Mix];
Wouldn't Change A Thing [The Espagna Mix];
Step Back In Time [Harding/Curnow Remix];
Shocked [Harding/Curnow Remix];
Word Is Out [Summer Breeze Mix];
Celebration [Techno Rave Mix];
Better The Devil You Know
[Movers & Shakers Alternative 12" Mix];
What Do I Have To Do
[Movers & Shakers Mix])

November 2003   *Body Language*   6
(Slow; Still Standing; Secret [Take You Home];
Promises; Sweet Music;
Red Blooded Woman;
Chocolate; Obsession; I Feel For You;
Someday; Loving Days; After Dark)

Release Date	Title (track listings in parentheses)	Highest UK Chart Position
September 2004	*Kylie Minogue: Artist Collection* (Confide In Me [Master Mix]; Limbo; Breathe [Radio edit]; Automatic Love; Dangerous Game [Dangerous overture]; Too Far; Put Yourself In My Place; Did It Again [Single version]; Take Me With You; Love Takes Over Me; Where Is the Feeling [Acoustic version]; Cowboy Style; Dreams)	N/A
November 2004	*Ultimate Kylie: CD1* (Better The Devil You Know; The Loco-Motion [7" Mix]; I Should Be So Lucky; Step Back In Time; Shocked; Wouldn't Change A Thing; Hand On Your Heart; Especially For You [With Jason Donovan]; Got To Be Certain; Je Ne Sais Pas Pouquoi; Give Me Just A Little More Time; Never Too Late; Tears On My Pillow; Celebration) *CD 2* (I Believe In You; Can't Get You Out Of My Head; Love At First Sight; Slow; On A Night Like This; Spinning Around; Kids [with Robbie Williams], [Radio Edit]; Confide In Me; In Your Eyes; Please Stay; Red Blooded Woman; Giving You Up; Chocolate [Radio Edit]; Come Into My World [Radio Edit]; Put Yourself In My Place; Did It Again; Breathe; Where The Wild Roses Grow [With Nick Cave])	4

Videos and DVDs

Release Date	Title
November 1989	*Kylie – The Vidoes 1* (I Should Be So Lucky; Got To Be Certain; The Loco-Motion; Je Ne Sais Pas Pourquoi)
November 1989	*Kylie – The Videos 2* (It's No Secret; Hand On Your Heart; Wouldn't Change A Thing; Never Too Late)
April 1990	*Kylie On The Go – Live In Japan* (Hand On Your Heart; The Loco-Motion; Made In Heaven; Got To Be Certain; Je Ne Sais Pas Pourquoi; Wouldn't Change A Thing; Tears On My Pillow; I Should Be So Lucky)
December 1991	*Let's Get To…The Videos* (Better The Devil You Know; Step Back In Time; What Do I Have To Do; Shocked; Word Is Out; If You Were With Me Now)
April 1992	*Kylie – Live In Dublin* (Step Back In Time; Wouldn't Change A Thing; Got To Be Certain; Let's Get To It; Word Is Out; Finer Feelings; I Should Be So Lucky; Love Train; If You Were With Me Now; Too Much Of A Good Thing; What Do I Have To Do; I Guess I Like It Like That; Shocked; Better The Devil You Know)

Release Date	Title
August 1992	*Kylie Minogue – Greatest Hits*

(I Should Be So Lucky; Got To Be Certain;
The Loco-Motion; Je Ne Sais Pas Pourquoi;
It's No Secret; Especially For You
   [With Jason Donovan];
Hand On Your Heart;
Wouldn't Change A Thing; Never Too Late;
Tears On My Pillow; Better The Devil You Know;
Step Back In Time; What Do I Have To Do;
Shocked [DNA Mix]; Word Is Out;
If You Were With Me Now
   [With Keith Washington];
Give Me Just A Little More Time; Finer Feelings;
What Kind Of Fool)

| August 1998 | *The Kylie Tapes 94-98* |

(Breathe; Did It Again; Some Kind Of Bliss;
Confide In Me; Where Is The Feeling;
Put Yourself In My Place)

| November 1998 | *Intimate and Live* |

(Too Far; What Do I Have To Do;
Some Kind Of Bliss; Put Yourself In My Place;
Breathe; Take Me With You;
I Should Be So Lucky;
Dancing Queen; Dangerous Game;
Cowboy Style; Step Back In Time;
Say Hey; Free; Drunk; Did It Again; Limbo;
Shocked; Confide In Me; The Loco-Motion;
Should I Stay Or Should I Go;
Better The Devil You Know)

| October 2000 | *Kylie Minogue – Live In Sydney* |

(Love Boat; Kookachoo; Hand On Your Heart;
Put Yourself In My Place; On A Night Like This;
Medley – Step Back In Time/Never Too Late/

Release Date	Title
	Wouldn't Change A Thing/Turn It Into Love/ Celebration; Can't Get You Out Of My Head; Your Disco Needs You; I Should Be So Lucky; Better The Devil You Know; So Now Goodbye; Physical; Butterfly; Confide In Me; Kids; Shocked; Light Years. Special DVD feature, Spinning Around)
November 2002	*Fever* (Prelude [Sound Of Music]; Come Into My World; Shocked; Love At First Sight; Fever; Spinning Around; More, More, More; The Crying Game; Put Yourself In My Place; Finer Feelings; Dangerous Games; Confide In Me; Cowboy Style; Double Dutch; Kids; On A Night Like This; The Loco-Motion; In Your Eyes; Please Stay; Rhythm Of The Night; Never Too Late; Limbo; Step Back In Time; Light Years; I Feel Love; I Should Be So Lucky; Burning Up; Better The Devil You Know; Can't Get You Out Of My Head)
July 2004	*Body Language Live* (Still Standing; Red Blooded Woman; On A Night Like This; Breathe/Je T' aime; After Dark; Chocolate; Can't Get You Out Of My Head; Slow; Obsession; In Your Eyes; Secret; Spinning Around; Love At First Sight)
November 2004	*Ultimate Kylie* (I Should Be So Lucky; Got To Be Certain; The Loco-Motion; Je Ne Sais Pas Pourqoui; Especially For You [with Jason Donovan];

Release Date	Title
	Hand On Your Heart;
	Wouldn't Change A Thing;
	Never Too Late; Tears On My Pillow;
	Better The Devil You Know; Step Back In Time;
	What Do I Have To Do; Shocked;
	Give Me Just A Little More Time; Celebration;
	Confide In Me; Put Yourself In My Place;
	Where The Wild Roses Grow
	[with Nick Cave];
	Did It Again; Breathe; Spinning Around;
	On A Night Like This;
	Kids [with Robbie Williams]; Please Stay;
	Can't Get You Out Of My Head; In Your Eyes;
	Love At First Sight; Come Into My World; Slow;
	Red Blooded Woman; Chocolate)

November 2005   *Showgirl – Greatest Hits Tour*
(Overture - The Showgirl Theme;
Better The Devil You Know; In Your Eyes;
Giving You Up; On A Night Like This; Shocked;
What Do I Have To Do; Spinning Around;
In Denial; Je Ne Sais Pas Pourquoi;
Confide In Me; Red Blooded Woman/
Where The Wild Roses Grow; Slow;
Please Stay; Over The Rainbow;
Come Into My World; Chocolate;
I Believe In You; Dreams; Hand On Your Heart;
The Loco-Motion; I Should Be So Lucky;
Your Disco Needs You;
Put Yourself In My Place;
Can't Get You Out Of My Head;
Especially For You; Love At First Sight)

Films

Release Date	Title
1989	*The Delinquents*
1994	*Street Fighter: The Movie*
1995	*Hayride to Hell*
1996	*Misfit*
1996	*Bio-Dome*
2000	*Cut*
2000	*Sample People*
2001	*Moulin Rouge*
2005	*The Magic Roundabout (voice)*

About the Author

Sean Smith is one of the UK's leading celebrity biographers whose bestselling books have been translated into more than twenty languages throughout the world. Since his internationally acclaimed biography of JK Rowling he has examined the world of the modern pop icon – Kylie Minogue, Robbie Williams, Justin Timberlake and Britney Spears.

Described by the *Independent* as a 'fearless chronicler', he specializes in meticulous research, seeking out the real person behind the star image.

Photo Credits

Index

Abba, 38
Adamson, Georgina, 43
Aitken, Matt, 77, 84–5, 88, 91–2, 96
  see also Stock, Aitken and Waterman
albums:
  Body Language, 27, 244–5, 247
  Enjoy Yourself, 11, 12, 146
  Fever, 24, 25, 216, 220, 227, 244, 245, 247
  Greatest Hits, 15, 132, 246, 247
  Hits +, 193, 247
  Impossible Princess, 19, 138–40, 142–4, 151, 174, 179
  Kylie, 10, 11
  Kylie Minogue, 16, 133, 177
  Kylie Minogue in Europe, 20, 143–4
  Let's Get To It, 14
  Light Years, 22, 186, 210, 211, 213, 216
  listed, 258–63
  Rhythm Of Love, 13–14, 130
  Ultimate Kylie, 28, 247
And the Ass Saw the Angel (Cave), 135
Anderson, Steve, 16–17, 133, 138–9, 141, 178, 181
Appleyard, Bryan, 2, 219, 221

Arias, *see* Australian Record Industry Awards
Ashley, Gary, 77, 81
Astley, Rick, 88, 94, 95
Audience with Kylie Minogue, An, 24, 219
Audience with Ricky Martin, An, 23
Australian Export Awards, 21
Australian Record Industry Awards (Arias), 19, 24, 26

Bad Seeds, 18, 135
Bailey, Chris, 129
Bailey, Pearl, 129
Baker, William, 16, 25, 28, 171–2, 175–81, 186, 194, 198–200, 210
  Kylie parts from, 246–7
  Kylie reunited with, 255
Baldwin, Stephen, 148, 166
Ball, Dave, 139
Bambi awards, 24
Bananarama, 88
Band Aid II, 12, 123, 247
Basinger, Kim, 156
Beckham, David, 159
Beckham, Victoria, 24, 159, 218, 255
Bennett, Michele, 117–18, 129, 172
Bertrand, Marcheline, 242

Best Arse competition, 221
Beyoncé, 27
Bhatia, Amit, 27, 235
Big Brother, 14
Big Day Out concerts, 18
Big Issue, 107
Billboard, 220
  Top 100, 25
Binoche, Juliette, 239, 244
Birthday Party (formerly the
  Boys Next Door), 134
Björk, 167, 168
Blamey, Terry, 9, 79–83, 92,
  99, 100, 103, 104, 121,
  128, 152, 229, 230
Blondie, 176
Bloom, Beverly, 226
Bonser, Damian, 46
Boyd, Eva (Little Eva), 74
Boys Next Door (later
  Birthday Party), 134
Boyz, 186
Bradfield, James Dean, 20,
  140–1
Bright, Spencer, 88, 90, 135,
  143
Brit Awards, 25, 26, 188, 220,
  226–7
Brothers in Rhythm, 16, 19,
  133, 138
Brown, Ethan, 245
Burchill, Julie, 199

Calder, David, 201
'Candle In The Wind', 142–3
Carey, Mariah, 153
Carlisle, Belinda, 130
Carrey, Jim, 157, 159
Cash, Pat, 161
Casta, Laetitia, 169–70
Cave, Nick, 17, 18, 126, 132,
    134–7, 138, 155, 167,
    174, 198, 199
Chairmen of the Board, 15
Chambers, Guy, 211
Charles, Prince, *see* Wales,
  Prince of
Charles, Ray, 19
Cher, 153
Children in Need, 24
Christensen, Helena, 130
Cleo, 106, 138, 169
Clubbed to Death, 139
Cobain, Kurt, 168, 172
Coleman, Cassius, 159, 201
Comic Relief, 19
Cooper Barr, Kelly, 194–5,
  200
Cosmopolitan, 167
Countdown Music Awards,
  118
Cowell, Simon, 205
Cox, Patrick, 186
Crowe, Russell, 153, 227

D Mob, 217
Dahl, Sophie, 226, 233
Dahlstrom, Kaj, 75–6
Daily Express, 98
Daily Mail, 105, 168
Daily Mirror, 5, 107, 147, 174
Daily Star, 160
Daily Telegraph, 105–6
Dale, Alan, 74
Dando, Evan, 159, 162
Davis, Rob, 217
De Souza, Steven, 148
Dead Or Alive, 185, 218
Dean, Hazell, 88
deConstruction, 15, 21, 133,
  139, 142
  Kylie parts from, 193

Deeley, Cat, 4, 29, 250, 252, 254, 255
Deevoy, Adrian, 126
Dennis, Cathy, 217
Depp, Johnny, 162
Diana, Princess of Wales, 9, 19, 86, 142–3, 151
Donovan, Jason, 7, 8, 11, 64–9, 71–2, 83, 88, 90–2, 94, 95, 100, 119–20, 124, 147, 158–9
    drugs and, 71, 125, 188–9
    Face affair and, 187–8
    gay audience of, 187–8
    Kermit replacement for, 220
    Kylie meets, 40
    Kylie's duet with, 11
    Kylie–Michael relationship and, 122–3
    Lloyd Webber role for, 97
Donovan, Terry, 65, 188
Dougan, Rob, 139
Douglas, Johnny, 209–10
Duck, Colin, 100
Duffy, Mike, 77, 78
Duran Duran, 21, 194

Eagles, 194
Easton, Sheena, 163
Edmonds, Noel, 86
Elle style awards, 20, 26
Ellis-Bextor, Sophie, 217
Esquire, 106
Evans, Chris, 159

Face, 107, 187–8, 229
Fame and Misfortune, 8, 59
Farnham, John, 19
Farrell, Colin, 242
Farriss, Andrew, 116–17

Farriss Brothers, 117
Farriss, Tim, 126
Fiennes, Ralph, 202
films:
    Bio-Dome, 17, 148–9, 166
    Cut, 21, 151
    Delinquents, The, 11, 12, 105, 126, 134, 145–8, 183
    Diana & Me, 151
    Hayride to Hell, 17, 149–50
    Justify My Love, 168
    listed, 268
    Magic Roundabout, The, 153
    Misfit, 150
    Moulin Rouge, 23, 60, 153
    Sample People, 152
    Street Fighter, 16, 17, 145, 148, 150
Fox, Samantha, 88
Friedman, Andrew, 70

Galliano, John, 248
Garbo, Greta, 154
Garcia, Adam, 24
Garland, Judy, 95
Garner, Nadine, 56–8 *passim*
Garrett, Leif, 64
Gary Puckett and the Union Gap, 33
G-A-Y, 171, 186, 255
Gaye, Marvin, 44
Gaynor, Gloria, 186
Geldof, Bob, 12, 172
Gerber, Mark, 149, 159, 165–6
Gere, Richard, 236
Ghosts … of the Civil Dead, 135
Gillespie, Bobby, 102–3
Glastonbury, 29, 256
Goffin, Gerry, 74

Gooding, David, 225
Gooding, James, 22, 23, 26–7, 43, 159, 223–7, 231–4, 246
GQ, 209
    Services to Mankind Award, 24
Graham, Marcus, 104
Grammy Awards, 235, 245
Grasset, Alain, 240
Grazia, 5
Guardian, 209, 249
Gudinski, Michael, 76, 152, 251

Hand, Derek, 172
Hardy, Alan, 56, 58, 60, 62, 73, 74
Harry, Debbie, 176
Hawke, Bob, 129
Hayek, Salma, 249
Heat, 27, 28, 104, 108, 244, 246
Heath, Chris, 229
Hello!, 204
Henderson Kids, The, 7, 8, 51, 56–60, 73, 227
    Kylie auditions for, 56
Henderson Kids II, The, 60
Hendrix, Jimi, 172
Hesketh-Harvey, Kit, 201
Heyman, David, 55
Hit Factory, 84–5, 94, 95, 132, 228
    see also Stock, Aitken and Waterman
Holt, Peter, 70
Home and Away, 92
Hurley, Liz, 127
Hutchence, Kell, 115
Hutchence, Michael, 2, 3, 12–14 *passim,* 42, 53, 67, 94, 113–31, 132–3, 134, 135, 147, 154, 158, 164
    birth of, 115
    Cave and, 136
    death of, 20, 171–4
    drugs and, 71, 119, 162
    funeral of, 174
    Kylie meets, 9, 118
    Kylie parts from, 14, 104
Hutchence, Patricia, 115, 116, 117–18, 120, 122, 130, 203
Hutchence, Rhett, 115
Hutchence, Tina, 115

Iley, Chrissy, 203
Independent on Sunday, 179
Interview, 236, 240
'Intimate and Live' tour, 177, 178–81, 193–4, 198
INXS, 116–17, 118, 119, 127, 129, 173, 215
    see also Hutchence, Michael
'I Will Survive', 186

Jackson, Janet, 232
Jackson, Michael, 24
Jackson, Samuel L, 242
Japan Radio Music Awards, 12
Jebb, Katerina, 176, 197, 199
Jeffries, Tim, 159, 165
John, Elton, 18, 19, 142, 186, 251
Jolie, Angelina, 242–4
Jones, Dennis (maternal grandfather), 34, 38
Jones, Millie (maternal grandmother), 34, 35,

38

Jonnie, 120

Jopling, Jay, 150

Joseph and the Amazing Technicolor Dreamcoat, 187

Just a Man (Hutchence, Glassop), 117–18

Kath and Kim, 28

Kay, Jay, 159

Kaydeebee, 80, 94, 103
  see also Minogue, Ron

Keane, Paul, 74

Keith, Penelope, 202

Kennedy, Nigel, 199

Kermit the Frog, 24, 220

Kick, 118

Kidd, Jodie, 200

Kidd, Johnny, 200

Kidman, Nicole, 232

King, Carol, 74

Kinski, Klaus, 116

Kinski, Nastassja, 115–16

Kiss, 219

Klum, Sharon, 173

Kravitz, Lenny, 159, 164–5

Kylie (Baker, Minogue), 21, 199–200

Kylie and Jason: Just Good Friends, 72

Kylie La La La (Baker), 171

LaBelle, Patti, 59, 60

Lagerfeld, Karl, 29, 248

Lane, Diane, 236

Langman, Chris, 56, 57–8

Laureus World Sports Awards, 27

Lavin, John, 148

Lee, Ben, 21

Lemonheads, 162

Lennon, John, 172

Lennon, Julian, 159

Leno, Jay, 220

Life Ball, 21

Limbo (website), 176

Little Eva (Eva Boyd), 74

Little, Jimmy, 23

Loaded, 18

Logie Awards, 9, 10, 76, 118

Lopez, Jennifer, 153

Lords, Traci, 140

Love, Courtney, 162

Love Kylie x, lingerie, 23, 26, 41

Luhrmann, Baz, 16, 153, 199

Lyne, Adrian, 237

M People, 133

McCall, Davina, 14

McCartney, Paul, 194

McDonald, Julian, 248

McIntyre, Sue, 65

McLachlan, Craig, 74

McMahon, Julian, 16, 204

McMahon, Sir William, 204

Macpherson, Elle, 165

Madonna, 3, 26, 99, 145, 153–6, 184

Major, John, 102

Malkovich, John, 129

Mandela, Nelson, 102

Manic Street Preachers, 19, 20, 139–41, 174, 178, 198

Marcolin, Paolo/Paul, 45–54, 57, 160

Martin, Ricky, 188

Martinez, Olivier, 4–5, 27, 29, 159, 235–44, 249–50, 251, 253–5, 256
  Kylie meets, 26, 235

Martinez, Robert, 237, 238
Mastroianni, Marcello, 238
Mel & Kim, 88
Mel C, 188
Melbourne Sun, 100, 105
Men Behaving Badly, 19
Metro Weekly, 245
Minogue, Brendan
        (brother), 7, 24, 35,
        219–20, 250, 253
Minogue, Carol (mother),
        26, 34–5, 37–8, 40, 42,
        81, 94, 171, 180, 195,
        230
    Hutchence and, 121
    Kylie's cancer and, 250,
        252
Minogue, Danielle (Dannii)
        (sister), 3, 9, 20, 24, 37,
        39–41, 50, 92, 127, 182,
        195, 204–6, 219, 227,
        231–2, 241, 251, 252–3,
        255
    birth of, 7
    clothing label of, 41
    fan mail of, 33
    wedding of, 16, 193, 204
Minogue, Kylie:
    anorexia rumours
        concerning, 101, 104
    birth of, 7, 33
    cancer all-clear given to, 4,
        29, 253
    cancer of, 1–2, 5–6, 28–9,
        250–6
    drugs rumours
        concerning, 125
    early life of, 34–63
    gay appeal of, 2, 13, 96,
        155, 172, 175, 182–7,
        212, 216

    thirtieth birthday of, 20
    Tussaud's waxwork of, 26
    twenty-first birthday of, 11
    world tours of, 23, 25
    see also albums; films;
        *individual programme
        titles*; songs
Minogue, Ron (father), 34,
        35, 42, 79, 149, 246
    cancer operation on, 230
    children's finances and,
        80–1, 93, 103
    Kylie's cancer and, 250
Minx, 107
Mittal, Vanisha, 27, 235
MixMag, 106
Mohan, Dominic, 226
Monroe, Marilyn, 154
Montand, Yves, 238
Morissette, Alanis, 168
Morrison, Jim, 172
Movie Magazine International,
        148
MTV Music Awards, 221
Mud, 217
Murder Ballads, 136
Mushroom Records, 76–8,
        80, 177

Neighbours, 8, 9, 10, 61–71,
        73, 77, 152, 153, 227–8
    background music to, 23
    gay staff on, 183
    Kylie auditions for, 61–2
    Kylie joins cast of, 39
    Kylie's last episode on, 87
    spoof of, 28
    UK popularity of, 85
Neill, Sam, 39
New York, 245
News of the World, 125, 223,

225, 226
Newton-John, Olivia, 38, 195
Night and Day, 24
NME, 141
Noel Edmonds Christmas Day Special, The, 86
Now, 108

Oasis, 90
O'Brien, Peter, 74
Oddy, Jane, 105, 228
O'Donnell, Zane, 159, 160–1, 165
OK!, 226
Olympic Games, Sydney, 22, 214–15
On A Night Like This tour, 23
One Hundred Great Welsh Women, 35
Osbourne, Ozzy, 153
O'Sullivan, Kevin, 174

Pack, Roger Lloyd, 159, 201
Paramour, Jordan, 244
Paris Motor Show, 26
Parlophone, 21
Passaro, Vince, 236
Pearce, Guy, 73, 74, 153
Pelman, Amanda, 77
Penry-Jones, Peter, 202
Penry-Jones, Rupert, 159, 201, 202–3
Pet Shop Boys, 152
Pete Waterman Limited (PWL), 84, 86, 92, 124, 127
   see also Hit Factory; Stock, Aitken and Waterman; Waterman, Pete
Petherick, Greg, 64–5, 74, 75

Piaf, Edith, 2
Poetry Olympics, 18, 132, 137–8
Portobello Café, 136
Presley, Elvis, 117
Price, Gwenda, 59
Prince, 15, 50, 159, 162–4, 164–5
Prince Albert of Monaco, 25
Principal, Victoria 156
Priscilla, Queen of the Desert, 215–16
Private Eye, 98
Punch, 89

Q, 125–6

Radcliffe, Daniel, 55
Rainforest Foundation, 15
Raven, Charlotte, 209
Red Hot Chili Peppers, 168
Rhythm of Life, 15
Richard, Cliff, 89
Riddiford, Dennis (great-uncle), 35
Ringwald, Molly, 152
Ritts, Herb, 129
Rob D, 139
Rodriguez, Michelle, 249
Rolling Stone, 107, 213
Rolling Stones, 33–4, 194
Rook, Jean, 10, 98, 99–100, 160
Russ, Jan, 61, 196

S Club 7, 24, 217
Scatena, Dino, 70
Schiffer, Claudia, 165
Schlatter, Charlie, 146
Scissor Sisters, 27
Seaman, Dave, 133, 138

Sednaoui, Stephane, 17–18,
    20, 136, 142, 159,
    166–70, 172, 197, 199,
    242
Select, 102
Shears, Jake, 27
Shore, Pauly, 17, 148, 159,
    166, 167
Showgirl Princess, The
    (Minogue), 254
Showgirl tour, 27, 28, 246,
    247–50, 255, 256
Simpson, Dave, 249
Sinitta, 88
Sky, 154
Sky, Rick, 101, 158
Skyways, 7, 40
Small, Heather, 133
Smash Hits, 56, 105, 115
    Awards, 17
Smashing Pumpkins, 168
Smith, Clinton, 152
Smiths, 90
'So You Want To Be a
    Rockstar' game, 79
Solo, 106
Some Kind of Kylie, 20
songs:
    'Better The Devil You
        Know', 13, 92, 123,
        128, 136, 180, 182,
        186, 194, 217, 248
    'Breathe', 20, 143
    'Bury Me Deep In Love',
        23
    'Can't Get You Out Of My
        Head', 10, 11, 23–4,
        216–18, 227
    'Celebration', 15, 132
    'Chocolate', 245
    'Come Into My World', 245

'Confide In Me', 16,
    133–4, 145, 180
'Count The Days', 13, 128
'Cowboy Style', 180
'Dancing Queen', 194, 214
'Dangerous Game', 133
'Did It Again', 20, 143, 174
'Do They Know It's
    Christmas?', 12
'Dreams', 139
'Enjoy Yourself', 12
'Especially For You', 11,
    67, 91, 118, 123, 138,
    249
'Finer Feelings', 161
'GBI', 168
'Give Me Just A Little More
    Time', 15
'Got To Be Certain', 10, 92
'Hand On Your Heart', 11,
    88, 123, 146
'I Believe In You', 247
'I Should Be So Lucky', 9,
    18, 85, 86, 92, 118,
    137, 179, 182, 227–8
'If You Were With Me
    Now', 14–15
'In Your Eyes', 25
'Je Ne Sais Pas Pourquoi',
    10–11, 87
'Jump, 141
'Kids', 22, 208, 211, 216
'Limbo', 140–1
listed, 257–8
'Loco-Motion, The', 8, 9,
    10, 11, 75–8, 118, 182,
    215, 249
'Love At First Sight', 249
'Loveboat', 211
'Made In Heaven', 11
'Never Too Late', 12

'Put Yourself In My Place',
      17, 134, 149
'Red-Blooded Woman',
      245
'Reflex, The', 21
'Shocked', 14, 92, 180
'Sisters Are Doing It For
      Themselves', 186
'Slow', 27, 244–5
'Some Kind Of Bliss',
      19–20, 140–3, 209
'Spinning Around', 22,
      137, 208, 209, 210,
      212, 216
'Step Back In Time', 14
'Tears On My Pillow', 13
'Time Will Pass You By',
      133
'Too Far', 139, 141, 179
'Turn It Into Love', 11
'What Do I Have To Do',
      14, 16, 92, 160, 175,
      182
'Where Is The Feeling',
      18
'Where The Wild Roses
      Grow', 17–18, 136–7
'Word Is Out', 14
'Wouldn't Change A
      Thing', 12
'Your Disco Needs You',
      211–13 passim
Sonia, 88, 89
Sonny and Cher, 75
Sorvino, Mira, 240, 244
Spears, Britney, 3, 99, 153,
      199
Spice Girls, 153
Spin, 116
Spooks, 203
Stark, Koo, 165

Stern, Bert, 16
Sting, 15
Stock, Aitken and Waterman,
      9, 12, 13, 15, 42, 60, 85,
      87–90, 94, 97, 128
   beginnings of, 87–8
   bestselling roster for, 89
   gay appeal of, 185
   Kylie splits with, 132
   see also Hit Factory; Pete
      Waterman Limited;
      Waterman, Pete
Stock, Mike, 77, 84–5, 88, 89,
      95, 96–7
   see also Stock, Aitken and
      Waterman
Sullivans, The, 39, 56
Summer, Donna, 44, 59–60
Sun, 22, 100, 189, 226
Sunday Times, 219, 234

T in the Park, 18
Take That, 211, 212
Taylor-Wood, Sam, 150
Tempest, The, 21, 200–1
Thomas, David, 105
Thorne, Angela, 202
Tiffany, 87
Timberlake, Justin, 26, 231–2
Time Out, 107
Time, 69
Times, 201
Tonight Show with Jay Leno, 25
Tonight Show, The, 220
Top of the Pops, 22, 24, 210
Towa Tei, 168
Townsville Theatre Royal, 34
Travolta, John, 38
Tricky, 168
Turner, Tina, 168
TV Hits, 108

TV Week, 69, 72, 76

U2, 168, 211
US Style, 106

V2001 Festival, 23
Van Damme, Jean-Claude, 16, 145, 148
Vicar of Dibley, The, 17
videos:
  'GBI', 168
  Kylie – The Videos, 11, 13
  Kylie Live, 14
  listed, 264–7
  'Live in Sydney', 26
  Scott and Charlene: A Love Story, 93
  'Shocked', 183
  'Some Kind Of Bliss', 209
  'Spinning Around', 208, 209, 210
Villeneuve, Jacques, 204–5
Vogue, 16, 196–7

Wales, Prince of, 9, 86
Wales, Princess of, 9, 19, 86, 142–3, 151
Walsh, Brian, 66
Waterman, Pete, 10–11, 24, 76, 77, 78, 83–5, 88–97 *passim*, 103, 154, 185, 220, 229

  see also Stock, Aitken and Waterman
Waters, John, 75
Watson, Paul, 184–5
Watson, Reg, 62–3, 66
Watt, Andrew, 101
Webster, Nikki, 214
Welsh, Irvine, 156
Whigfield, 134
Who, 4
Who Weekly, 107
Wilde, Kim, 198
Williams, Robbie, 3, 21, 159, 194, 208, 210–12, 226, 232
Wilson, Brian, 194
Windsor, Barbara, 221
Wings of Desire, 135
Wire, Nicky, 140
Woman's Day, 124–5
Wood, David, 43–4
World Music Awards, 14
World Tour (2002), 229–30

Yates, Paula, 118, 130, 136, 172, 173, 174
Young Talent Time, 7, 40, 41, 50, 59–60
Young, Jenny, 225
Young, Simon, 79

Zoo Family, The, 8, 59, 61